D0622433

Why Have Children?

Basic Bioethics
Arthur Caplan, editor

A complete list of the books in the Basic Bioethics series appears at the back of this book.

Why Have Children?

The Ethical Debate

Christine Overall

The MIT Press
Cambridge, Massachusetts
London, England

© 2012 Massachusetts Institute of Technology
All rights reserved. No part of this book may be reproduced in any form by any electronic
or mechanical means (including photocopying, recording, or information storage and re-
trieval) without permission in writing from the publisher.

MIT Press books may be purchased at special quantity discounts for business or sales pro-
motional use. For information, please email special_sales@mitpress.mit.edu or write to Special Sales Department, The MIT Press, 55 Hayward Street, Cambridge, MA 02142.

This book was set in Sabon by the MIT Press. Printed and bound in the United States of
America.

Library of Congress Cataloging-in-Publication Data

Overall, Christine, 1949–
Why have children? : the ethical debate / Christine Overall.
    p.   cm. — (Basic bioethics)
Includes bibliographical references (p.) and index.
ISBN 978-0-262-01698-8 (hardcover : alk. paper)
1. Human reproduction—Moral and ethical aspects. I. Title.
QP251.O85   2012
176—dc23
                                                            2011024312

10   9   8   7   6   5   4   3   2   1

For Tabitha Bernard
and her daughter, Arden Noor Khan,
with love and appreciation

Contents

Series Foreword

Glenn McGee and I developed the Basic Bioethics series and collaborated as series coeditors from 1998 to 2008. In fall 2008 and spring 2009, the series was reconstituted, with a new editorial board and under my sole editorship. I am pleased to present the thirtieth book in the series.

The Basic Bioethics series makes innovative works in bioethics available to a broad audience and introduces seminal scholarly manuscripts, state-of-the-art reference works, and textbooks. Topics engaged include the philosophy of medicine, advancing genetics and biotechnology, end-of-life care, health and social policy, and the empirical study of biomedical life. Interdisciplinary work is encouraged.

Arthur Caplan

Basic Bioethics Series Editorial Board
Joseph J. Fins
Rosamond Rhodes
Nadia N. Sawicki
Jan Helge Solbakk

Acknowledgments

Writing this book has been an exciting and difficult challenge, and many people as well as two institutions have provided input, support, and help. In 2006, Mount Saint Vincent University in Halifax, Nova Scotia, appointed me the tenth Nancy's Chair in Women's Studies for a year. The university offered the ideal environment to begin work on this project. Queen's University, which awarded me a University Research Chair in 2005 and renewed it in 2010, has made it possible for me to continue writing while also teaching and supervising graduate students.

To my friends and Queen's University Philosophy Department colleagues Susan Babbitt, Jacqueline Davies, and Adèle Mercier, thank you for your support, understanding, and courage. Your political acuity, personal warmth, and wisdom have been invaluable. In the department's main office, Marilyn Lavoie and Judy Vanhooser are always patient, kind, and knowledgeable sources of assistance.

Unbeknownst to herself, Tabitha Bernard, a master's student at Mount Saint Vincent University, played a big role in this book. Her brave and groundbreaking work on the ethics of planned unassisted childbirth reminded me that reproductive ethics is still a huge field with many unexplored questions. Thank you, Tabitha, for helping me to return to some of my academic origins. And I am delighted about the birth of your beautiful daughter, Arden Noor.

I have also been inspired along the way by Tanya (Oja) Watson, who wrote her Queen's master's thesis on childlessness and the concept of woman, and by Queen's PhD student Katherine (Kassy) Wayne, whose insights into bioethical issues always open my eyes to new ways of seeing.

As a philosophy PhD student at Queen's, Christopher Lowry, now at the Chinese University of Hong Kong, gave me detailed comments on

---

parts of the book. At two of the annual meetings of the Canadian Philosophical Association, Nicholas Dixon of Alma College, Michigan, and Wesley Cooper of the University of Alberta provided helpful and encouraging comments on early drafts of parts of the book. And the undergraduate students in my course Philosophy 204, "Life, Death, and Meaning," in 2007, 2008, and 2009 prompted me to think carefully both about whether coming into existence is always harmful and about whether human extinction is inevitably a bad thing. Vishaal Patel, Matthew Kersten, and Rian Dewji, students in this course in 2007 and 2009, were especially insightful about the work of David Benatar.

I am fortunate to have had the support of Clay Morgan of the MIT Press while I finished and revised this book. I also thank Deborah Cantor-Adams and Annie Barva for their excellent work in editing my manuscript.

I am very grateful for the feedback I received from the three external reviewers of this manuscript: Dena Davis of Cleveland State University; Laura Purdy of Wells College, New York; and Nadia Sawicki of Loyola University, Chicago. I am indebted to them for the time they devoted to reading and responding to my work; each one helped me to rethink crucial parts of the book. Any remaining problems or weaknesses are, of course, entirely my responsibility.

I am deeply appreciative of all that I am learning at Kingston's Path Yoga. Thank you to Carolyn Johanson and all the instructors for teaching me that yoga is about strength and flexibility of the mind as well as of the body, that the yoga mat reflects what is going on in my practice and my life, and that I don't have to push myself to the point of injury or exhaustion.

I also thank my friends Kathy Silver and Bob Cadman. Bob is always game for a philosophical discussion, and his hospitality and kindness are heartwarming. Kathy, my Big Sister, wise woman, and dancing queen: I'm so glad you are in my life.

Nancy Chapple has been an excellent writing companion (and "trophy guest") at several stages in the writing of this book. Evan Alcock, my friend for fifty-something years, provides the best possible example of devotion to research, love of learning, and staying forever young. Gisela Braun and Dave Beavan have been supportive by taking me back to my high school roots.

Tom Russell always reminds me that teaching is important and deserves all the time and attention I can give it. Ruth Dubin's personal strength and her commitment to science and scholarship are inspiring. Beth Morrison shows me how an enlightened life might be lived, and Sylvia Burkinshaw was a strong example of living life well for more than nine decades.

My friend and former student Sue Donaldson is one of the very best philosophers I know; her insights are immeasurably helpful. My colleague and friend Sue Hendler, whose death in 2009 was a devastating loss, always supported me in rethinking problems and believing in myself.

I am thankful to my mother, Dorothy Overall, for choosing to have children despite her fears about global dangers. I am grateful to Julie Mayrand and Mike Ashton, whose intelligence, kindness, and sense of fun have immeasurably enriched our family.

My cat, Ozzie, accompanied me through the writing of four books. This one was her last. She was stalwart and brave, gentle and sweet, until the very end. I miss her very much.

Above all, I am forever appreciative of my life partner, Ted Worth, and of our children, Devon Worth and Narnia Worth. Choosing to have children was a decision to change our lives forever—and I'm so glad we did.

1

Introduction

I call heaven and earth to record this day against you, that I have set before you life and death, blessing and cursing: therefore choose life, that both thou and thy seed may live.
—Deuteronomy 30:19.

Why Have Children?

I suspect that most people eventually ask themselves the question "Why have children?" at least once or twice during their lives.

Back when I was much younger than I am now, I was trying to decide whether I wanted to have children or not. I eventually did choose to have two children, whom I adore. I am fortunate and blessed to have them. Along the way, I learned a few things about the decision whether to have children.

First, if you wait to have children until you are absolutely sure that it is the right decision, then you may wait forever, and you may never have children.

Second, as Onora O'Neill remarks, a decision to have a child is not merely a choice to beget or bear a child, but rather a decision "to undertake the far longer and more demanding task of bringing up a child or arranging for its upbringing, to at least that level which will minimally fit the child for independent adult life in its society" (1979, 26). But you cannot know ahead of time what it will be like to become a parent or what sort of child you will have. You cannot entirely know what is good and what is hard about the process of creating and rearing until well after you have the child.

And third, the decision to have a child is a decision to change your life forever. It is irreversible and for that reason more significant than most other life decisions, including those related to education, romantic commitments, work, or geographical location. As one author puts it, "Motherhood is a threshold that, once crossed, cannot be eradicated. . . . Ironically, it's like death—'the bourn from which no traveler returns' as Hamlet says. In becoming a mother, a woman goes to a new place" (Fertile 2006, 187).

Choosing whether to have children may not seem like the sort of decision that is deserving or even capable of analysis. The novelist Margaret Laurence once wrote, "I don't really feel I have to analyse my own motives in wanting children. For my own reassurance? For fun? For ego-satisfaction? No matter. It's like (to me) asking why you want to write. Who cares? You have to, and that's that" (quoted in Sullivan 1998, 244). Philosopher Diana Tietjens Meyers similarly observes, "When asked why they want or don't want to have children, most people are flummoxed. Highly articulate individuals lose their fluency, grope for words, and stumble around, seizing on incompatible explanations and multiplying justifications" (2001, 752).

How one decides whether to have children and the ethics of choosing to procreate are topics that I have been pondering for decades.[1] In this book, I explore questions that are at the heart of the "why have children?" issue. I am asking what we might talk about if we were not "flummoxed" and inarticulate about having children.

Why Choosing to Have Children Is an Ethical Issue

In contemporary Western culture, it ironically appears that one needs to have reasons *not* to have children, but no reasons are required to have them. People who are childless[2] are frequently and rudely criticized and called to account for their situation. One woman who wrote about her decision not to procreate was "denounced as bitter, selfish, un-sisterly, unnatural, evil" (Kingston 2009, 39). It is assumed that if individuals do not have children, it is because they are infertile, they are too selfish, or they have just not yet gotten around to it. In any case, they owe their interlocutor an explanation. They cannot merely have decided not to procreate. In contrast, no one says to a newly pregnant woman or the proud father of a newborn,[3] "Why did you choose to have that child? What are your reasons?" The choice to procreate is not regarded as needing any thought or justification.

Indeed, the philosopher Rosalind Hursthouse says, "Just as a special context is needed to make sense of 'What do you want to have health (or knowledge, or pleasure or virtue) for?' so is one needed to make sense of 'What do you want to have children for?'. Unions are 'blessed' not cursed with issue; those who have children are 'favoured by fortune'; the childless are 'unfortunate'; to be unable to have children is a lack, a privation, a misfortune" (1987, 309).[4] In other words, Hursthouse thinks it does not make sense, outside of special contexts, to inquire into the motives or reasons for having children. This view suggests that having children is the default position; not having children is what requires explanation and justification.

These implicit assumptions, I suggest, are the opposite of what they ought to be. The so-called burden of proof—or what I would call the burden of justification—should rest primarily on those who choose to have children. That is, the choice to have children calls for more careful justification and reasoning than the choice not to have children simply because in the former case a new and vulnerable human being is brought into existence whose future may be at risk.

Thus, I think Laurence's "Who cares?" attitude is mistaken. The lack of acknowledgment that childbearing can be a moral choice may be due to its assimilation to other processes thought to be normal parts of human life—for example, the phenomena of "falling in love" or being sexually attracted to another person. These aspects of human life are often regarded as the product of drives or instincts not amenable to ethical evaluation. For example, James Lenman claims that asking why we want children is "foolish," for "it is partly just because we're programmed that way much as we are for sex. It just seems to be a part of our biological dispensation that most of us aspire to parenthood, feel pleased when we attain it and are more or less unhappy when it passes us by. It's not altogether a matter for rational consideration" (2004a, 325).

Some people, women in particular, believe that there is a "biological clock" inside them that generates a deep drive to have a child. It appears to be more than a simple desire to have a child; it is felt more like a biological force and is therefore very compelling. This drive is sometimes explained in evolutionary terms: our very biological constitution determines that we bear children. The popular press likes to refer to the existence of a supposed "mommy gene." Biologist Lonnie Aarssen writes about an apparently nongendered "parenting drive," which he describes as "an explicit desire to have children in the future" and which involves "an anticipated experience of contemporaneous pleasure derived directly from 'real-time' parenthood per se" (2007, 1772).

The questions we should ask are whether such a desire is either immune to or incapable of analysis and why this desire, unlike virtually all others, should not be subject to ethical assessment. There are many urges apparently arising from our biological nature that we nonetheless should choose not to act upon or at least to be very careful about acting upon. Even if Aarssen is correct in postulating a "parenting drive," such a drive would not be an adequate reason for the choice to have a child. Naturalness alone is not a justification for action, for it is still reasonable to ask whether human beings should give in to their supposed "parenting drive" or resist it. Moreover, the alleged naturalness of the biological clock is belied by those growing numbers of women who apparently do not experience it or do not experience it strongly enough to act upon it. As Leta S. Hollingworth wisely noted almost a century ago, "There could be no better proof of the insufficiency of maternal instinct as a guaranty of population than the drastic laws which we have against birth control, abortion, infanticide, and infant desertion" (1916, 25).[5]

After all, human beings are thoroughly social entities. Our sheer survival means we have been socialized; we live not as individual "islands, entire of ourselves," in John Donne's words, but as a "part of the main," an acculturated segment of the whole that is humanity. Because we are social beings, we do not just see the world; we instead see the world *as* we have learned to see it and as we sometimes choose to see it. All human behavior (except perhaps simple reflex actions, such as the movement of the leg in response to a hammer tap on the knee) is a reaction to the world as perceived. Once past the age of early infancy, we do not just respond like automatons to inner promptings. Instead, what and how we perceive and feel are at least in part a function of our experience and our learning. In seeing, hearing, tasting, feeling, or smelling something, we are engaged in a process of interpretation, a process that we have gradually learned as part of our socialization into our particular culture.

The inevitability of interpretation applies to our inner as well as our external environment. Thus, for example, if I experience a certain fluttering in my midsection, I may variously interpret it as anxiety, fear, anticipation, happiness, or just the need for a snack. Whatever inner promptings we may experience, they "always already" contain a social message, and they are "always already" open to reinterpretation. This description applies to the desire to have a child. Because of the inevitability of interpretation, it does not make sense to blame or credit instinct as the source of behaviors such as having children.

If we fail to acknowledge that the decision whether to have children is a real choice that has ethical import, then we are treating childbearing as an unavoidable fate and a mere expression of biological destiny. Instead of seeing having children as something that women *do*, we will continue to see it as something that simply *happens* to women or as something that is merely "natural." But whatever our biological inclinations may be, we do have some control over our fertility, and the rapidly declining birthrate in most parts of the world is evidence of that fact.

But I myself stressed at the beginning of this chapter that there are many things about having children that one cannot know until one actually has them. It might similarly be argued that one cannot know what a childless life will be like until one commits to living it. Given the unknowability of the outcomes of a decision to have a child or not have a child, it may seem unfair to elevate the decision to the level of ethics.

However, I would argue that many significant ethical decisions are similar to this particular decision: we cannot know or know well all the possible outcomes of the choices we consider. Some things do just have to be experienced. Nonetheless, the indeterminate results of human freedom do not relieve us of the responsibility to consider carefully the moral aspects of our decisions. Moreover, although our own experiences of and reactions to having a child or remaining childless may be difficult to predict, it *is* possible to observe the effects on other people who have made those decisions. We are surrounded by people who have had children or have chosen not to. As with many important life decisions, we can learn something about the nature of the choices by observing others who have already made them. So the difficulty of making the choice whether to have a child or not and the unknowability of the outcome in one's own case do not preclude seeing procreation as an ethical decision.

Nevertheless, it might be objected that the question whether to reproduce or not is merely prudential, not ethical—that it is like other major life decisions, such as whom to marry (or whether to marry), where to live, what career to choose, and so on. These decisions affect primarily the chooser's welfare; hence, they are not inherently ethical issues.

But I suggest that virtually every area of human life has ethical dimensions, including seemingly pragmatic choices of what to eat, what form of transportation to use, how to heat or cool one's home, and so on. We can no longer assume that so-called private life is only personal and therefore in principle immune to ethical examination. Questions about choosing whether to have children are of course prudential in part; that is, they are in part practical in nature, and they are concerned about what is or is not in one's own interests. But they are *also* ethical questions, for they are about whether to bring a person (in some cases more than one person) into existence—and that person cannot, by the very nature of the situation, give consent to being brought into existence. Such questions therefore profoundly affect the well-being both of existing persons (the potential parents, siblings, grandparents, and all the other people with whom the future child may interact) and of potential persons.

Children are both vulnerable and dependent; they will have a "lifelong emotional interdependence" with their parents (Cassidy 2006, 44). Procreation decisions are about whether to take on responsibility for a new life or new lives. Questions about choosing to procreate are also closely tied to how we define our own lives and how we interact with our social and physical environments.

These decisions also have profound implications for the community or communities in which we live. Mianna Lotz argues, "There exists a (generally unacknowledged) distinctly collective interest *in procreation being undertaken with a seriousness, intent and purposiveness that reflects and expresses concern or regard for the moral community itself*, understood at its broadest level as comprising both moral agents and moral subjects." Lotz 2008b, 9, her emphasis). This collective interest requires us to "relinquish our relatively recent yet now widespread preoccupation with procreation as principally, even exclusively, a private and individual matter. . . . Questions of procreative morality are not posed exclusively within the sphere of private individual morality or the procreator–child relationship, but always fall also within the scope of collective morality" (2008b, 12).

Lotz suggests several possible explanations of why our specific reasons for procreating matter morally. One possibility is that our reasons are "predictive of the quality of parenting, and derivatively of the quality of life or welfare of the future child" (2008a, 294). However, Lotz says, the empirical information available does not suggest much of a connection between "procreative motivations" and "parenting capacity." Instead, factors such as parental mental ill health, domestic violence, alcohol and drug abuse, and socioeconomic deprivation better predict bad parenting, including the abuse and neglect of children (2008a, 295).

But notice that some of these factors might in certain cases also affect parental motivations. For example, a woman who is the target of domestic violence might want to have a child because of the illusion that doing so will eliminate the abuse. Or a woman who is addicted to alcohol might think that having a child will somehow help her to stop drinking. Because children generally do not solve their parents' problems, the implausibility of these reasons suggests that a motive for procreation might in some cases predict potential problems in how the child is treated. That is, some parental motivations might be indirect predictors of bad parenting. In chapter 5, I argue that at least one motivation for parenting—the quest for a "savior sibling" for an existing child who is ill—does have a substantial effect on how the new baby will be treated. More generally, we cannot be indifferent to the potential implications of procreative motives for parenting behavior.

A more plausible explanation, Lotz says, for why our reasons for having children matter lies in what children "express": the "meaning or message" (whether it is intended or not) that is conveyed by one's procreative motivation, whether it is conveyed to family members, to people outside the family, or even to the child herself (2008a, 297). I agree that our procreative motivations may have this signaling effect. And even if this particular effect is small, our motives for procreating (or not) remain morally significant for the other reasons I have suggested.

In this book, then, I investigate not only what *actual* reasons women and men might have for procreating or what reasons they may *say* they have, but also reasons that people do not recognize or that they fail to acknowledge. So in part I am attempting to recover those reasons. But this investigation is normative rather than empirical; it is concerned with values and not only with facts. Many of the standard reasons for procreation are, I think, mistaken, but they are worth attending to for the sake of what can be learned about whether there are *good* reasons (as well as bad ones) for having children and, if so, what they might be. When it comes to choosing whether to have children or not, there *is* a moral right and wrong to the choice or at least a moral better and worse.

My aim, I hasten to add, is not to argue for policing people's procreative motives or for creating disapproval (or approval, for that matter) of particular procreative decisions. I'm not interested in being a moral disciplinarian. Nor am I interested in telling people what they ought to do or what I think is right for them to do. My aim is simply to explore some ways in which we might think systematically and deeply about a fundamental aspect of human life.

And I want to insist that this aspect *is* something about which we can, do, and should think. Although choosing to have children or not to have children may involve many feelings, motives, impulses, memories, and emotions, it can and should also be a subject for careful reflection. Whereas in the past procreation was not a matter to which women's will or ideas or decisional capacity had much application, now it is something that women can potentially control, that they can make truly their own. As Lori Leibovich points out, "Couples can opt out of parenthood, women can have children into their fifties, single women can procreate on their own, and gays and lesbians can start families—or not. All of the old rules about childbearing no longer apply" (2006, xv). Moreover, the decision whether to have a biologically related child or not is one that may be made repeatedly over a period of years. Many women (and men) do not simply choose once and for all whether to become parents; rather, they make decisions about their life goals and parenting plans on several occasions, including during pregnancy itself.

The Gendered Nature of the "Why Have Children?" Issue

Any discussion of the ethics of procreation must include feminist perspectives because choosing whether to have children is gendered; it cannot be discussed as if men's and women's very different roles in procreation are irrelevant to the issue. Some parts of the discussion must be unique to women themselves because of women's role—despite recent technological developments—in conception and gestation. For a woman, the decision whether to have a child may include the decision whether to conceive a child; whether, once it is conceived, to carry it to term; and whether, once it is born, to rear it. A woman[6] may (that is, has the ability to) accept or reject motherhood at any of these three stages; hence, the reproductive decision she makes is not a unitary once-and-for-all choice, but rather an ongoing process of assenting to or rejecting motherhood.[7] In this book, I focus primarily on the decision whether to conceive or not. This book is not about abortion or about choosing to give up one's child for adoption. Nonetheless, I make a few comments about abortion in chapters 7 and 8.

Unlike men, who can literally walk away from the results of their procreative behavior, women must literally bear the procreative consequences of their heterosexual activity. To prevent conception, the woman is the one who must worry most about using contraception successfully; all forms of contraception lodge in or are ingested by her body, and she runs the health risks that some forms of contraception create. It is the woman who undergoes the physical consequences of conception and pregnancy. Even if she has an abortion and hence decides against motherhood (at least of the particular individual the fetus would eventually otherwise become), she must bear the moral, pragmatic, and medical weight of making that decision. If she continues the pregnancy, she must care for herself as her body changes radically and must take into account all the consequences of her actions for the fetus. During labor and delivery, she undergoes an experience that can be uniquely demanding and often severely painful.

Just as important, women are still defined socially in terms of their relationship to children. Hence, the context of the procreation decision is political—that is, it is imbued with differences in power, authority, prestige, wealth, and future prospects. Although considerable progress has been achieved in the past century, most of the responsibility for children is still automatically assumed to rest upon mothers rather than upon fathers. Women much more than men pay the price of bad decisions to bear children, whether that price is in terms of the women's education, their employment, their money-making potential, their health and the care they receive for it, their relationships, or their personal fulfillment. Because the context of procreation is political, reproductive decision making cannot realistically be discussed outside of a feminist framework. That framework must include a deep understanding of the differences gender creates in human lives—differences in personal experiences, belief systems, material resources, access to power, and opportunities. Later chapters show that failing to take seriously the gendered nature of society, including our procreative behavior, results in analyses of procreative choices that are not only unrealistic, but also profoundly immoral.

In order for any procreative decision to have ethical significance, the woman involved must have moral agency, authority, and freedom. A woman's choice whether to procreate can be made independently of being in a relationship with a man—indeed, with the assistance of insemination, it can be made independently even of any sexual interaction with a man. Nonetheless, the ethics of men's reproductive decisions is also interestingly complex and worth considering, comprising not only the decision whether to take part in conception, but also whether to support the woman's pregnancy and delivery and whether to raise the child. Meyers points out that "many child-bearing decisions are collaborative decisions that bring into play the peculiar psychodynamics of particular couples and, in many cases, the power imbalances that shadow heterosexual relationships as well" (2001, 744). I believe she is right, but I do not focus directly on the power imbalances themselves. I instead assume a situation in which women, whether in a relationship or not, are able to be self-determining decision makers. I do not think this assumption is farfetched; indeed, many women, though certainly not all, with access to effective contraception are able to make autonomous procreative decisions. The rapidly declining birth rate in every culture in which women have good access to education and health care is evidence of their capacity to make such decisions. In doing so, they may collaborate with another person, male or female, in making procreative decisions, or they may make these decisions alone. Meyers is considerably more pessimistic than I, arguing, "While it would be wrong to claim that *no* woman ever makes a fully autonomous reproductive decision—either to have children or not to have them—the evidence of women's testimony suggests that the women who do are *exceptional*" (2001, 746, my emphasis). I'm not convinced she's right, for as philosopher Lisa Cassidy observes, "Even though . . . pressures [religious, legal, and cultural] may subject many of us to emotional strain, it would be wrong to say the very *existence* of such social pressures wholly co-opts every reproductive choice we make" (2006, 42, my emphasis).

However, I would not go as far as Corinne Maier, the author of a sardonic book that offers "forty good reasons not to have children" (Maier

2007). Maier claims, "Ever since the pill and the IUD, most of the children who have been born have been *wanted* children. They are no longer the unavoidable consequence of a sexual act but the product of willpower under scientific management. The unforeseen has been eliminated. Long live planning!" (2007, 5, her emphasis).[8] The notion that most babies, even in the West, are the outcome of careful planning assisted by "scientific management" is implausible, though. Many teen mothers and mothers of a little "baby bonus" arriving in their menopausal years can attest to its falsehood.

Procreation is not always a choice. In a few cases, a couple may want one child but end up with multiples (particularly if they have used the "scientific management" of in vitro fertilization [IVF] with the implantation of multiple embryos); hence, one child is chosen, but the others are not, even if they are not actively unwanted. In some cases, contraception is simply not used, whether because it is not available, because the individuals are unaware of it or the need for it, or because of a failure to take responsibility for birth control. In other cases, heterosexual intercourse is voluntary, but although children are not wanted contraceptive methods are inadequate or are incorrectly used. And sometimes conception is not chosen because sex is the result of coercion or violence.

All of these facts are deeply problematic. In some of these cases, there is no moral responsibility, as, for example, when multiples result "naturally"—that is to say, without the intervention of reproductive technology. There is sometimes moral culpability on the part of both partners (for example, when contraception is omitted out of laziness or misused out of culpable ignorance). But in cases of rape or cases where the man refuses to use contraception and the woman acquiesces out of fear, there is a clear violation of the woman's rights and integrity. Moreover, there is a growing social scientific and philosophical body of evidence about the various social forces that have acted, primarily on women,[9] to induce or compel people to have children or in some cases to persuade or prevent them from having children. The literature on pronatalism, antinatalism, and women's autonomy (e.g., Hollingworth 1916; Peck and Senderowitz 1975; Gimenez 1983; Meyers 2001) is fascinating. Although it is undeniable that procreation is often unchosen, I am nonetheless interested in cases where whether to have children is voluntary.

I am therefore setting aside any discussion of childlessness that is not deliberately chosen. That is not to say that unchosen childlessness is not a topic of interest in itself, including as it does issues related to infertility, women's relationships with men, and socioeconomic status, among others. But I am interested in cases where a true choice is made.

Ethical questions arise both in procreating one's own children and in adopting. Both are interesting and important topics, and they have some themes in common. Ethically speaking, however, the two are not entirely the same, largely because in the case of adoption the child already exists (or at least is in utero), whereas in the case of procreation one is deciding whether to bring a child into existence.[10] In adoption, there are also several social policy issues—such as the nationality of the baby, the role that religion and race should or should not play, the adoptive parents' age and sex/gender, their supposed fitness for parenting, and so on—that are different or at least thought to be different from the issues about having one's own biologically related child. Much has been written about the ethics of adoption, and it is a huge topic in its own right. Rather less has been written, as far as I can tell, about the general ethical dimensions of procreating—a choice that millions of people presumably make quite frequently.

Self-help books on the market purport to assist would-be parents in making a practical choice about whether to have children. There are also informal discussions in nonphilosophical books, on Web sites, in newspapers and magazines, and in blogs. Yet despite the significance of biological offspring both to an individual's self-concept and life plans and to the broader community's well-being, the ethical nature of this choice is seldom recognized, even—or especially—by philosophers.

There is an extensive academic literature[11] about the use of IVF, egg and embryo donation, and pregnancy. There is also considerable debate about choosing whether to procreate when there is a strong possibility that the resulting child(ren) will have physical or mental impairments (I return to this issue in chapter 8). But although bioethicists have had much to say about "new" reproductive technologies and practices, about procreation and disability, and about pregnancy and childbirth, they appear to assume that simply choosing whether to procreate is a pragmatic decision, not one with moral repercussions. And although population ethicists discuss abstract utilitarian issues concerning overpopulation, quality of life, and how many people there should be in the world, they usually fail to explore the " why have children?" question as an individual moral issue for which multiple arguments, for and against, are relevant.[12] I believe these discussions are radically incomplete, and this book shows how this large gap in philosophical thought can be filled.

I focus primarily on the choice to procreate via heterosexual intercourse or insemination, but not via other technologies. I am concerned not so much with *how* people do or ought to procreate, as with *whether* they should procreate and how many children, if any, it is morally legitimate to have. (The latter is in effect a question about repeated "whethers"—whether to have a first child, whether to have a second child, whether to have a third child, and so on.) Nonetheless, issues related to "assisted reproduction" using reproductive technologies cannot be entirely ignored. Let me give just one example for now. To the extent that ectogenesis (growth of a fetus outside the uterus) becomes possible and available, it may dramatically change the "why have children?" question, for pregnancy (or at least part of pregnancy) would no longer be necessary.[13] If ectogenesis becomes widely and readily available, it may have wide-ranging effects on our ideas about rights and obligations with respect to procreation (I discuss this possibility further in chapter 3).

In discussing the ethics of choosing whether to procreate, my focus is primarily on the context of twenty-first century North America. The book is not about legal issues concerning procreation. Nonetheless, there is a relationship. First, the laws of the society in which one lives may either constrain or encourage one's procreative decisions; the legal environment is part of the context that needs to be considered when individuals are deciding whether to reproduce. Second, one's conclusions about the ethics of choosing whether to procreate may have implications for what the law should be. So, for example, if there are certain rights with respect to procreation, then society's legal framework may need to reflect and reinforce those rights. Existing reproductive laws may well be illegitimate and in need of modification or abolition. More generally, a society's social policies should support morally justified reproductive needs and choices and provide assistance in acting on them. Individuals making choices about procreation should not and cannot be regarded as acting in a social void, independent of other people and relationships or outside of the broader culture in which they live.

Main Questions

At least six general ethical questions should be considered in the ethics of choosing whether to have children:

1. What are good reasons for having a child?
2. Under what conditions is having children morally justified?
3. Do women ever have a moral obligation[14] to have a child?
4. What are good reasons for not having a child?
5. Under what conditions is having a child not morally justified?
6. Do women ever have a moral obligation not to have a child?

Notice that these questions are quite distinct. You might, for example, have good reasons to have a child without having any obligation to have a child. You might have good reasons not to have a child without having an obligation not to have that child. For example, one of your good reasons for having a child might be that you are "good with" children. But that fact in itself does not give you an obligation to have a child. One of your good reasons for not having a child may be the fact that you have a demanding career, but that reason in itself does not mean you have an obligation not to have a child.

In discussing these six questions, I for the most part set aside questions about what *kind* of child to have. An extensive literature discusses, pro and con, the ethics of choosing to have particular sorts of children, whether by embryo selection, cloning, or genetic enhancement (e.g., J. Harris 2007). Such questions are complex and fascinating. But this book examines the choice prior to deciding what kind of child to have and is concerned simply with whether to have a child or not. The discussion of children's own characteristics arises primarily in chapters 7 and 8, when I discuss the potential obligation not to have children.

Looking Ahead

The first important consideration in answering the six main questions is reproductive rights, in particular the reproductive rights of women. Chapter 2 is devoted to canvassing the scope and limits of reproductive rights with respect to the ethics of choosing to have children. I distinguish between the right to reproduce and the right not to reproduce, and I suggest that there are two different types of right to reproduce. I argue that simply appealing to reproductive rights by itself does not constitute a complete justification for choosing to have children. Yet acknowledging and respecting women's reproductive rights is essential to protecting women from procreative exploitation. In chapter 3, I discuss the situation in which prospective biological parents disagree about whether to continue a pregnancy that has already been initiated. Whose wishes should prevail? Is there a solution that attends to the interests of both prospective parents?

Chapters 4 and 5 are concerned with reasons for having children. The various purported justifications for having children that I investigate derive from historical sources, from contemporary culture, and, in a few cases, from philosophical debates. One list of putative reasons, for example, comes from a study undertaken by a then-philosophy graduate student, Leslie Cannold, of childless and so-called child-free women in the United States and Australia. The reasons these women suggested for having children include "the desire for the responsibility and commitment children require, the desire to take risks and to face new life challenges, to satisfy and/or keep their partner, to fulfil their (positively viewed) imagined future as a mother, . . . to love and to be loved by a child, to confirm their femininity and adulthood, to remain 'in-step' with their peers, to avoid loneliness, to affirm existing relationship bonds (like those with their own mothers), and to find existential meaning and fulfillment in their lives" (2003, 279).

For the most part, these reasons fall into one or the other of two familiar categories of ethical theory: deontology and consequentialism.[15]

Deontologists believe that certain acts or the practices and rules to which these acts are related—for example, keeping a promise—are right in themselves and that other acts—for example, murder—are wrong in themselves, independent of the consequences of the acts. Outcomes are not what make our choices morally justified; it is their conformity to certain moral rules. If you are a deontologist, you regard it as important to make the "why have children?" decision on the basis of doing what is inherently right and avoiding doing what is inherently wrong. Deontological reasons include what are, for some people, core values: the values of lineage, name, and property; religious duties; marital and familial duties; and even duties to the state. I discuss these reasons in chapter 4.

By contrast, consequentialism is the ethical theory that the rightness and wrongness of actions are entirely a function of their outcome. If you are a consequentialist, you regard it as important to make the "why have children?" decision on the basis of the anticipated consequences of having a child or not having a child. You would try to minimize the harmful consequences and to maximize, or at least to optimize, the good consequences. So, for example, some people have said that the justification for having children lies in benefits to the society or the benefits to the would-be parents and other members of the family, such as would-be grandparents and already-existing siblings. I discuss these reasons in chapter 5. Together, chapters 4 and 5 show that the reasons typically given for having children are not very strong and are insufficient to constitute an obligation to procreate. Indeed, most typical justifications for procreation implicitly or explicitly involve using women or children for others' purposes.

Now some might say that even if most reasons for having children are inadequate, there is usually at least one important and valid consequentialist reason for procreation: that children themselves are benefited by coming into existence. This idea is controversial. Some philosophers believe that individuals are neither benefited nor harmed by coming into existence and that, as a result, all reasons for procreation must necessarily be "other referring"; that is, they cannot have anything to do with the child's well-being because before being created, no one exists who can be affected by coming into existence. Other philosophers argue that coming into existence has the potential to be a benefit, but it can also be a harm, particularly if the child is born into severe poverty or abuse. Indeed, in a recent book tellingly titled *Better Never to Have Been: The Harm of Coming into Existence*, philosopher David Benatar argues vehemently that "coming into existence is *always* a serious harm" (2006, 1, emphasis added). If he is correct, then there appears to be a well-nigh insuperable reason that makes having children morally wrong. I think he is mistaken. In chapter 6, I point out various problems in Benatar's arguments and suggest that it is *not* always "better never to have been."

In chapter 7, I consider some possible reasons not to have children,[16] which are mostly consequentialist in nature, and I discuss whether there are cases where one might have an obligation not to have children. Potential reasons for the moral wrongness of having children include concerns such as the repressive effect of motherhood on women within cultures where being a woman is still a social disadvantage and the dangers of bringing a child into a severely impoverished, oppressive, or perilous social environment or of exposing a child to war or to life-threatening environmental threats. In chapter 8, I discuss the complicated questions of whether the risk of passing on serious disease or physical or mental impairments generates a responsibility not to procreate and whether persons with impairments of their own can justifiably choose to procreate.

On a global scale, the dangers of procreation go far beyond the individual: they include growing overpopulation and the strain on planet Earth's carrying capacity. The "why have children?" decision is, therefore, a big issue, having to do with fundamental institutions such as education and health care, the way we do business, our stewardship of the environment, our consumption of resources, and our care for each other. It more broadly raises questions about the value of humanity and the future of the planet. Should we care whether the human race persists or be sanguine about the possibility of human extinction? Both overpopulation and the possibility of extinction are the focus of chapter 9. Our procreative reflections raise deep-seated issues about the importance of human existence and the value of what we do and who we are, with all our frailties as well as our virtues.

Based on the discussion in the first nine chapters, I come to the conclusion that an approach to the ethics of choosing to have children that relies on reproductive rights, on deontological reasons, or on consequentialist reasoning is inadequate or incomplete. In chapter 10, I examine the possibility that the procreation decision, weighty as it is, ought to be seen as a kind of wager. Rejecting that approach, I then explore what procreation means to human beings in terms of our central values and our sense of identity. In becoming a parent, one not only creates a child but also re-creates oneself. To become a biological parent is to generate a new relationship—not just the genetic one, but a psychological, physical, intellectual, and moral one. I conclude by exploring the nature of the parent–child relationship at its best and argue that the formation of that relationship is the best possible reason for choosing to have a child.

2

Reproductive Freedom, Autonomy, and Reproductive Rights

The ground of the right to become a parent is indeed the interests of the potential parents. Becoming a parent is something that lends shape and meaning to one's life and often to a life that one shares with another parent; and evidence suggests that the interest is one that is very widely shared. So it is a natural candidate to ground a right. That right cannot be absolute, for two reasons: first, the standard feasibility test may in some cases be a problem, and it would be unreasonable to demand that unlimited medical resources be devoted to solving it; second, there are issues about the suitability of potential parents that worried (for example) J. S. Mill, who believed that the responsibilities of parenthood were beyond the capacity of some potential parents. So not everyone can, or should, become a parent.

—Sarah Hannan and Richard Vernon, *Parental Rights*

There are three main reasons for starting this exploration of the ethics of procreation with an examination of rights. First, moral rights are fundamental to much ethical debate, and reproductive rights have typically been emphasized in traditional discussions of procreative issues such as abortion and IVF. But as the quotation from Sarah Hannan and Richard Vernon suggests, reproductive rights are more complex than is often recognized. It is therefore necessary to delineate the scope and limits of reproductive rights; this discussion provides background for the rest of the book. Second, some people might assume that deciding to have a child is easily justified on the grounds that doing so is simply an expression of reproductive rights.[1] I examine whether this assumption is correct. Third, like many other rights, reproductive rights may also play a protective role, providing a moral defense against social and legal demands for certain kinds of procreative behavior. If a person has a right to do X, then it is morally wrong to prevent the person from doing X. If a person has a right not to do Y, then it is morally wrong to force the person to do Y. The protective function of reproductive rights must be clarified.

In this chapter, I develop a taxonomy of reproductive rights—what they are, how they are justified, and what their limits might be. My focus here is on *moral* rights, not legal rights. A moral right is an entitlement that we have good reason to accept, an entitlement that is an expression of one's humanity and that belongs to an individual by virtue of her or his being a human person. A moral right may or may not be legally recognized; that is, a moral entitlement may or may not be encoded within the laws of the state in which an individual lives, but it is no less real and morally significant even if it is not recognized by the state (Kates 2004). For example, the 1994 United Nations International Conference on Population and Development (UNICPD) affirmed "the basic right of all couples and individuals to decide freely and responsibly the number, spacing and timing of their children and to have the information and means to do so, and the right to attain the highest standard of sexual and reproductive health. It also includes the right of all to make decisions concerning reproduction free of discrimination, coercion and violence as expressed in human rights documents" (quoted in Kates 2004, 57). Even in the most repressive regimes, where there are few or no reproductive services or protections, individuals nonetheless still possess *moral* reproductive rights, despite their not being legally recognized.

I both identify our moral reproductive rights and discuss the kinds of state resources, services, and protections that those rights may indicate. A state that provides the resources, services, and protections supported by our moral reproductive rights is in fact according to its citizens legal reproductive rights, even if those legal rights are not formally stated and acknowledged.

Carol A. Kates claims that there is no need to recognize any special fundamental reproductive rights; we can be content with "a general right to liberty" (2004, 63). But subsuming reproductive rights under a general right to liberty may not be adequate both because of the profound value of reproduction to most individuals and societies as well as because of the far-reaching impact of procreation particularly on women. We might therefore say that reproductive rights have both a consequentialist and a deontological foundation.

First, having children is, for many people, deeply definitive of their identity and their life's value. For others, remaining childless is equally essential. Failing to have a child when one wants to be a parent can be a source of immense sorrow and regret. Becoming a parent against one's wish can be a lifelong burden. Hence, the protection of procreative choices by means of the recognition of reproductive rights is necessary both to ensure that people's lives go well and to prevent the misery, deprivation, and even oppression that results when people have little or no control over their procreative behavior. In addition, the well-being of children is dependent on the recognition of reproductive rights. Children may suffer if they are unwanted. Within families, unwanted children may be handicapped by scarce material resources, lack of attention, and stressed parenting. Within society at large, as we know from the past, unwanted children are likely to face inadequate provisions for their education, health care, and eventual employment. There are thus strong consequentialist reasons for articulating and protecting reproductive rights.

Second, women are particularly vulnerable with respect to procreation. Most women are fertile from their early teens until their late forties. Women conceive, gestate, deliver, and breastfeed their babies. Women are still expected to be the primary caregivers for their children. As a feminist, I therefore take women's bodily freedom (the absence of physical, legal, or social constraints on one's decisions about one's body) and autonomy (the capacity to be self-determining, especially with respect to one's body) to be the sine qua non for women's equality and full citizenship. The deontological basis for reproductive rights is that they are indispensable to protecting women's personhood. Without moral recognition and legal protection of their bodily freedom and autonomy, women are little more than procreative slaves. It is essential to respect women's bodily freedom and autonomy because it is simply wrong to subject women to forced reproduction; it is wrong to use women as a means to others' reproductive goals. Such treatment violates their personhood. (A similar claim might also be made about men with regard to the use of men's gametes, but the fact that gestation is a female condition makes respect for bodily freedom and autonomy particularly significant for women.)

Thus, there are both consequentialist and deontological justifications for reproductive rights. Those rights, properly delineated and understood, provide the foundation for the ethics of procreation. They are a necessary (though not sufficient) criterion for evaluating procreative decisions. And, as I argue in later chapters, because reproductive rights are foundational, they cannot be disregarded or voided.

Nonetheless, to say that essential reproductive rights must be recognized does not imply that there is an unlimited right to reproduce. Respect for bodily freedom and autonomy does not constitute a license to procreate. For example, as Onora O'Neill points out, if, like Jean-Jacques Rousseau and his mistress, individuals simply produced infants and then abandoned them at a foundling hospital, we would not be inclined to say such persons were justifiably exercising their right to procreate (1979, 25).

I propose that the general idea of reproductive rights should be analyzed in terms of two distinct prima facie rights—that is, rights that are "conditional on not being overridden by other relevant moral principles" (Frankena and Granrose 1974, 80). These prima facie rights are the right to reproduce and the right not to reproduce. Prima facie rights are strong entitlements that make legitimate calls on the behavior of others—either individuals or the state (or both)—but they are not defeasible. They can sometimes, though perhaps only rarely, be superseded by other moral requirements—for example, when rights are in conflict with each other.

Let's look first at the right to reproduce. In my early work on reproductive ethics and social policy (Overall 1987, 1993), I distinguished between two different kinds of right to reproduce: the positive or welfare right and the negative or liberty right.

The Right to Reproduce in the Positive or Welfare Sense

The prima facie right to have children in the positive or welfare sense is an entitlement to have a child by any means one may choose and to be provided with all possible assistance in reproduction. Although there arguably is such a right, and it provides important protections, it is nonetheless limited in some important ways.

Reproductive services should be seen for what they are: a category of health care. As a category of health care, reproductive services ought to be available to and accessible by potential patients on medical grounds. Social discrimination in the provision of reproductive services is just as unfair and unjustified as social discrimination in the provision of other forms of health care, and anyone who opposes social discrimination for the latter should oppose it for the former. Hence, an individual patient's gender identity, race, sexual orientation, marital status, and other identity characteristics are not justified criteria either for providing or for refusing medical treatment because they are not relevant to health care for the individual's medical condition. For example, if a married heterosexual woman is entitled to reproductive treatment X, then so is a single woman or a lesbian woman. The single woman and the lesbian woman should not be denied access to donor insemination or IVF just because of their marital status or sexuality.

In general, the social identity of potential patients is irrelevant to whether they should be permitted reproductive services. For a number of reasons, it is morally wrong for the medical profession to use social identity criteria to determine who is entitled to become a parent, who is competent to become a parent, or, for that matter, who lacks the characteristics for parenthood.

First, physicians are not trained or qualified to determine who is and is not competent to become a parent. A physician's role is to provide medical care, not to serve as a gatekeeper to parenthood. There is no reason to believe that physicians have a special ability to discern parenting capacities. Moreover, attempting to be such a gatekeeper would compromise physicians' moral responsibilities to serve their patients' best interests because it would make reference to standards that are independent of and even incompatible with the patient's health care.

Second, individuals who do not seek reproductive services are not subjected to any test or qualification for parenting. If there is no screening system for prospective parents who do not need reproductive services, it seems unjust to subject to screening those who have the misfortune of needing medical help. Although some philosophers have argued that there should be a licensing system for prospective parents (see, for example, Tittle 2004), such a system would be a severe imposition on people's bodily freedom and autonomy, would be grotesquely unwieldy, would consume enormous resources that can better be used to support good health and good parenting, and would not likely improve the care of children.

Third, there is no clear empirical method for predicting which individuals will be good parents and which will not. Certain factors no doubt make parenting easier (perhaps training about children's development and needs) or harder (serious socioeconomic deprivation). If so, then instead of requiring physicians to make ad hoc predictions in individual cases, it would be better for a society that is concerned about the quality of parenting to provide good education, health care, and socioeconomic support for all its citizens, including children, parents, and prospective parents.

Fourth, there is no empirical evidence that social identity in itself either compromises or enhances parenting abilities. It is unjustified to generalize about all persons with a particular identity. Contrary to social conservatives' protests, single women have been successfully rearing children in greater and greater numbers for the past half-century. The evidence shows that lesbians' children turn out fine (Gartrell and Bos 2010). And, in contrast, some married, heterosexual parents physically and psychologically abuse their children.

One's age, impairments, and health history are similarly in principle relevant to one's eligibility for reproductive services *only* on medical grounds—that is, if these characteristics demonstrably make such services either ineffective or dangerous to the individual seeking them. It is not up to physicians to make judgments about whether a patient's age or impairment renders her ineligible for motherhood. (In chapter 7, however, I discuss the significance of one's age for the moral justification of one's procreative choices, and in chapter 8 I say more about parenting decisions by persons with impairments.) Thus, if a person is simply not healthy enough to undergo a particular medical treatment, if there is little or no prospect that the medical treatment will help the individual, or if it in fact will even harm the individual, then it is legitimate not to provide the treatment. For example, if the body of an older woman or a woman with an impairment does not respond to hormonal hyperstimulation, then it is medically unjustified to persist in attempting to extract ova from her. The cessation of treatment would be based on empirical evidence of likely ineffectiveness or harm, not on the mere fact that the patient is a certain age or has a particular impairment.

Hence, the right to reproduce in the positive sense can be construed as protecting individuals against unjustified discrimination in access to reproductive services, which ought not to be denied to individuals on any grounds but medical ones.

However, because the positive right to reproduce draws upon others' material resources and services, it cannot be boundless. To what sorts of reproductive services might a positive right to reproduce allow access? My answer here should be considered somewhat tentative and suggestive only, for much depends on two factors: a society's general level of affluence and the resulting availability of money and resources for health care, and the kinds of decisions the society may make about health-care goals and priorities. For example, societies with scarce resources are entitled to decide whether they will provide IVF services. In some societies, other services may legitimately be considered more immediately valuable, including preventive health services, pregnancy care, infant and maternal care, medical treatments for various impairments, and so on. I do not attempt here to determine how such priorities might be evaluated. The issue is complex and difficult; debating the relative value of different health-care goals and priorities would require a book of its own. My discussion in the rest of this section is intended simply to indicate the kinds of considerations that would be relevant to determining the health-care implications of the positive right to reproduce, given adequate resources and a careful assessment of priorities.

I suggest that the right to reproduce requires minimally the provision of health-care services for healthy pregnancy and delivery, including well-supported home birth and midwifery when these options are chosen. Depending on the society's assets and resources, the positive right to reproduce may also entitle patients to reproductive services that alleviate infertility, including the surgical repair of damaged fallopian tubes in women, the reversal of a vasectomy in men, and, for women, intrauterine sperm injection or trials of IVF with a willing, competent, informed, and autonomous partner.[2] All of these procedures increase the likelihood that an individual may become a parent, although of course they do not guarantee anyone a baby, especially in the case of IVF, for which success rates are still much less than 50 percent.[3]

A society may nonetheless be entitled to place appropriate limits on *how* some reproductive services are provided. IVF is a good example. Having access to IVF does not automatically entitle a woman to determine how the procedure will be carried out, for that issue is a medical matter. Being provided with IVF does not give a woman patient the entitlement to have as many embryos as she wishes inserted into her uterus. Although inserting a large number of embryos increases the woman's chances of becoming pregnant, it also exacerbates the probability of higher-order multiples (HOM)—triplets, quadruplets, quintuplets, sextuplets, and more. Such pregnancies are dangerous for the woman and for the fetuses; HOMs require vastly more health-care services—during gestation and birth, in the neonatal period, and often beyond—than do singletons. (Think of the case of American "Octomom" Nadya Suleman, who after IVF ended up gestating and delivering eight fetuses.) Hence, a hospital is entitled to set a policy limiting the number of embryos implanted—perhaps to two or three.

Second, access to IVF does not include an automatic entitlement to use the procedure at any age. Despite the fact that some women have become pregnant and given birth, thanks to IVF, at the age of sixty or older, there are good medical reasons, related to the woman's health risks, her ability to sustain a pregnancy, and perhaps her offspring's prospective physical health, not to permit IVF for every postmenopausal woman who may want it. I am not saying that no "older" woman should ever have access to IVF; I am simply reiterating my earlier point that health-care professionals are entitled to use *medical* criteria to determine the patient's suitability for the procedure. The situation must be decided on a case-by-case basis according to the woman's medical condition.

Third, there is no automatic entitlement to have as many individual IVF treatments as the patient may wish for. In some cases, a large number of treatments may turn out to be medically futile. If so, then there is a significant question of health-care resource allocation. If a society does determine that it will offer IVF, as I have argued, it must not discriminate on irrelevant grounds in providing access to such services, but it is entitled to place limits on the number of treatments an individual woman may have. Doing so is in part a matter of medical effectiveness, but in part also a matter of straightforward fairness with respect to a limited and expensive service. A woman may have no more than x treatments simply because other women also need IVF treatments, and if one woman has many treatments, then others will have fewer. Thus, issues of fairness among individuals with similar needs dictate that no woman can just demand a large number of IVF treatments as part of her right to reproduce and expect automatic compliance.

So far, then, I have suggested that there is a positive right to reproduce and that in a society with good health-care resources exercising that right might include access to a variety of treatments intended to support pregnancy and birth and to enhance, repair, or restore fertility. Access to these services should not be denied based on social identity characteristics such as marital status or sexual orientation, nor should it be denied on the basis of age, health status, or impairment unless the latter are *medically* relevant to the provision of services.

But the right to reproduce in the positive or welfare sense has one additional important and indefeasible limit: it does not and cannot include an *entitlement* to consumerlike activities such as buying and selling gametes or purchasing the services of a contract procreator because no one has a right to the use of others' sperm or ova or a right to have another woman gestate and give birth to a baby for them. There can be no *entitlement* to such activities because to satisfy such supposed entitlements would require that one or more other people must provide bodily products or services. There cannot be a moral requirement for anyone to provide sperm or eggs or to serve as a gestator; such a requirement would violate other women's or men's bodily freedom and autonomy.[4] Respect for women's and men's bodily freedom and autonomy obviates the possibility of compelling some women to provide ova or to undergo pregnancy or of compelling men to provide sperm, even to facilitate procreation by other women.

Some individuals may (for whatever reasons, including perhaps the dubious desire for genetic "immortality") wish to donate their gametes (sperm or ova). Such donations can be very helpful to people who are struggling with infertility. But the donor cannot expect a guarantee that the gametes will actually be used or even that a health-care facility should have to take the gametes if there are medical reasons not to.

If a particular jurisdiction offers sperm or egg banks, donors to which have given willing, competent, informed, and autonomous consent, then women who are candidates for using donated sperm or eggs ought not to be discriminated against on irrelevant grounds if they seek access to them. But no individual has an obligation to donate or sell their gametes; hence, no other individual has a right to be given them or buy them. If a particular society does not offer gamete donation, or if it does offer the service and no one chooses to supply gametes, then, nonetheless, the rights of those who may want or need others' gametes have not been violated.

There is never a guarantee that an individual will be able to have a baby, and it is a mistake to say that a woman (or a man) has a "right to a baby" or a "right to a family." This claim is true for several reasons. There is no guarantee of obtaining a baby biologically even through the use of one's own gametes and pregnancy, for some women cannot conceive, some pregnancies end prematurely, and some births fail to yield a live infant. But there are also no guarantees morally and politically, for people are not entitled to keep a child, even a child that came out of their body, whom they abuse. There is no guarantee through adoption because no one has a *right* to someone else's baby, although at times some women are generous enough to give up their infants for adoption. There is no guarantee through the use of someone else's gametes because no one has a *right* to someone else's gametes, and no one owes an in-need person their gametes. There is no guarantee through contract pregnancy because no one has a *right* that a woman will provide gestational services, and no woman owes another person the child of her pregnancy. Insofar as reproduction for some people requires the use of and access to other individuals' bodies and bodily products, there is no positive right to reproduce in that manner.[5] Saying this does not mean that all of these activities are necessarily wrong, only that they cannot be justified as the exercise of a moral right, for no one has an obligation to provide gametes or gestational services.

An additional limit to the prima facie right to reproduce in the positive sense is that individuals do not have a right to the best possible baby or even to the kind of baby they most want. Although women certainly are entitled to good prenatal and neonatal care, there can be no guarantees about the characteristics of the resulting infant. Ben Bova claims, "An individual's desire to produce offspring that are as close to the ideal that the parent can envision seems well within the rights of any citizen" (1998, 194). He makes this claim by contrast to the idea that a government would be entitled to run a eugenics program, an idea that he rejects. But individuals don't have an *entitlement* to engage in their own private eugenics program either. Although there is a strong case for helping people with infertility to increase their chances of procreating, the case for helping people to obtain a "designer baby" is much weaker.

People are, of course, free to choose among consenting adults with whom to reproduce—or they should be. Such decisions in themselves have an effect on the kind of child they will have. But whether they are entitled to the complex genetic services—including IVF and embryo screening—that would enable them to make more precise choices is a further issue and a complicated one. Much depends on the costs of such services compared to other health-care costs. Societies have to make policy decisions as to which kinds of health care should be provided. Consider, for example, the possible funding of hearing aids for the hearing impaired, prostheses for those missing all or part of a limb, and wheelchairs for those whose mobility is reduced. It is not at all obvious that these items are less important than funding the capacity to choose the best baby possible. Even in a nation where health care is not publicly funded, there will still be questions as to what sorts of medical research, education, and training should be supported and encouraged; as I pointed out earlier, choices about health-care priorities have to be made.

The potential justification of seeking to produce the best possible baby also depends on the reason that screening is needed. It would be far more controversial to screen embryos for intelligence, beauty, or athletic ability than it would ever be to screen them for the presence of diseases, such as Tay-Sachs, that will cause unrelieved suffering. In chapter 7, I discuss whether parents have any *obligation* to enhance their offspring by choosing the best available embryo, and in chapter 8 I return to the topic of prenatal screening when I explore whether there is an obligation in some circumstances *not* to procreate because of the fetus's condition.

The Right to Reproduce in the Negative or Liberty Sense

Although there are several actual and potential limits on the right to reproduce in the positive sense, there are no comparable limits on the prima facie right to reproduce in the negative or liberty sense. This right is the entitlement not to be interfered with in procreation, and it is primarily this reproductive right that is asserted in the consensus statement from the UNICPD quoted earlier. The right to reproduce in this sense means the freedom to decide when, where, and with whom one will have one's biological children and how many. Of course, no man is *entitled* to have his female partner produce a baby for him, any more than a woman has an entitlement to be given her male partner's sperm. But if two people agree to reproduce together using their own gametes, they are entitled not to be interfered with or prevented by third parties.

What, then, about the right to reproduce in the negative sense with respect to women in a same-sex relationship? They have the same reproductive rights as persons in heterosexual relationships; the state has no right to prevent them from having children if they choose. But their situation is, of course, *reproductively* more complex. They need the collaboration of one more person. As I explained earlier, no one has an entitlement to another person's reproductive gametes. But if a third person agrees willingly, competently, and autonomously to collaborate by providing his sperm, then women in a same-sex relationship are entitled not to be interfered with in their decisions about when, where, and with whom to procreate or about how many children to have.

Honoring the right to reproduce in the negative sense would also require the provision of at least a minimally healthy physical environment and working conditions that do not damage or compromise one's procreative capacities. People are entitled to be protected from environments and employments that are dangerous to their health, including their reproductive health. It would also mean no interference in or limitation of one's biological procreative behavior. Thus, respecting the negative right to reproduce requires that there can be no forced sterilization, no coercive contraception,[6] no forced marriage or prostitution, no racist marriage or domestic partnership laws, no forced abortions, and no forced caesarians (all of which are, of course, wrong on other grounds, too).

The Right Not to Reproduce

Women and men also have a clear right *not* to reproduce. The right not to reproduce means that human beings are entitled not to be compelled to reproduce against their will. No one should be compelled to give away or sell their gametes or embryos against their will. No woman should be compelled to undergo pregnancy or continue it against her will. This right is implicit in what I said earlier, in discussing limits on the right to reproduce, about the absence of entitlement to other people's reproductive resources and services. Indeed, I suggest that the right not to reproduce is morally more basic than the right to reproduce, at least in the sense that it is strongly unethical to violate one individual's right not to reproduce in order to serve another individual's right to reproduce.

As I noted in chapter 1, pregnancy sometimes results because contraception is simply not used, whether because it is not available or not chosen or because the individuals are unaware of it or the need for it. In other cases, heterosexual intercourse is voluntary, but although children are not wanted, there is no effective contraception, or contraceptive methods are inadequate or are incorrectly used. And conception is sometimes unchosen because it is the result of rape. Therefore, respecting the right not to reproduce requires comprehensive education about sex and procreation, access to safe and effective contraception and to timely and effective abortion services, and protection from compulsory heterosexual intercourse, whether by assault or by forced marriage. Of course, just as there is no guarantee that one will receive a baby after pregnancy and birth, so also there is no guarantee that contraception will work. That is a fact that women must always take into account. It is also a fact that men must accept, as I show in chapter 3.

The justification for recognizing the negative right to reproduce is simply that if it is not respected, then women especially, but men too, have no choice of or control over their biological reproductive behavior, and therefore their bodily freedom and autonomy are violated. All women, like men, have a right *not* to reproduce—that is, a right not to be forced to reproduce, whether through sexual slavery, denial of access to contraception, or lack of access to abortion.[7] Because some women have historically been forced against their will into marriage or prostitution, women's right not to reproduce is important whatever their sexual orientation may be. Part of what is morally wrong about forced marriage and prostitution is that it makes women vulnerable to unwanted procreation; it violates their right not to reproduce.

Any violation of the right not to reproduce is serious. No individual should be forced to provide her or his gametes to another person, whether for procreation or for research. No woman should ever be forced to undergo pregnancy against her will. In the words of D. S. Hutchinson, in unwanted pregnancy "the body is being altered for a purpose that does not belong to the person. But this is a case where the body is not just used, but transformed. The transformation is different in kind from the bodily changes involved in ordinary actions, for it is a transformation of a very special nature. It results in two people where there was previously only one." In unwanted pregnancy, the woman's body "is treated as a means to a project that is alien to [her;] it involves an alienation of the body from the person." It thereby undermines her integrity because "a commitment to one's body is given in the human condition" (1982, 71). If the right not to reproduce is not respected, then the result is reproductive slavery: the compulsory and unwilled use of people's bodies for procreative purposes—whether they are other individuals' or the state's purposes.

(Reproductive coercion—the production of babies through the forced, often violent use of women's bodies—is a standard feature of enslaved societies and is part of what makes enslavement morally execrable.) People need to be able to protect their reproductive capacities and not have them exploited or coerced to serve purposes that are not their own. As I argued at the beginning of this chapter, genuine reproductive freedom is one of the essential building blocks of a just and flourishing society.

Conclusion

What does this discussion of reproductive rights tell us about the "why have children?" ethical decision?

The right not to reproduce and the right to reproduce in the negative sense (the entitlement to freedom from interference) are grounded in general human interests; people need protection from compulsory procreation as much as (or perhaps even more than) they need protection from denied procreation. The appeal to the right not to reproduce also provides important protections to women (as well as to men) insofar as it provides a strong prima facie argument against any obligation to procreate. If a woman has a right not to reproduce, then she is prima facie not obligated to reproduce. In chapters 4 and 5, I investigate whether there are any factors that can create such an obligation despite the prima facie right not to reproduce.

Moreover, the appeal to the right to reproduce in the negative sense is inadequate to serve as a complete ethical justification for choosing to have children because, as subsequent chapters show, many other factors are morally relevant to procreative decisions. The fact that interfering in an individual's procreative behavior violates the individual's right to reproduce does not by itself morally justify the individual's decision to reproduce. At the same time, the right to reproduce in the positive sense is limited by a variety of factors and does not guarantee a baby to anyone.

In other words, a general appeal to reproductive rights cannot be used to vindicate a wholesale entitlement to procreate, to be given a baby, or to parent. Among the reasons for this claim, the most obvious is that in making the decision to procreate, a new human being will be brought into existence. As S. L. Floyd and D. Pomerantz put it in regard to a putatively unlimited right to self-determination, "It does not take into account the impossibility of a being's actual or hypothetical consent to becoming a child" (2004, 232). Of course, by the very nature of the situation, the prospective child cannot consent. And the impossibility of the child's consent does not make all procreation wrong. At the very least, however, the prospective well-being of the child-to-be is surely relevant to the ethics of choosing to have children. That issue is one to which I return several times.

A second reason that the right to reproduce, whether positive or negative, is not by itself sufficient to justify procreation has to do, broadly speaking, with resource issues, including the constraints generated by the growing human population and the planet's limited carrying capacity. I explore this latter set of issues in the penultimate chapter.

A third reason that the right to reproduce is not by itself sufficient to justify procreation is provided by the need for a procreative partner. It still takes two to make a baby, if not by sexual intercourse, then by other means of combining egg and sperm. Several times in this chapter, I have added the caveat that one must have a willing, informed, competent, and autonomous reproductive partner. No one has a *right* to another person's sexual services or procreative capacities, and no one has a *right* of access to another person's gametes. No one is entitled to obtain them by force or by subterfuge. Consent to providing reproductive capacities and gametes is essential.

The content and structure of reproductive rights leave open the possibility that there might sometimes be an obligation not to reproduce. Acting on one's rights, including the right to reproduce, is not always morally justified. One may have the right to do something that is nonetheless not morally justified. Reproductive rights are a necessary but not sufficient condition for justifying choosing to have children.

Therefore, the next topic to be considered is the situation where potential parents disagree—in particular, where they disagree as to whether to continue a pregnancy or not. In such cases, one or the other partner does not consent to procreate. How might such disputes be resolved?

3

When Prospective Parents Disagree

What is the morally justified path when the two individuals in a couple disagree about whether to continue their pregnancy or not?[1] Various approaches have been proposed to resolve such disagreements. Some aspects of these disagreements have been explored in the recent work of several American philosophers, and I try to make sense of what I think are patterns in their work. Here I am not discussing the question of *whether* to conceive a child or not, but rather the question of forming a morally justifiable resolution when two people disagree, particularly in the context of a pregnancy that is already in progress.

In the standard case, the two partners would be the male and the female, and that is the situation on which I focus. I sometimes refer to them as the "inseminator" and the "gestator"—not "father" and "mother," the use of which I think begs the question. I should also point out, however, that some of the issues I'm interested in here may also occur in the case of two female partners, one of whom is pregnant.[2]

There are two themes to this debate: (1) the reproductive freedom of both women and men—but especially of women because without it women's lives and prospects are severely limited; and (2) the inseminators' rights—or at least, inseminators' *alleged* rights, which have turned out to be the focus of much debate both in academic and nonacademic publications.

The Disagreements and How Some Philosophers Resolve Them

Consider table 3.1. Quadrant 1 is presumably uncontroversial. For feminists and others with progressive politics, Quadrant 4 also seems morally straightforward, assuming that one is not opposed on moral grounds to abortion[3] or adoption.

Table 3.1
Prospective Parents' Attitudes toward Pregnancy

	She wants the baby.	She doesn't want the baby.
He wants the baby.	1. Gestate and raise it.	3. ???
He doesn't want the baby.	2. ???	4. Abort the fetus. Or gestate it and surrender the infant for adoption.

In Quadrant 2, the male (the inseminator) does not want to be a parent, but his female partner is pregnant, and she wants to be a parent. Among other things, this means that she has no interest in having an abortion. And in Canada and the United States, he cannot legally *force* her to abort. In Quadrant 3, the male *does* want to be a parent, but his female partner who is pregnant does not. She can choose to have an abortion; in Canada and the United States, he cannot legally prevent her.

Several philosophers have recently explored the dilemmas raised by Quadrants 2 and 3—among them Steven D. Hales (1996a, 1996b), Elizabeth Brake (2005), Jennifer S. Bard (2006), Bertha Alvarez Manninen (2007), Dien Ho (2008), and Don Hubin (2008).[4] Their primary philosophical concern is the protection of what they see as the inseminator's needs and rights rather than the protection of women's reproductive freedom.

Resolving Quadrant 2
According to American philosopher Dien Ho, couples' disagreements about their reproductive plans are morally troubling because of what he calls "procreative asymmetry" (2008, 1). The problem of "procreative asymmetry" is that women can make unilateral procreative decisions (insofar as they can legally choose, on their own, whether to continue the pregnancy or abort), but men cannot because they can legally neither prevent nor compel an abortion. This asymmetry generates a problematic limitation, according to Ho, on the scope of the male's reproductive freedom because men may become fathers against their will: "Considering the harm done by allowing the asymmetry to exist (i.e., giving gestating women a unilateral right to determine procreation for their unwilling partners), there is a moral imperative to attempt to achieve parity through

some compensatory mechanism" (2008, 13–14). Steven D. Hales expresses the problem, as he sees it, even more unambiguously:

The father, having participated in conception, cannot escape the future duties he
will have toward the child. The father can decide that he cannot afford another
child, that he is not psychologically prepared to be a parent, that a child would
hinder the lifestyle he wishes to pursue, and so on, to no avail. He is completely
subject to the decisions of the mother. If she decides to have the child, she thereby
ensures that the father has certain duties; duties that it is impossible for him to
avoid. Even more, the mother is solely in charge: If she wants to have an abortion
and the father does not want her to, she may anyway. If she does *not* want to have
an abortion and the father does want her to, it is permissible for her to refuse
to have one. If there is any conflict between the mother and the father here, the
mother's wishes win out. (1996a, 8, his emphasis)

Moreover, both Dien Ho and Don Hubin are concerned about what
they see as the dangers of deceptive women.[5] Both worry about the woman who lies to her male partner, saying that she takes the contraceptive pill
but then conceives even though her male partner has been absolutely clear
that he does not want to have children with her (see Ho 2008, 16). Such
a woman, they say, is violating the inseminator's reproductive freedom.[6]
Ho writes, "No one should be *allowed* to make procreative decisions for
another competent individual who is unwilling to procreate" (2008, 16,
my emphasis). Hubin also worries about cases such as that of the "purloined sperm," in which a woman offered a man oral sex provided he
used a condom. She then used the sperm from the condom to inseminate
herself (2008, 31). Hubin writes, "We do not generally hold people morally responsible for the consequences of other actions that they performed
as a result of malicious deception" (2008, 26).

With respect to resolving the disagreement in Quadrant 2, Ho distinguishes procreative autonomy from bodily autonomy. He argues that
women's unilateral right to terminate pregnancy is an instance of the latter, not the former. Women, like other human beings, are entitled to have
dominion over their bodies (2008, 14); hence, they can obtain abortions.
Women do not, however, have procreative autonomy, he says, if that
means making unilateral procreative decisions for other people: "No one
should be allowed to make procreative decisions for another competent
individual who is unwilling to procreate" (2008, 16).

Hales also acknowledges women's bodily autonomy. He admits that
no woman should be compelled to have an abortion against her will.

Hence, he argues that in order to preserve what he regards as each partner's equal procreative rights, the nongestating partner (usually male, but possibly female) has no obligation to provide support for the resulting infant:

> In order for us to satisfy our goal of achieving equality as best we can, we should not only admit that fathers have a right to avoid future duties, but there needs to be some mechanism by which they can, by personal fiat, exercise that right. . . . Perhaps it will do to say that, sometime during the span of time that a mother may permissibly abort, a father may simply declare that he refuses to assume any future obligations. . . . Let us put it this way: A man has the moral right to decide not to become a father (in the social, nonbiological sense) during the time that the woman he has impregnated may permissibly abort. He can make a unilateral decision whether to refuse fatherhood, and is not morally obliged to consult with the mother or any other person before reaching a decision. Moreover, neither the mother nor any other person can veto or override a man's decision about becoming a father. He has first and last say about what he does with his life in this regard. (1996a, 11–12)

The principle of equal rights requires, Hales argues, that the woman can't be compelled to abort a fetus that she wants and the man can't be compelled to raise a child he does not want. Thus, Hales interprets the situation as a matter of respect for reproductive rights. In Hales's view, by means of his resolution both preferences are respected: that of the gestator who wants to have a child and that of the inseminator who does not. In effect, the inseminator declares himself to have no moral, psychological, social, or material connection to the resulting offspring. In the words of George W. Harris, the man in these cases "has not given his consent to the use of his body for the pursuit of her interest in procreation" (1986, 597). Hence, the fact that he is the biological father "is not sufficient either to give him rights to the child or to put him under an obligation to it or to the mother" (1986, 598 fn. 1).

Elizabeth Brake likewise argues for what she regards as complete parity of reasoning between women and men: "If women's partial responsibility for pregnancy does not obligate them to support a fetus, then men's partial responsibility for a pregnancy does not obligate them to support a resulting child," particularly in a case where a man uses contraceptives in a nonmarital relationship (2005, 56). Mel Feit, the director of the US-based National Center for Men, similarly says that when contraception fails, men should have a choice about whether to continue their legal and financial responsibilities to the future child. Then "women have a right to know what that choice is as they decide how to proceed" (quoted in Gibbs 2006). Feit calls this choice a "financial abortion" (quoted in Gibbs 2006).

Resolving Quadrant 3

In Quadrant 3, the pregnant woman does not want to be a parent, but the man who impregnated her does. Bertha Alvarez Manninen writes, "To have an abortion in these circumstances will probably result in great emotional harm for the man, for it robs him of the child he so desperately desires" (2007, 3). Manninen believes that women should not be compelled to gestate; a man has no right that she should do so against her will. Nonetheless, in order to resolve their disagreement, a virtuous woman who does not want her baby should, at least in some circumstances, be willing to take the pregnancy to term for the sake of an inseminator who does want the baby. In effect, Manninen is advocating a form of altruistic contract pregnancy in which the woman agrees to continue a pregnancy (but without payment, as in the case of commercial contract motherhood) in order to bestow a child on the biological father, a child that she herself does not want. So that is one proposed resolution of the conflict in Quadrant 3.

Another possible resolution would have the couple resort to ectogenesis.[7] Ectogenesis is the gestation of a fetus outside the female body. The woman who does not want to be a parent may satisfy her goal not to be a parent by having the fetus removed from her uterus; it can then be placed in an artificial uterus to be brought to maturity for the man to raise. As far as I know, no one has directly defended the use of ectogenesis in cases where the inseminator wants a baby that the gestator rejects. Nonetheless, in recent discussions at conferences and in published papers it has been suggested that ectogenesis will resolve or transform related dilemmas about care of the fetus and parental obligations. Therefore, although ectogenesis is not yet practically possible, it is in the philosophical air (so to speak).

And it is certainly well within the purview of Ho's thinking; he not only argues against prohibiting ectogenesis but also speculates that ectogenesis "might permit the traditionally non-gestating partner to share the responsibility of fetal development in a more equitable fashion" (2006, 145). Jennifer S. Bard similarly argues that with ectogenesis "there is no longer any reason to priviledge [*sic*] a mother's right to terminate a pregnancy over the father's since both mothers and fathers have made biologically equivalent contributions towards the creation of a new life." She adds: "It seems a short leap from the ability to continue a pregnancy in an artificial womb to the *requirement* that every unwanted pregnancy must be completed in an artificial womb" (2006, 150–151, 152, my emphasis).

A defender of the ectogenesis solution might also point out that if the fetus is removed from the unwillingly pregnant woman's body, her bodily autonomy appears to have been respected. As Ho writes, "The bodily autonomy move draws the right line in that what distinguishes gestating women from their non-gestating partner is not gender but geography" (2008, 18). Once again, according to Ho, bodily autonomy does not imply procreative autonomy if the latter involves making another person a parent against his will.

We can now add to table 3.1 the various philosophical views I have briefly described here (see table 3.2).

Note that if we admit the possibility of ectogenesis as a resolution for disagreement in Quadrant 3, then ectogenesis may also become relevant to the situation in Quadrant 4, wherein there is no disagreement between gestator and inseminator simply because a new outcome for the fetus is then imaginable.

In the rest of this chapter, I discuss whether these philosophers are correct in their assessment of the morality of disagreements between the gestator and the inseminator. I also present and defend an approach to the situations in Quadrants 2 and 3 that is different from those presented so far. The primary questions are: What are the prospective parents' moral obligations, if any? And how can reproductive freedom and rights for both women and men best be respected and promoted in cases where their intentions or goals conflict, while minimizing harm, especially to the woman as gestator and to the potential infant?

Evaluating Solutions to the "She Wants the Baby and He Doesn't" Dilemma

The "procreative asymmetry" identified by Ho is generated, he thinks, because we have a justified moral commitment to both women's and men's

Table 3.2
Philosophers' Proposed Solutions to Disagreements between Prospective Parents

	She wants the baby.	**She doesn't want the baby.**
He wants the baby.	Gestate and raise it.	*Manninen:* To avoid the man's potential suffering, the virtuous solution is for the woman to gestate and give the infant to the male parent to raise. *Ho:* She can abort. But ectogenesis, as a possible solution, should not be prohibited. *Bard:* Ectogenesis might be morally required.
He doesn't want the baby.	*Ho:* She is entitled to bodily autonomy but not to procreative autonomy. *Brake:* Men's causal responsibility for pregnancy is not sufficient for moral responsibility for the child. *Hubin:* Men should not be victimized by women who become pregnant via deception. *Hales:* If she has the baby, the male parent has no moral obligation to support it.	Abort the fetus. Or gestate it and surrender the infant for adoption. Or possibly resort to ectogenesis.

equal moral rights and duties (2008, 2). But equality need not mean "sameness," and in the context of procreation sameness is, in some respects at least, impossible. On the contrary, because the biological roles of women and men are so different, both in the past and at present, the burden of justification rests upon anyone who says that the practical expression of women's and men's reproductive rights and duties must nonetheless in practice be precisely the same. The fact is that there are huge differences in what we might call "sweat equity" between what women contribute and what men contribute in ordinary procreation. A man, on the one hand, merely needs to produce viable sperm and be capable of erection and ejaculation. A woman, on the other hand, must be able to produce viable ova and sustain a pregnancy. Her body devotes nine months to the creation and nourishment of the fetus, after which she labors and delivers the baby. The amount of work and physical and psychological "investment" by the woman and the man, respectively, is staggeringly different in quantity and quality. Therefore, there should be no prima facie assumption that in practice the reproductive rights and duties of women and men must be expressed in exactly the same way.

So what is the morally correct solution if a woman and a man disagree about whether to continue the pregnancy or not? To make the problem as stark as possible, let us suppose, in line with Hubin's worries, that the woman used deception in order to become pregnant.

The woman clearly is morally wrong to have deceived her sex partner, and in no way would I defend her for that. I would insist both that she is wrong in what she did and that she had no right to do it. But Hales's solution, absolving the inseminator of any parental responsibilities if he does not want them, simply means that the child pays for the gestator's deception. The infant had no involvement in or choice about coming into existence. It is also not in the baby's interests for the inseminator to be absolved of all moral and economic responsibility resulting from sexual activity in which the inseminator chose to participate. I suggest that the child's interests in being well supported and cared for must trump the inseminator's interests in not being a parent. Hence, it is not fair to the future child to allow his future father to have what Feit calls a "financial abortion." As a social practice, it makes sense to hold men materially responsible for the children they help to create. Women's entitlement to abort a fetus is, contra Brake, in no way analogous to men's supposed entitlement not to support their offspring, even if those men used contraception, because a child is not morally analogous to a fetus.

Now it might be objected that it cannot be good for the child to be on the receiving end of obligations owed by a reluctant, dissenting, perhaps even angry father. True. For that reason, it seems implausible that the inseminator would be morally required to interact with the child and play an active role in raising it if he genuinely does not want to. Nonetheless, it is entirely plausible to expect that the man should be held both legally and morally responsible for at least the financial support of the child to the degree that he is capable of it and notwithstanding the mother's own obligation to contribute to the child's financial support.

It is of course essential that the scope and limits of the man's capacity to pay be taken into account if a formal determination is made of his finances. Brake makes much of the possibility that a man might be unfairly burdened by paying child support. She imagines an oil-field worker or welder or other laborer expressing his feelings about being a mere resource for the child he is supporting: "'A good percentage of my labor does not benefit me; it is like slavery. And I face another seventeen years of this, with no chance to better myself'" (2005, 65–66). I am not advocating that any man be placed in a situation of destitution, extreme suffering, or servitude in order to support his child. However, no child should have to experience destitution, extreme suffering, or servitude because of the negligence of the man who fathered her. A man who fears that the costs of child support will prevent him from "bettering himself" should take every possible step to avoid fathering children.

There are two legitimate exceptions to the general practice of holding men materially and morally responsible for the children they create. First, my argument does not imply that donor-insemination arrangements, in which the sperm donor has no responsibility for the resulting child, are immoral.[8] Donor insemination is a legitimate exception; women who obtain donor insemination acknowledge, in most cases, that the inseminator will have no material or moral responsibility for the resulting child. The basis for this exception is the formal prior agreement in writing, which is entered into freely, autonomously, and informedly by both the gestator and the inseminator, that the inseminator will be materially and morally detached from his offspring. The significance of the "purloined sperm" cases, however, is that there is no prior agreement whatsoever; hence, the male is not absolved of his responsibility.

The second legitimate exception to the general practice of holding men materially and morally responsible for the children they create arises when the male has not been able to make an informed, free, and autonomous choice about the sexual activity itself. Both women and men are entitled to bodily autonomy, and part of that entitlement is the right to choose whether, when, how, and with whom to engage in sexual behavior. An informed, free, autonomous choice to engage in sexual activity is a necessary condition for holding a man responsible for the offspring he engenders. There are at least two main categories of males who are not able to give an informed, free, and autonomous choice to sexual activities.

One such category is pubescent boys of twelve, thirteen, or fourteen, especially if they are offered sexual intercourse by a woman who is no longer an adolescent. The other category is males of any age who suffer from mental impairments that compromise their autonomy. We cannot assume that males in either of these categories are capable of making an informed, free, and autonomous choice about their sexual behavior; hence, they cannot be held morally responsible for the outcomes of their sexual behavior.

It might be argued that if the justification for holding the man responsible in the case of deception is the interests of the child, then we should also hold men and boys responsible even in cases where they are not competent to choose sexual activity. But I am suggesting that, in addition to the conceived children's interests, we also have to take into consideration the well-being and capacities of pubescent boys and of men with cognitive impairments. Individuals who are unable to act freely and autonomously cannot be held responsible for their actions. Moreover, even if we attempted to hold them responsible, it is unlikely that pubescent boys or males of any age with mental impairments would be capable of discharging the responsibilities that follow from procreative sexual activity.

Now it might be objected that the man in the purloined sperm case did not consent freely, autonomously, and informedly to having oral sex because he did not know his sperm would be used to inseminate the woman. Brake construes the idea that men who have been deceived should nonetheless pay child support as making a claim along the following lines: "They [men] knew when they decided to have sex that they could be ordered to pay child support, [and] they accepted this risk when they decided to have sex rather than abstain." She then points out that, as a matter of fact, it is highly unlikely that some men ever consented to support a child and that it is inappropriate to impute tacit consent. "This makes a mockery of the notion of consent, since surely consent, to be a meaningful moral concept, must be something more than foresight" (2005, 59, 60). But holding men morally responsible for a child that results from their consensual sexual activity is not an empirical claim that men always do in fact consent to supporting a child when they consent to sex. Rather, the claim is that when consent is knowledgeable and unconstrained, unimpaired adult men do in fact know that *a child might result* from their sexual activity, and therefore they *ought* to be held responsible for its consequences. The claim is in part an empirical one about what men know (or should know) about the consequences of sexual intercourse. But it is also a normative claim, a claim about moral responsibility for the very serious outcome that is the creation of a child.

Now, this sort of language may be worrying because it appears reminiscent of the kind of language used by antiabortionists in an attempt to prevent women from getting abortions. "If you have sex," they say, "you must pay the price, including the price of pregnancy. And you cannot get out of paying that price by having an abortion." In one respect, they are correct: women do sometimes "pay the price" by becoming pregnant. It is a risk that fertile women always take. It does not follow, however, that they cannot have an abortion. A fetus is within the woman's body, hence legitimately within her control as to whether it stays there. An infant, on the other hand, is a person and no longer in anyone's body; hence, supporting it is not optional for the inseminator.

So my response to Hubin and Ho is simply that men, too, must take the kind of responsibility that women routinely have to take and must recognize, as women always have, just how risky heterosexual activity can be. No contraception is foolproof, and sexual activity, even nonstandard sexual activity, can result in pregnancy. In the "purloined sperm" case, the fact that a man does not anticipate a pregnancy as a result of oral sex is not a defense. In general, we have a greater responsibility to be careful with our gametes than with our other bodily parts and fluids. (If it were possible for urine or blood to be used to make a new human being, a similar caution would be incumbent upon us regarding them.) Our gametes are potentially powerful materials, and it is every competent person's responsibility to be careful about what he or she does with them. This is also why sperm and ova donation (which are protected by a mutual agreement about the eventual use of the gametes) must be treated as the morally significant activities that they are.

I am arguing, then, that provided a man genuinely chooses to take part in sexual activity, the inseminator's desire and intention, even his clearly stated intention, not to be a parent is not, contrary to Hales, enough to release him from part of his role as a biological parent. Nor, contra Brake, is his use of a condom, if in fact he did wear one. Nor, contra Hales, is the fact that the woman chose to continue the pregnancy by not having an abortion and thereby willingly took on the challenges of child rearing or the fact (when it is a fact) that the mother enjoys child rearing and does not find it burdensome (Hales 1996b, 47). Nor is the evidence that the gestator will be a good mother and provider. Instead, men ought to be aware of the empirical risks and realities that are always attendant upon even consensual sexual behaviors—just as women must be and are.

What about cases where sperm is generated outside of shared sexual activity? The following imaginary cases have been suggested to me. A man needs to get a sperm sample to a laboratory and asks a female acquaintance to store it in her fridge for him overnight, whereupon she uses it to inseminate herself. Or a woman asks a man for a sperm sample for a science experiment and then inseminates herself. Once again in these cases I do not condone or defend deception. Although I am very skeptical that purloined sperm cases are as frequent as philosophers' concern about them appears to indicate, nonetheless, stealing sperm samples—whether obtained through mutual sexual activity or acquired, as in these hypothetical examples, as lab samples from a trusting colleague—is wrong. But if a baby results in these cases, it's important to ensure that that baby is cared for; the inseminator should be responsible, to the extent he is able, for contributing to its support.

It might be objected that by taking such a strong stance I am condoning the violation of men's right not to reproduce, which I discussed and defended in chapter 2. I disagree. Men can protect their right not to reproduce by being prudent about their ejaculatory behavior and protective of the use of the sperm they produce. If they were forced into ejaculating, the situation would be a different one. But no one coerced any of the men in the purloined sperm cases, both real and imaginary, to produce sperm, and no one compelled them to hand it over. The men had a choice about the disposition of their semen. The man in the oral sex case agreed to have sex and agreed to the use of the condom. He could have kept the condom afterward and disposed of it himself, but he chose not to. In the hypothetical lab cases, the men also make autonomous and free choices, and they are responsible for their own negligence. Gametes, because of their baby-making potential, should be treated with great care and caution—hence, probably not handed over for experimentation or left in someone else's refrigerator.[9]

It might be objected that holding men to this standard even in cases of deceit is setting the moral bar too high. It means that men must be constantly on the lookout for possible misuses of their semen. It means that men must always worry about being responsible for the outcome of their sexual activities. I agree; that is exactly what it means. With this requirement, men are placed in the same sort of situation that most women are in whenever they engage in heterosexual activities. From puberty to menopause, women (unless they know for sure that they are infertile) must always worry about the chance that they might become pregnant. They must always be concerned about the possibility that even the most reliable form of contraception may fail. And if they do become pregnant, they are always responsible for dealing with the pregnancy—whether by obtaining an abortion or by gestating and giving birth to the baby. Holding men responsible does not put them in any more difficult a position than women are in, and, for the most part, their position is less difficult, given that men never get pregnant.

This way of resolving the dilemma in Quadrant 2 in table 3.1 protects the children of unwilling fathers. It also protects mothers. Because of women's role in gestation (along with their subsequent role in breastfeeding), which can entail physical and psychological risks and can compromise women's work roles at least early in the infant's life, and because of women's relative disadvantages generally in pay and work opportunities, it makes sense not to allow men off the hook when it comes to supporting the children they father. But even if the gestator were independently wealthy or very successful and earning a spectacular salary, it still makes sense to see the inseminator as morally responsible at least for his share of the financial support of the infant, for, as a general practice, it is important not to give the message to men that they are not responsible for the consequences of their voluntary sexual behavior. Sexual activities can have serious consequences; even in an age of growing sexual liberation, the potential connection between heterosexual behavior and procreation cannot be overlooked. It is better for children, for women, and perhaps even for men themselves[10] to hold men both legally and morally responsible at least for the financial support of the offspring they engender.

It might be objected that requiring men to support children they have been deceived into creating rewards the women who deceive them. It might therefore be argued that in cases where the man has been deceived, there should be a backup mechanism whereby the state takes responsibility for supporting the child rather than unfairly saddling the inseminator with the financial burden.

I agree with the general point that society collectively should provide more support for children and for child rearing. This imperative applies to all children and all parents. Children grow up to be the adults of the future, who will contribute the labor, create the material goods, and grow the food to enable society to continue. Children become adults who provide education and health care to other citizens; who create art, music, films, and books; who develop science and engineer and construct the built environment. Childbearing and child rearing are social goods, not merely individual enterprises. The importance of childbearing and child rearing to society should be recognized by providing social support for them. There should be a social safety net that ensures, at a minimum, that no child goes hungry or without adequate health care and that all parents are able to raise their children with an assurance that the family will not suffer if one or both parents is or becomes unemployed, ill, or disabled. That social safety net should of course protect single mothers and their children. It is wrong that women would have to (or think they have to) deceive men in order to obtain child support.

The question is whether there should be a special mechanism just to support the children of deceitful women in order to let the deceived father off the hook. If the objection is focused on the inappropriate rewarding of deceitful women by requiring inseminators to support their children, note that state support of the child would equally be a reward—if child support can be considered a "reward." So the problem, if it is a problem, of rewarding deceitful women is not obviated by state support.

In any case, however, the number of purloined sperm cases is likely to be quite small. I have focused on them only for the sake of argument, not because they are a serious social problem. And I argued that in instances of disagreement between a gestator who wants to continue her pregnancy and an inseminator who wants either a real or a "financial" abortion, the inseminator should, to the extent he is able, be expected to support his child. Such a requirement is not in any way incompatible with having a broader social system that provides support for all children—and their parents—who are in need.

Having a special backup system just for the children of deceitful women is unworkable and may have undesirable results. First, in order for such a mechanism to be available, there would have to be legal procedures by which it could be determined that the pregnancy was the result of the gestator's deception. Such procedures would be intrusive and difficult; much of the time the situation would come down to deciding between the gestator's word and the inseminator's word. Such a situation would be similar to investigations of cases in which women report rape or sexual assault; the kinds of interventions into their lives and sexuality that result are unlikely to be worth duplicating in a procreative context. Moreover, if there is a widely recognized procedure for dealing with supposed cases of deceit by gestators, I worry that such a practice would open up the possibility for some inseminators to claim deceit even in cases where it has not occurred. Generally speaking, it would not be good for children or women (and maybe not for men, either) to create a practice whereby the state offers men who engage in heterosexual activity an escape clause from parental responsibility should they care to exploit it. A society in which this behavior is permitted would surely be less desirable than a society in which every person takes responsibility for behavior that can result in procreation.

Moreover, with respect to the potential for deception, the male is not more disadvantaged with respect to responsibility for offspring than is the female, for it may well be that some men have deceived some women by telling them that they have had a vasectomy or that they are otherwise infertile in order to induce women to engage in sexual activities without contraception. If a woman who does not want to become pregnant agrees to sex on the assumption that she is protected from pregnancy but then becomes pregnant, she undergoes a profoundly unwelcome bodily condition. She can of course obtain an abortion because the fetus is within the domain of her body, and the woman is entitled to make her own choices about her bodily domain, but abortion, as offered under current conditions, can have its own costs. And if she does not have an abortion, then she has the entire experience of pregnancy, labor, and birth to contend with.[11] Thus, male sexual deception can and does have serious and irrevocable consequences for women.

Both the woman and the man can, of course, decide jointly to give up the baby for adoption.[12] However, what the man cannot do, with moral justification, is to make an individual, unilateral decision during the pregnancy to reject all responsibility for the infant.

Evaluating Solutions to the "She Doesn't Want the Baby, but He Does" Dilemma

Two solutions were put forward for the Quadrant 3 dilemma: Bertha Manninen's "virtuous" solution, and the ectogenesis solution. I discuss them in that order.

The "Virtuous" Solution

In her defense of taking an unwanted pregnancy to term for the sake of an inseminator who wants to be a father Manninen writes, "As women, we must understand that we have great power over men in this area, and thus we should try to ensure that we exercise this power in the most virtuous manner possible" (2007, 3).[13]

I don't agree that the capacity to become and remain pregnant constitutes "great power *over* men" (my emphasis).[14] It *is* power of a sort: an ability possessed by no men and by only a subset of women (those of reproductive age who do not have overriding fertility problems). Whether the ability to become and remain pregnant is anything more than that depends on the social context. I suppose the ability to get and remain pregnant is a "great power" for a particular woman if the infant is wanted, if the culture puts a genuinely high value on women's reproductive labor and on infants and children, and if the man who inseminated her is supportive. But there are far too many contexts in which becoming pregnant is a liability: for women who are considered "too young," "too old," or "too impaired"; for women who are considered to lack the right sexual orientation, the right socioeconomic class, the right gender identification, or the right marital status to be pregnant; for women who are not allowed or not able to do paid work while pregnant; for women who already have enough (or more than enough) children; for women whose bodies are barely adequately nourished to sustain their own lives; and for women who do not have the money to support another child. Indeed, far from constituting a power over men, pregnancy in fact puts many women in a situation where they are *under* the power of a man—if they become ill or vulnerable, if they lose the capacity to support themselves, if they need the man's income to support the child, and so on.

According to Manninen, the circumstances relevant to determining if a woman who is unwillingly pregnant should take a pregnancy to term for the sake of an inseminator who wants to raise the baby include the following:

- Whether the fetus is the product of consensual sex
- Whether gestating the fetus would cause "many emotional or physical burdens on the woman"
- Whether the woman and man were or are in "an intimate relationship already built on trust and love"
- Whether the potential father can care for the potential infant
- Whether the pregnant woman will suffer "any emotional or long-term damage" if she gives the infant to the inseminator (2007, 10)[15]

Hence, it would be virtuous of the woman to continue an unwanted pregnancy in those situations where *all* of the following are true: the fetus is the result of consensual sex; continuing the pregnancy will not burden the woman; the woman and man are or at least were in a trustful and loving relationship (Manninen 2007, 15); the potential father can care for the infant, presumably in the absence of the infant's mother; and the pregnant woman will not suffer from giving the infant to the inseminator. I submit that the simultaneous coincidence of these five conditions would be rare indeed. And although Manninen concedes that, in general, giving away a child can be a source of life-long pain to the gestator (2007, 18), we must also consider the kind of pain that may be involved for the gestator in surrendering the infant at the end of her pregnancy to a man who was her former lover and perhaps partner. The woman would then have the choice either of being partially involved in the child's life (and handling all the awkwardness and pain of a relationship like that, in particular explaining and justifying it to the child himself or herself) or of giving up all contact with the child forever, knowing that the child is being raised by someone with whom the woman herself deliberately decided no longer to be in a relationship. In either case, I suspect there would be much worry, uncertainty, pain, awkwardness, and perhaps guilt (whether justified or not).

I'm willing to concede that there might be some cases where a woman's getting an abortion might be sad and disturbing to the man who inseminated her. But as Manninen herself notes, "A woman who brings a fetus, whom she initially wanted to abort, to term in order to give a good man a chance to be a good father is courageous, fair, kind, empathetic, selfless, and very noble indeed" (2007, 15). Pregnancy is not usually a pleasant condition if it is not wanted.[16] Thus, although Manninen couches this choice in terms of moral virtue, it will usually be supererogatory in the sense of being considerably above and beyond the call of ordinary virtuous behavior. It is never morally *obligatory*, as Manninen herself agrees (2007, 16), to continue a pregnancy in order to accommodate the inseminator's desires, and the woman never loses her moral right to terminate the pregnancy.

The Ectogenesis Solution

In evaluating the ectogenesis solution, I don't want to imply that I think ectogenesis is morally unproblematic. I set aside debates about the moral value of ectogenesis. I also set aside most of the practical issues and assume, simply for the sake of argument, that ectogenesis would be as safe or almost as safe as ordinary human gestation.[17]

In evaluating the ectogenesis solution to the Quadrant 3 dilemma— she doesn't want the baby, but he does—it is essential first to note that ectogenesis, as a potential technology, is *not* gender neutral. There is a tendency in the existing philosophical literature to assume that it is: that it requires no more (and no less) procreative labor from a woman than from a man. Thus, Brake speaks of "effortlessly transfer[ring] the embryo to a mechanical womb" (2005, 65). Indeed, you will recall that Bard says, "Both mothers and fathers have made biologically equivalent contributions towards the creation of a new life" (2006, 150–151). Ho assumes that if two people agree to ectogenesis, then it would be "plainly unfair if only one party has a unilateral right to terminate gestation based on nothing but gender." He writes, "The minute we place gestation in a bodily neutral place (as in ectogenesis), we no longer believe that either procreative party has the right to determine unilaterally to terminate or to continue gestation" (2008, 15, 16).

If ectogenesis, that supposed "bodily neutral place," were available, then it would involve one of two of the following processes. First, an ovum would be removed from a woman's body and fertilized; then the embryo would be gestated in an artificial uterus. In the alternative process, a fetus already gestating inside a woman's body would be removed from it and placed in an artificial uterus. Given these two possibilities, ectogenesis would be entirely gender neutral, requiring no more and no less procreative labor from the woman than from the man, *only if* the two following counterfactuals were true: (1) the process of removing ova from a woman's body were no more painful, difficult, intrusive, or invasive than the process for men of ejecting sperm; and (2) there were no pain, stress, or invasiveness associated with the removal of the fetus before maturity, intact and unharmed, from the woman's uterus.

It is hard to see how either of these counterfactuals can be made true. Unless ova can one day be manufactured (in which case I am not sure whether we are any longer talking about producing *human* beings), it will always be necessary to remove them from the woman's body.[18] This process can presumably be made somewhat easier, less painful, and less invasive, while needing the use of fewer drugs, than it is now, but the process will presumably never be analogous to the ejaculation of sperm. Moreover, a fetus that is unwanted after several weeks or months of gestation would have to be removed from its gestator's uterus, and doing so would likely involve pain, stress, and invasive procedures for the gestator. The physical burdens of so doing may presumably be reduced, but it is unlikely that they can be eliminated. Thus, ectogenesis, if it were to be feasible, would still involve more "sweat equity" and potential pain from the female parent than from the male parent. Ectogenesis thus would not and cannot be, contrary to its supporters' assumptions, a gender-neutral reproductive process,[19] and it would not obliterate all biological reproductive asymmetries. As a result, the psychological and physical costs to the gestator would mean that having the fetus removed from her body and put in an artificial uterus in circumstances where the inseminator wants the baby would not just be "virtuous" (to use Manninen's term) on the woman's part; it would be positively heroic, and it would therefore be in no way morally obligatory.

What if removing the fetus in an abortion procedure and removing the fetus for deposit in an artificial uterus were exactly the same in terms of the demands and effects on the gestator? Even then, because she is entitled to bodily autonomy, the gestator has no moral obligation to submit to having the fetus removed for purposes of ectogenesis. It would be her choice which operation is performed on her body. As long as it is within her body, it is subject to her bodily autonomy.[20]

Another important reason for not choosing ectogenesis to resolve the disagreement in Quadrant 3 is that ectogenesis for fetuses unwanted by

Table 3.3
Morally Justified Solutions to Disagreements between Prospective Parents

	She wants the baby.	She doesn't want the baby.
He wants the baby.	Gestate and raise it.	She is morally entitled to abort. Neither continuation of the pregnancy nor ectogenesis is morally required.
He doesn't want the baby.	She is not morally required to end the pregnancy. The child's interest in receiving financial support must override the fact that the male parent did not want a child. This outcome is better for children and mothers.	Abort the fetus. Or gestate it and surrender the infant for adoption. Ectogenesis is not morally required.

their gestators is a poor use of resources. I have deliberately side-stepped the general question whether ectogenesis is desirable, worth developing, or deserving of resources and funding.[21] Here I simply want to suggest that it is questionable whether a fetus that has, in a way, already received one negative vote (from its gestator) should be gestated in an artificial uterus.[22] If ectogenesis is to be used—and this "if" is huge—it might be preferable to save the process for fetuses that are wanted by both their gestators and their inseminators.

Thus, given its burdens on women, ectogenesis cannot be a morally obligatory solution to the Quadrant 3 dilemma. These arguments would also defeat any moral requirement to use ectogenesis in Quadrant 4, where neither biological parent wants the pregnancy.

Table 3.3 lists the main evaluative claims for which I have argued regarding the Quadrant 2 and Quadrant 4 dilemmas.

Conclusion

I have endeavored to provide morally justified resolutions for situations in which a male and a pregnant female disagree about whether they want to be parents, resolutions that are different from those recommended by Bard, Brake, Hales, Ho, Hubin, and Manninen. In the case where the woman wants the child and the man does not, I argue that the woman is entitled to continue the pregnancy and the man is obligated to provide at least financial support, to the extent that he can, for the resulting child. The child's interests in being well cared for and the mother's potential vulnerability trump the man's interests. In the case where the woman does not want the child and the man does, I argue that she never has an obligation to continue the pregnancy, and only very rarely would it be a virtuous choice for her to continue gestation; the choice is mostly supererogatory in the sense of being above and beyond the call of moral virtue. Moreover, the woman has no moral obligation whatsoever to make use of ectogenesis to preserve and develop the fetus, whether or not the inseminator wants the child.

It might be protested that I described myself as being concerned with women's and men's reproductive freedom, yet the solutions I offer honor women's reproductive freedom without honoring men's. My response draws upon Ho's concepts of bodily autonomy and procreative asymmetry. Like women, men are entitled to autonomy over their own bodies. Hence, men are always entitled to a choice as to whether to engage in sexual activities with a woman. But men are not capable of pregnancy, and that fact undermines any claim about "gender neutrality" or "moral symmetry" in human reproduction.

4

Deontological Reasons for Having Children

Whenever human beings decide to reproduce, the decision has at least two foundational and morally relevant features. First, children themselves do not choose to come into existence; by the very nature of procreation, their consent is not possible. Hence, in cases where pregnancy is the result of choice, the decision that a new human being will come into existence is inevitably made for them by others. Second, no child can be brought into existence for its own sake. What I mean is that there is no *previously existing* entity that is given material human existence via reproduction.

Some people believe that having a child may be, in part, an expression of gratitude that one exists oneself. They say they give the "gift of life" because others gave it to them. However, J. David Velleman argues that life is not a gift at all because the gift has "no intended recipient. It is a 'gift' that is launched into the void, where some as-yet nonexistent person may snag it. Such untargeted benefits do not fit our usual concept of gift-giving" (2005, 372 fn. 7).

That's not quite right, though, for "untargeted" benefits can sometimes also be gifts. Consider monetary donations to charities. These gifts have no specific intended recipients; they are "launched into the void" in the sense that one does not know and is likely never to know who are the specific people who are helped. I think what makes procreation an odd "gift" is not that it is "untargeted" but the fact that the recipient does not yet exist. In this one case, the gift *creates* the recipient, and there is no particular being on whom the "gift" of existence is bestowed. As David Benatar puts it, because procreation is not a matter of bringing "the benefit of life to some pitiful non-being suspended in the metaphysical void and thereby denied the joys of life," children are never brought into being for their own sake (2006, 129–130).

Given, then, that children never consent to coming into existence and cannot be brought into existence for their own sake, this chapter begins the inquiry into whether there nonetheless are good reasons for procreation. Israeli philosopher Saul Smilansky goes so far as to argue that "under certain conditions many people are under some moral *requirement* to attempt to bring children into being (in order to raise them)" (1995, 41, my emphasis). Despite the fact that women's and men's roles in reproduction are significantly different, he does not distinguish between what he takes women's and men's procreative obligations to be. He simply states a series of arguments in favor of an obligation to procreate, arguments that include the value of children, the value of loving relationships with children, the need for new persons who will "support the economy and provide all care and services in society," the need to supply "future voters and concerned individuals," and the importance of fulfilling others' pronatalist expectations, preserving a cultural form of life, and perpetuating a genetic and cultural familial pool (1995, 46, 47).

If the taxonomy of rights in chapter 2 is correct, and women and men have a moral right not to have children, then there is a prima facie very strong reason for believing that they are seldom or never under an obligation to have children. This claim, I show, can further be defended through a critical examination revealing the inadequacy of each of the reasons that might be put forward to support such a putative obligation, including those presented by Smilansky. Smilansky's reasons are a mix of deontological and consequentialist approaches. In this chapter on deontological arguments for procreation and in chapter 5 on consequentialist arguments, I engage in an examination of his reasons and others. The various reasons traditionally offered for having children turn out to be surprisingly inadequate.

As I stated in chapter 1, deontologists believe that certain acts or the practices and rules to which these acts are related—for example, keeping a promise—are right in themselves and that other acts—for example, murder—are wrong in themselves, independent of the consequences of the acts. Outcomes are not what make our choices morally justified; it is their conformity to certain moral rules. A deontologist regards it as important to make the "why have children?" decision on the basis of doing what is inherently right and avoiding doing what is inherently wrong. The main deontological arguments in support of procreation pertain to heeding the supposed intrinsic value of childbearing; passing on a name, genetic link, or property; fulfilling a duty to others; keeping a promise; and discharging religious duties or duties to the state. I discuss each of these arguments in turn.

Bearing Children as Intrinsically Worthwhile

Unlike most male philosophers who write on the subject, Rosalind Hursthouse is aware of the special responsibilities and risks that procreation inevitably places on women but not on men. She says that men and women (and especially women who have borne a child) are not "morally equal" because women are better: "In bearing children, Mrs. Average does something morally significant and worthwhile which Mr. Average does not match, whereby they are not morally on a par." Hursthouse compares pregnancy and labor to going "into battle" and says that they require "courage, fortitude and endurance." She questions why women are not "praised and admired" for all of this. After all, she says, "a man who goes through something like what women go through in childbearing (such as a painful illness or operation) with the same unthinking courage, fortitude and endurance is counted as particularly admirable" (1987, 299, 300, 304).

Thus, Hursthouse emphasizes the burdensome aspects of pregnancy and delivery, and sees childbearing as (usually) a heroic endeavor. She romanticizes women for their sheer capacity to gestate and give birth to children. She writes, for example, that "women are, in one respect, born superior to men—superior in the straightforward sense that they are born with a capacity to do something worthwhile, *viz.* bear children (and no corresponding incapacity, such as being unable to think logically) which men lack." She even goes so far as to suggest, at least tentatively, that anyone who has not "borne children well" might have to say, "I haven't done anything with my life really" (1987, 298, 318).

It's a rather pleasant change to read the work of a philosopher who so powerfully values childbearing. Nonetheless, in her enthusiasm for women's procreative capacities Hursthouse goes too far. It is implausible and even sexist to suppose that merely possessing a biological capacity makes women superior to men. Some women never exercise that capacity; being the possessor of a uterus does not make them better human beings. Yet using one's capacity to gestate and give birth is also not automatically value conferring. If it were, then the more children one had, the better and more moral a person one would be. Mere numbers of offspring do not make multiparous women morally superior to those who are childless or who have only one; the mother of five is not more advanced than the mother of two. The fact is that some women, depending on their medical condition and the available medical resources, are heroic in pregnancy and delivery, and some are not. Most simply get through it, and most are fairly gracious about it. Although pregnancy and delivery are significant, even more important is how one raises the child, for that endeavor requires at least an eighteen-year moral commitment.

To claim that persons who have not "borne children well" have not done anything with their lives is preposterous, given all the other valuable, even heroic activities that many human beings engage in. The idea is especially dangerous for women. It might be used to get women to give up other activities on the grounds that all that matters is having a baby. To suppose that every single childless person has "not done anything" with her or his life is to devalue our human history of creativity and achievement.

Hursthouse describes childbearing as "intrinsically worthwhile." The basis for this notion is not, she says, that human beings in general are intrinsically valuable. Rather, the idea that childbearing is intrinsically worthwhile expresses important ideals with respect to "the value of love, of family life, of our proper emotional development through a natural life-cycle and what counts as enrichments of this emotional development." Hence, it is more accurate to think of having one's *own* child as intrinsically worthwhile to oneself (1987, 311, 312).

But if the supposed intrinsic value of childbearing is actually a function of certain other values, then it is not in fact worthwhile for its own sake, but for the sake of other values. We therefore need to assess those values and see whether they are indeed connected to procreation in the way that Hursthouse believes. We can and should ask not only whether childbearing is connected to love, family life, and emotional development, as Hursthouse believes, but also whether all or any of these elements is sufficient to justify childbearing. I explore some of these alleged connections in this chapter, some in chapter 5 in looking at consequentialist reasons to choose to have children, some in chapter 9 in the discussion of resisting extinction, and some in the final chapter in the examination of procreation, values, and identity. The notion that childbearing is intrinsically valuable is unfounded.

Name, Property, Genetic Link

One traditional basis for childbearing is lineage: to carry on the family name and family line. Some people also want to keep property "in the family," whether the property is land, housing, artworks, mementos, or money. Some people believe that there is a *duty* to perpetuate one's name, one's genetic line, and one's family property. People often express concern that a family name may "die out" or that a family line will end if a particular individual or couple does not have children. Such persons, and there are quite a few of them, assume that the sheer perpetuation of a particular bloodline is of intrinsic value. For such people, having children is also a way of achieving a kind of vicarious immortality: "Humans are probably unique among species in their cognitive awareness of mortality, and particularly their conspicuous anxiety in anticipation of it. Humans are presumably also uniquely aware that 'leaving something of oneself' for the future (despite mortality) can be accomplished by leaving genetic descendants" (Aarssen 2007, 1769).

The idea of a genetic duty to have children is sometimes expressed in a form that is directed at particular individuals. For example, women in the sciences or the professions occasionally receive the message, "Women like you should be having children." The idea is that they ought not to devote their entire lives to their careers. Because their offspring are believed likely to be particularly talented and intelligent, they are thought to have an obligation to perpetuate their genes.

I'm skeptical about using the genetic link as a reason for having a child, let alone about claiming that it may constitute the basis for an obligation. Is anyone's biological composition so valuable that it must be perpetuated? Let's assume that you *are* a great human being (that is, you are enormously intelligent, skilled, or talented or have strong sports abilities or leadership capacities). You need not have children of your own: much of your genetic material will be perpetuated as long as your siblings have children. Some of it will even be passed down if your cousins procreate.

The not-so-subtle assumption underlying the focus on the genetic link is that it is better for educated women (who of course are also likely to be white and relatively well off) to increase their fertility rates rather than for women whose offspring supposedly are less valuable to society and to humanity—women who are likely to be poorer, less educated, impaired, or not white. Canada and the United States have a sorry history of engaging in the compulsory sterilization of members of certain groups, including some native people, poor people, people of color, and people with impairments, having judged that such persons were unfit to perpetuate their own genes.[1] The wrongness of those negative eugenicist policies is now recognized and in need of no further arguments, but so also should be the wrongness of positive eugenicist policies that favor reproduction by some persons more than others. Such expectations and policies are ableist, classist, and racist.

But the assumption itself that one's genetic inheritance is inherently good and worth preserving no matter one's identity is itself questionable. For one thing, it's conceited. I'm reminded of the infamous sperm bank founded in the 1980s to which Nobel Prize winners were supposed to donate their sperm (Plotz 2001). Of the many things wrong with that idea, one main problem is the assumption that Nobel Prize winners' sperm is so much more valuable than other men's sperm. After all, given the size of the human population, there are millions of people with great intelligence and talents. In that respect, no one is unique. Moreover, there is no guarantee that offspring will inherit their parents' abilities or that, even having inherited them, they will decide to act upon them. We all know of famous writers, scientists, and athletes whose children lack either their parents' talents or the motivation and perseverance to follow through on them. And although nature undeniably plays a role in how people turn out, so does nurture. So it is possible to pass on some of one's gifts and abilities not only by having one's own biologically related children, but also by adopting and raising children, by mentoring nieces and nephews or the children of friends, and by teaching and coaching within an educational environment.

The implication of all these arguments is that the perpetuation of a genetic link is not a very good basis at all for having children. Moreover, emphasizing genetic connectedness may have undesirable consequences. I raised concerns about this problem more than twenty years ago, when reproductive technologies were still genuinely new[2] (Overall 1987). People seek out these technologies in many cases because they're determined to have a genetic connection to their offspring—so determined that they spend thousands of dollars, commit hundreds of hours, and take medical risks to have a genetically related child. They see their child as a product who must and will reflect well on them. The undesirable consequence of such an outlook is that parents can have unrealistic expectations of their children. If I have a child because I'm a marvelous clarinet player, and I want a son who will also be a marvelous clarinet player, then I'm setting myself up for disappointment, and I may put a great deal of pressure on my son that he will neither appreciate nor benefit from—especially if it turns out he'd rather be a potter or a plumber. Children have enough pressures on them as it is; they don't need parents who expect them to be little replicas.[3]

Moreover, the practice of having children in order to "pass on" a name is sexist because in most cultures only males can carry on the family name; females give it up at marriage and take on their husbands' names. "Carrying on the family name" is, then, an illusion founded on the implicit assumption that the mother's name and lineage contribute nothing to the offspring.[4] Even if the child is given a double surname reflecting both parents, in practical terms it cannot be maintained through future generations: when a double-surnamed person procreates with another double-surnamed person, a name or names are bound to be dropped, if only for convenience and simplicity. A surname certainly has cultural and personal value—it is part of our identity from birth—but perpetuating one's own particular branch of the family with that name is hardly an adequate justification for bringing a child into the world. Indeed, it makes the child into a mere vehicle for the name.

It is unsurprising that many people want to pass on their property and money to their children, but to have children only for this purpose puts the cart before the horse. Handing down an inheritance benefits the children, but to have children *in order* to hand down an inheritance means that one is having children in order to benefit the inheritance. Such arrangements treat women as mere instruments for reproducing the family. They also treat the child as a means to an end (whose importance is overestimated) and not as valuable in himself. Surely such treatment is morally unjustified. If I'm wealthy and I have a baby in order to keep my wealth in the family, then I am using that child as a mere instrument for maintaining the family fortune. Instead of acquiring money and possessions in order to support one's offspring, one acquires offspring in order to support one's money and possessions. Having a child only for that purpose seems selfish and almost fetishistic: Why must the money be kept in that way? A person who has considerable wealth can usually do far more good by donating much of it to museums, libraries, schools, or charities that benefit people in need.

Whether it is a matter of perpetuating a genetic link, carrying on a name, or passing on wealth and property, none of these deontological arguments can legitimately be regarded as the basis of an obligation to have children or even as an adequate justification for choosing to procreate.

Duties to Others (and the Problems of Pronatalist Pressures)

Can an obligation to have a child or at least a good reason to have a child be founded upon a duty to other people? Perhaps having a child should be seen as a way to honor one's family and one's upbringing.

Some people long to become grandparents. Such people may put pressure on their adult children to "start a family." Pronatalist pressures are still ubiquitous, and the resulting tendency to define womanliness in terms of procreation and manliness in terms of begetting has not disappeared. In some communities at some times, one cannot even be a "real" woman unless one is a mother. Having children thereby becomes a means to conformity, a way of giving the community the gendered behavior it expects. Married persons who are childless, whether by choice or by virtue of infertility, are then subjected to many invasions of their privacy and bombarded by suggestions that they should "get busy and have a baby."

The creation of such pressures is morally unjustified. Although would-be grandparents are often thrilled when their adult child has a baby, they should not impose their grandparental goals on their children. To have a child out of a sense of duty to family is to use the child as a kind of currency in the family exchange, a repayment of a debt. Except where pronatalism is overwhelming, leaving no alternative (as surely happens for women in some subcultures), for the most part one is not justified in having children just to please one's parents or to accede to pronatalist pressures from other sources.

Even in the absence of pronatalist pressures, having a child to honor one's parents is of doubtful value. To do so is once again to use the children as means to an end rather than as ends in themselves. It may lead to disappointment (since grandchildren don't always turn out the way one might hope). And it doesn't seem to be adequate motivation to sustain the great amount of commitment, work, and devotion that go into child rearing—even if the grandparents will be around to help (and many of them will die before the children are grown). Choosing to have a child only to fulfill a duty to others is also unlikely to be good for the child himself. If the parents otherwise wanted to remain childless, they may even end up resenting their offspring rather than appreciating him for himself. Finally, if honoring one's parents is an important goal, there are other ways to do it: by encouraging one's parents in their own life endeavors; by supporting one's parents to perpetuate their own values and achievements; by caring for one's parents when they need it; and by making a good life for oneself.

Keeping a Promise

But might one have an obligation to have children that is based on one's commitment to one's partner? People have at least a prima facie responsibility to honor their promises. In the context of procreation decisions, Y may have married X on the condition or at least with the implicit understanding that X agreed to have children. In that case, there is a promise—a kind of moral contract—between the two individuals.

Is a woman who fails to live up to that promise morally wrong? It is not the sort of promise that should be made lightly; procreation is of great significance to some people, and the outcomes of that promise will affect the lives of several people, including the child, if there is one. But if the woman made the promise under coercion or at a time when she was not autonomous or lacked crucial knowledge, then she is not wrong to break the promise. And even if her promise was autonomous, free, and informed, she remains entitled to govern her own body. Breaking her promise may cause disappointment and even grief to the person to whom she made the promise, and in that respect her promise breaking is regrettable. Indeed, the relationship may not survive the sundering of the commitment to procreate, and the disappointed partner may understandably want to leave her. Yet if she truly does not want to be a mother, she does not have an obligation to donate the services of her body for the sake of another person's project to be a parent, even when she previously entered into an agreement to do so.

The keeping of a promise is not enough to justify being a parent. A promise is at best a defeasible basis for having a baby. If an individual becomes a mother only out a sense of contract with her partner and in the absence of any other reasons, she might resent not only the partner, but the child. If the promise is the only reason for having a child, then one wonders how the child would be treated and whether the parent would care about the child. The child would yet again in this case be treated as a means only—a means of keeping a promise.

Not every promise should be kept. In the absence of any other motivation for being a parent, a promise of this sort, which materially affects the well-being of a young and vulnerable human being, may be one of them. Better still, no one should promise to have a child unless (a) one has no doubts about one's willingness and capacity to have a child; (b) one will love and care for the child for its own sake, not merely out of a sense of being beholden to a promise; and (c) one is not using the promise for emotional or material gain.

Religious Duties

Some might argue that we have a moral duty to reproduce because that is precisely what God commanded human beings, his creatures, to do. According to the book of Genesis, God blessed Adam and Eve, the supposed first human beings, and said to them, "Be fruitful, and multiply, and replenish the Earth, and subdue it: and have dominion over the fish of the sea, and over the fowl of the air, and over every living thing that moveth upon the Earth" (Genesis 1:27–28). The value of children is reinforced in an often-cited passage found in the book of Psalms: "Lo, children are an heritage of the Lord: and the fruit of the womb is his reward. As arrows are in the hand of a mighty man; so are children of the youth. Happy is the man that hath his quiver full of them: they shall not be ashamed, but they shall speak with the enemies in the gate" (Psalms 127, 3–5). Thus, children are a blessing, a sign of God's favor, and procreation is a manifestation of religious obedience.

The question of divine justification for moral choices is long-standing and complex, and I do not intend—and do not have space—to analyze all the questions associated with basing moral decisions on religious belief. There are, however, two main objections to this argument for procreation that I think are insuperable.

There is first an epistemological argument: it is not possible to know that God wants human beings to procreate, or at least it is not possible to know to what extent God wants us to procreate and whether God would sanction any limits on procreation. Is God happy with a family of two children? Or does God want us to have nineteen children, as Michelle Duggar and Jim-Bob Duggar of the reality television show *Nineteen Kids and Counting* have done? Does God disapprove of the use of contraception? Or is God perhaps pleased when human beings make careful choices about controlling their fertility?

We can't know. No one has direct access to the mind of God. There are also many questions about the alleged authority of the Bible and other religious scriptures. Fundamentalists who cite scriptures as the source of their insights about God's wishes never provide any independent reasons for thinking one scripture is more reliable than another or for interpreting scriptures in a particular way, reconciling the inconsistencies within particular scriptures, or applying texts that are thousands of years old to the moral questions of the twenty-first century. Of course, many people would add that it is difficult, perhaps impossible, even to know whether God exists, let alone what God wants. For that reason, the discussion in this book is agnostic with respect to the existence of God and God's alleged preferences and actions with respect to human procreation.

But set aside the epistemological doubts. Let us suppose that somehow we do know both that God exists and that God commands human beings to be fruitful and multiply—whatever that might mean for practical procreative decision making in this century. But then a type of dilemma originally set forth in Plato's *Euthyphro* (1941) dialog arises. Does God command us to be fruitful and multiply because it is morally right to do so? Or is being fruitful and multiplying right because God commands it? If the first disjunct is correct—that is, God commands us to be fruitful and multiply because doing so is morally right—then there is some other moral standard or purpose that is independent of God's command and forms the basis for God's supposed command to procreate. That is,

God's say-so is not the final word on our moral duty to procreate; there is some value that we are supposed to be attaining or living up to when we reproduce. We should therefore look for that other moral standard or purpose, whatever it might be, evaluate it, and see whether and to what extent it still applies to twenty-first-century life and how we make our reproductive choices.

If the second disjunct is correct—that is, being fruitful and multiplying are right just because God commands that we do so—then God has no reason for God's commands, and the supposed duty to procreate is founded only upon God's fiat. But if God uses no moral touchstone for determining what to command human beings to do, then God might just as well command murder and torture, and God's commands are morally arbitrary. God might command us to be fruitful one month and the next month command every pregnant woman to have an abortion. God might require all men to get vasectomies one week and forbid all contraception the next week. Without any other moral standard, there is no assurance about the direction that God's commands might take. If that is the case, then human beings can have no more reason to obey God and in this instance to go on having children than they would have to obey a capricious human dictator. One might, of course, obey out of fear of God and dread of the consequences for disobedience, but one would not have any *moral* reason to obey, only a pragmatic one. Obedience to a divine dictator, under threat of reprisals, is a sadly inadequate justification for choosing to be a parent.

The *Euthyphro* dilemma shows us, then, that either we need to look for a further foundation to justify procreation, one that is beyond divine command—the foundation that God himself supposedly uses—or we need not automatically obey God's injunctions to procreate because God is no more than an arbitrary dictator. Because of this dilemma, I take religious duties as an inadequate justification for procreation. People's procreative decisions should not be based on claims about what God allegedly wants.

Duties to the State

Can there be a duty to the state or the nation to have children? What I'm interested in here is the idea that producing children for the benefit of society might be considered a material manifestation of one's moral indebtedness as a citizen to the society that provided one's own education, one's opportunity to make a living, and one's civil, political, and legal rights. From this point of view, having children is a patriotic duty, an expression of loyalty to one's nation.

This idea is different from the consequentialist argument that procreation is justified because children will grow up to be contributing adults who will benefit society. Children are said to be a public good; they are the engines of progress, the workers of tomorrow, the producers of goods and services, the sources of tax dollars, and the potential supporters of an aging population. This description is of course accurate in most cases, although what follows from it is not immediately self-evident. But I am not considering here the forward-looking argument that people should procreate for the sake of the economic value that children will one day bring to their society when they are adults. (In chapter 5, I discuss consequentialist arguments about producing children for the sake of the benefits they bring. And in chapter 9, I examine the claim that procreation is justified in order to avoid underpopulation.) Instead, I am considering a backward-looking argument that says, "Because your society provided an environment in which you could get an education, find employment, and participate as a citizen, you owe it to the society to contribute to the creation of new citizens."

Questions about the duties of citizenship are complex and multifaceted, and I cannot deal with them in any detail here. Nonetheless, it is appropriate to question whether one has a specifically procreative duty to the state. Suppose the society in which a citizen lives has not treated her well; she was consigned to grow up in poverty, subjected to racism or sexism, deprived of an equal education, and excluded from opportunities for good employment and participation in civil society. In such a case, there seems to be little or nothing that the citizen owes to the society in which she finds herself. In fact, such a person might even reason that the refusal to provide more beings to oppress is both a fitting response to living within an oppressive society and a way of protecting children who would otherwise exist from being the targets of continuing oppression. And even if one is treated fairly and has opportunities equal to those of other citizens, it might be argued that one is not inevitably indebted to one's society. After all, no one chooses where they are born and grow up or the particulars of the society in which they live. Perhaps one cannot incur a debt if one did not choose any of the events that led to that debt. And even if one feels a sense of obligation to one's society, there are many other ways of repaying the debt, if that is what it is: by working productively, paying taxes, being law abiding, voting and participating in other political activities, supporting community organizations, doing volunteer work, and so on.[5]

But the strongest reason women do not have an obligation to have children for the state is that such an obligation would make women into procreative serfs. It would mean that women are instruments for furthering the state good, a cause that most women never explicitly agree to. Moreover, a sense of duty to the state is not a strong foundation for having children because one's moral focus is then not on the children themselves, but on the society. A person who feels no great interest in or liking for caring for children but procreates out of a sense of civic duty would likely be an inadequate parent at best.[6] Such an approach might also be dangerous for the offspring, for it would mean treating children primarily as potential instruments of the state, whose labor can be used for military, industrial, economic, or intelligence purposes.

A General Comment on Deontological Arguments

I have shown that the standard deontological arguments advanced to support procreation—heeding the supposed intrinsic value of childbearing; passing on a name, genetic link, or property; fulfilling a duty to others; keeping a promise; and discharging duties to religion or to the state—are not morally compelling. They do not defeat the right not to reproduce; hence, they do not generate an obligation to have a child. Moreover, to the extent that these arguments purport to create a moral requirement that women serve as breeders or that children function primarily to fulfill the needs of dynasties or political regimes, then none of them is a good reason for procreation. The systemic moral problem with deontological arguments in support of choosing to procreate is that such arguments both require and validate the use of women or children and often both as mere means to the implementation of some duty or the perpetuation of some supposed intrinsic value. Using people as mere means to the accomplishment of a goal—a goal that is not inherently related to their own well-being—is a fundamental violation of their personhood.

5

Consequentialist Reasons for Having Children

If the criterion for the moral evaluation of our behavior is the consequences it produces, then we should act in a way that will produce good and avoid causing harm. It then appears that one is justified in having a child when the positive consequences of bringing the child into existence outweigh the negative consequences of doing so. This view, in its most minimal form, is the consequentialist justification for procreation. In this chapter, I examine various consequentialist arguments for procreation and show that they do not provide an adequate foundation for procreative choices. Indeed, in some cases, such arguments result in egregious unfairness.

Philosophers have often remarked that there is a philosophically interesting asymmetry in our assumptions about procreation. This asymmetry is that "while there is a duty to avoid bringing suffering people into existence, there is no duty to bring happy people into being" (Benatar 2006, 32).[1] In general, we think making *people happy* is rather a good thing. Why then should we not recognize an obligation to make *happy people*?

In fact, why not go further? As a version of consequentialism, the theory of utilitarianism says that one should not only produce good but produce as much good as possible, maximizing the balance of good over bad. Utilitarianism then appears to imply that we have an ethical *obligation* to bring children, perhaps many children, into the world, provided that doing so will increase net well-being. Torbjörn Tännsjö, for example, argues, "The mere addition to the world of a person leading a life worth living makes the world better" (2004, 232).

Suppose you are a woman with two children, each of whom has a good life. Then you have created double the amount of good that you would have created by having only one child. And if you have three children, then you have tripled the amount of good you would create by having only one child. The implication then appears to be that you have very good reasons for having a large number of children (Hutchinson 1982). Perhaps, like reality star Kate Gosselin, you should even use medical assistance to increase the likelihood that you will give birth to many children simultaneously. Of course, at some point the law of diminishing returns kicks in. Once you reach the fifteenth child—or for some of us it might be the tenth or the seventh—you would no longer be so capable of giving that child a very good life. You might be overworked and stressed; your resources would not go far; you might have trouble feeding, clothing, sheltering, and educating them all.

You might think, then, that you do not have reasons to have more than the number you can comfortably handle; you certainly have no obligation to do so. But that is not true, if utilitarianism is correct. For any child you have—even number eleven or twelve or higher—will probably still have a reasonably good life, and that life will constitute a net gain for the world's fund of happiness. The child may not be as happy as she would have been if you had only five children, but she will still experience a lifetime of at least some well-being. If the child never exists, though, then the well-being the child would have had will not exist at all.

Of course, the older a woman gets, the greater her risk becomes of having a child with impairments—for example, Down syndrome. Although some people believe that a life without disease or disability is better than life with either one, nonetheless, as disability activists remind us, we who are temporarily nonimpaired should never assume that impaired people's lives are not worth living. And in fact, on average, many people with Down syndrome seem to be remarkably content and happy. So the possibility of creating children with impairments may not be enough to release you from the utilitarian obligation of creating more children. (I say more about impairments in chapter 8.)

Perhaps after the twentieth child, you might be running the risk, if you are the woman having the children, of doing severe harm to yourself. According to utilitarianism, you are not entitled to value your well-being to the exclusion of that of others, but you are entitled to include it in the calculation. Nevertheless, you might be forgiven for wondering if there are reasons to stop having children long before the point that you make yourself very ill or even drop dead from bearing large numbers of them.

Taken to its extreme limit, the consequentialist justification for procreation famously results, on a global scale, in what philosopher Derek Parfit calls the "Repugnant Conclusion," which he defines as follows: "Compared with the existence of very many people—say, ten billion—all of whom have a very high quality of life, there must be some much larger number of people whose existence, if other things are equal, would be better, even though these people would have lives that are barely worth living" (2004, 10). In other words, if the goal is simply to produce as much good as possible, then we would have to produce as many people as possible, even if their individual lives are not very good, because the total amount of good would thereby be maximized.

This uncomfortable but nonetheless bizarrely plausible idea has spawned an entire generation of debate.[2] The debate is concerned with overpopulation, quality of life, and the current generation's obligations to future generations, yet it is mostly unrelated to individual moral decision making by women and men and oblivious to the reproductive labor by women that is necessary to produce future generations.

For fans of the "Repugnant Conclusion" debate, the main question is whether it is better for there to be more people who are less well off or fewer people who are better off. Tännsjö thinks we should simply accept the Repugnant Conclusion and comments, "Such a want of generosity, if we do not welcome such a creature [a newborn infant]!" (2004, 233). But generosity does not require us to create the baby in the first place. Although some children end up having very good lives, we do not have an obligation to nonexistent beings to bring them into existence. If a nonexistent individual is never conceived, no one has been wronged.

Moreover, Tännsjö never thinks about who the "we" are who would have to do the welcoming by conceiving, gestating, delivering, and breastfeeding these new creatures. The question is not only "How many children must be produced to reach maximum utility?" but also "Who will gestate and raise those children, how, if at all, will the gestators benefit from their own reproductive labor, and what sacrifices will they be expected to make?" Women all over the planet choose to have fewer children as their education and resources increase. This preference is a clear indication that women are unlikely to agree to maximize the population and will have to be treated coercively and denied education to compel them to do so. The Repugnant Conclusion is repugnant in part because it does not direct adequate moral attention to the women who would have to do the reproductive labor to generate the millions of new human beings. It is mistaken because the premises that lead to it are insidiously gender neutral. That gender neutrality at best ignores and at worst mandates injustice to women, first by requiring disproportionate sacrifices from women for the sake of the alleged goods to be obtained through procreation and second by ignoring women's right not to reproduce.

Any theory about the ethics of having children cannot overlook the necessity of both concern for women's well-being and respect for women's autonomy. Only by regarding so-called population ethics in utterly abstract and impersonal terms can these fundamental aspects of the "why have children?" decision be overlooked. An unmitigated devotion to the maximization of good by the production of more and more children is likely to ignore the right not to reproduce, instead seeing the hardships and lack of freedom experienced by a woman whose life is devoted to reproduction as outweighed by the prospective well-being of the children she produces.

As many critics have noted in other contexts, what utilitarianism routinely expects of us is supererogation—going above and beyond the call of duty. Maximization in population ethics requires women to go way above and beyond the call of duty at the expense both of their right not to reproduce and of their health and well-being. But none of us has an obligation to create the greatest possible amount of good at every point. If we were constantly trying to create the largest possible amount of good, we would be forced to lead very different lives, sacrificing ourselves almost to the point of collapse and ignoring many of our basic human rights. We might very well have to neglect our own relationships, commitments, and work. Perhaps some of us ought to give away our children to other people because other adults can make them happier or would be made happier than we are by raising our children.[3] The fact that we are not doing these things means, according to utilitarianism, that we are almost never doing what is right—a counterintuitive implication that suggests that utilitarianism demands too much.

Of course, a utilitarian might respond that if in fact we can do more good by attending to our own relationships, commitments, and work than by helping others, then of course we should not neglect them. But my point is a different (though not new) one: that we ought not to neglect our own relationships, commitments, and work *even if* there are other ways by which we can produce more good. A woman may have a particular commitment to a job, an artistic project, or a relationship; she may have dedicated herself to politics, science, or the care of younger siblings. These commitments are a core part of her sense of herself and her views about how to live her life; they are, for her, a matter of integrity (Smart and Williams 1973, 99). In many cases, it would simply be wrong for her to abandon these commitments in order to create babies, even if those babies will grow into happy and fulfilled adults.[4]

Rather than maximizing good across the board, our moral obligations for several reasons tend to be strongest in relation to those closest to us—our family members, our friends, our colleagues, our neighbors, our coworkers. First, we have usually made a commitment, explicit or implicit, to care about their well-being. Second, we can be more effective in doing good for those who are close to us. We are more likely to know their needs, wants, and abilities. We are more likely to interact directly with them.

Moreover, a principle that requires maximizing good does not work as a general moral rule even for one's own self. As Michael Parker points out, any attempt to achieve the best possible life "would need to factor in the effects of perfectionism itself" and might make "even the achievement of the good enough difficult." Perfectionism is likely to render people dissatisfied with the lives they have and to engage them in a "constant drive for self-improvement which would inevitably be both exhausting and unlikely to lead to stable, satisfying or deep interpersonal relationships" (2007, 282).

For all of the reasons I have discussed (respect for women's well-being and autonomy; supererogation; obligations to one's existing relationships and commitments; and the dangers of perfectionism), it is implausible to claim that women have an obligation to have large numbers of children because of the potential net good that children may experience or contribute. In other words, a simplistic utilitarianism is wrong about the ethics of having children.

To return to the question with which I started this chapter, we can most easily explain the absence of any duty to make happy people (as opposed to making people happy) by reference to the injustice, especially to women, that such a duty would create. Women and men have a right not to reproduce. That is, men do not have to provide sperm, and women are entitled to control their bodies and their reproductive functions in order to protect themselves from the sacrifices that procreation may demand. Those rights militate against any supposed duty or obligation to reproduce in any way, even if entirely happy people would be the result.

In chapter 9, in a discussion of the possibility of human extinction, I say more about consequentialist arguments regarding the general value of children to society. For now, I turn to an examination of consequentialist arguments regarding the putative benefits children may bring to their own parents and siblings.

Economic Benefits for Parents

One traditional consequentialist reason for having children is to help support the family. In the past (and even today in some parts of the world), children were the parents' only form of old-age pension. Children were needed for their labor—in the fields, the stable, the barn, the workshop, and the house. Once past the age of seven or so, a child would quickly go from being an economic liability to being an economic asset, even in fairly well-off families (see, e.g., Ariès 1962, 365–369). Children were valuable— not intrinsically valuable, but valuable in terms of their labor power.

By the mid–twentieth century in the West, children were becoming in economic terms mostly a liability and a growing one at that. As a result, the economic argument for procreation now looks implausible. It takes several hundred thousand dollars to raise children—money spent not only in feeding, clothing, and housing them, but in giving them the necessary education that will enable them to survive and thrive in economies where knowledge and technologies play greater and greater roles. Moreover, children are also expensive in terms of "opportunity costs": the foregone income that their parents give up to raise them. Someone must care for the children. Parents must either do it themselves or pay others to do it. If they do it themselves, they are foregoing the income they can otherwise earn in the labor market. It is usually the mother who foregoes this income, along with the pension that she might otherwise accumulate. Moreover, as is well known, women who participate in the labor market after having children often pay an additional price for motherhood in terms of having fewer chances for advancement, being regarded as "not serious" about their careers, falling behind in experience and current knowledge, being regarded as casual or expendable labor, and so on.

And even if one hopes that decades down the line one's children will be a source of support in one's old age, present observations show that this support cannot be counted upon. In a few cases, it's a matter of willful neglect by adult children of their aging parents. In some cases, it may be that the adult children feel they owe their parents nothing. In other cases, it's a matter of the adult children's having multiple familial and economic allegiances, so that precisely when their elderly parents may need support, the adult children are also being called upon to pay for the education of their adolescent children. And in some cases, for a host of reasons, adult children barely have enough money to support themselves, let alone their parents.

Therefore, anyone who has children for the sake of the supposed financial support they can provide is not only not justified in so doing but probably deluded. The economic value of children to parents is not a reason that in these days can make having children an obligation or even serve as the sole justification for procreation.

Psychological Benefits for Parents

I knew that children could teach you how to pay attention, but by the same token so can shingles, and I knew that children gave you so many excuses to celebrate, only half of them false. You will have to forgive me for using these terms: Children can connect you to the child inside you, who can still play and be silly and helpless and needy and capable of wonder. (Lamott 2007, 184)

Barring wartime or other social or political crisis, it is hard for me to understand any woman deciding not to have a child if she could (financially, physically, emotionally). There is nothing in my own life that could possibly have been more important or a greater source of joy and fulfillment. (Nedelsky 1999, 312)

When people are asked informally to explain why they want to have children or why they had the children they had, they often speak in consequentialist terms of potential benefits for themselves: "I love children"; "I love being pregnant"; "I will not be fulfilled unless I have a child"; "I don't want to miss out on the experience of parenting;" "To relive my own childhood"; "So I won't be lonely"; "I just want someone to love me." The Planned Parenthood Association says that people explain their desire for children as follows: "To give someone the opportunities I never

had. To have a child to be like me. To keep me company. To pass on beliefs, values and ideas to" (quoted in Bergum 1997, 29). More cynically,
Corinne Maier remarks, "We procreate in order to exact revenge on a dis-
appointing life. We are convinced we can save our child from the mistakes
that we believe victimized us" (2007, 62–63).

Many people believe the best reason for having a child is simply that
doing so will make the parents happy. But the evidence in support of that
belief is not very strong. There is not room here to survey all the data,
but the fact that so much of it fails to support a connection between
parenthood and happiness should give pause to anyone who thinks procreation will inevitably make them happier. Indeed, Nattavudh Powdthavee writes, "There is an almost zero association between having children
and happiness" (2009, 308). The *belief* that having children will bring
happiness is transmitted to later generations much more readily than the
belief that children will bring unhappiness because persons who hold the
latter view will likely not have children and hence transmit the belief,
whereas those who hold the former belief will procreate and pass it on
(Powdthavee 2009, 309). The belief's transmissibility, however, does not
make it true. Powdthavee states that the empirical evidence shows that
parents "often report statistically significantly lower levels of happiness
. . . life satisfaction . . . marital satisfaction . . . and mental well-being ...
compared with non-parents" (2009, 308). As Daniel Gilbert points out,
the research indicates that heterosexual couples start out happy in their
marriages "and then become progressively less satisfied over the course of
their lives together, getting close to their original levels of satisfaction only
when their children leave home" (2005, 243).

One of the few academic dissenters to this message is economist Bryan
Caplan, who argues that the gap between the happiness of those with
children and those without is small; parents, he believes, are almost as
happy as nonparents. Moreover, he says, empirical studies indicate that
if childless adults had their lives to do over, most would choose to be
parents. Parenthood, he says, "wins hands down" (2010). He also argues
that we need not see weak parenting as costly to children because parents' influence is overstated. Twin studies suggest that nurture has few
long-term effects: "If you think that your kids' future rests in your hands,
you'll probably make many painful 'investments'—and feel guilty that
you didn't do more. Once you realize that your kids' future largely rests

in their own hands, you can give yourself a guilt-free break" and hence enjoy parenthood to a greater extent. In fact, Caplan urges that his hedonic calculus actually implies "Buy more"—that is, have more children. The costs of raising children are "frontloaded, and the benefits are backloaded"; that is, babies are a great deal of work, but parents will one day be begging for time with their offspring.

However, many people do not accept Caplan's message. In an article scarily titled "All Joy and No Fun: Why Parents Hate Parenting," Jennifer Senior (2010) cites a variety of empirical evidence that "parents are less happy than nonparents." Children generate "unrivaled moments of frustration, tedium, anxiety, heartbreak." Although children provide their parents with "moments of transcendence," they are nonetheless "all joy and no fun."

Perhaps the reason for the alleged paucity of fun is that "raising children is probably the toughest and the dullest job in the world" (Powdthavee 2009, 310)—hyperbole to be sure: coal mining, garbage collecting, and human-waste processing can easily compete with and surpass child rearing in terms of toughness and dullness. Nonetheless, in prosperous regions in the twenty-first century children are "not only a great expense but subjects to be sculpted, stimulated, instructed, groomed" (Senior 2010), all of which takes a lot of work. Parents are spending more time with their children than they did in 1975, despite the fact that women are doing more paid work than in the past (Senior 2010).

As a result, it's a mistake to rely on procreation as a guarantor of happiness, at least in the short term. As Judith Timson trenchantly puts it, "Parents today need to get over expecting to be intrinsically happy or rewarded doing what people have dutifully done for millennia under sometimes astonishingly adverse conditions: create and raise the next generation. The search for perfect happiness through parenting is not only counterproductive, it's a luxury that only the affluent can afford" (2010, 3).

Not only is it risky to have a child to make oneself happy; it is also inconsiderate of the child. Childless people are sometimes said to be selfish, but the standard reasons people give for *having* children sound rather selfish or at the very least self-oriented. Interestingly, the childless women in Leslie Cannold's empirical study found it difficult to come up with what they considered to be truly adequate reasons for having children. Instead, they generated a list of self-oriented reasons that they regarded as bad or wrong—such as "to quell boredom; to remedy dissatisfaction at work; to do what everyone else is doing (stay 'in-step'); because time is running out; to avoid loneliness in old age; to hold a relationship together; to adhere to female socialization to mother; to experience pregnancy; [and] to have a child to satisfy one's own needs without adequate consideration of the child's need" (2003, 280).

Most people would probably agree that these reasons are weak. They are weak in part because, like procreating to become happy, they are impractical: there is no guarantee whatsoever that having children will hold a marriage together, resolve one's personal problems, or alleviate loneliness in old age. More important, however, they are weak because they are selfish: they propose to use a child to enhance one's own well-being without concern for the child's well-being. It is hardly fair to use a vulnerable, dependent, nonautonomous person to fix an adult person's life. This notion—using the child for purposes that have nothing to do with the child's welfare—is unfortunately characteristic of many reasons typically given for having children. We saw this in chapter 4 in the discussion of the deontological arguments for procreation, and we see it now with respect to the consequentialist arguments. To have a child in order to benefit oneself is a moral error. It risks a future child's happiness and well-being in order to promote good for oneself. If the child's own life is unhappy, then the child has been sacrificed to the parent's well-being. Even if the child is happy, he is still being used as a means to satisfy the parent's goals.

But perhaps it is inevitable that, whatever one's reasons for having a child, the child will end up serving as a means to some end (Gibson 1995, 236). Some argue that the main question is whether there are reasons for having children that do not treat them *only* as a means, but just in part (Cannold 2003, 286). British philosopher Susanne Gibson, for example, suggests that what are needed are reasons for having children that are "compatible with treating them at the same time as an end, or to put it another way, with respecting them as an equal human being" (1995, 237).

Gibson is saying that whatever an individual's original motive for procreation, selfish or self-oriented though it may be, if the child is treated with respect once it exists, then we need not worry about the reasons for creating it. I don't find this suggestion convincing. I think the motives for creating a child do matter, and they matter at least in part for consequentialist reasons, as I attempt to show in the next section.

"Savior Siblings"

Consider the possibility that the needs of an existing child might provide a good consequentialist reason for having a baby who will be a sibling to her. By definition, of course, this reason can never apply to the first child, only to subsequent children. Some parents have a second child just because they want their first to have the experience of a sibling. But a more pressing case is the one in which the first child has an apparent *medical* need for a "savior sibling."

"Savior sibling" is the media name for a child who is conceived, gestated, and delivered in order to provide umbilical cord blood, or, even more contentious, bone marrow desperately needed by the parents' older child (Mills 2005, 2). Without the stem cells obtained from the blood or bone marrow, the ill elder sibling will die. In order to try to ensure that the savior sibling is a close genetic match for the ill older child, IVF, preimplantation genetic diagnosis (PGD), and tissue typing are usually carried out (Boyle and Savulescu 2001).

Contrary to the majority of opinions expressed in the bioethical literature (e.g., Boyle and Savulescu 2001; Robertson, Kahn, and Wagner 2002; Sheldon and Wilkinson 2004; Spriggs 2005), I believe that creating a child to serve as a savior sibling is not justified. That is, the consequentialist argument that it is morally justified to have a child for the sake of her potential medical benefit to an existing sibling is unsuccessful. To show this, in the following six sections I present and evaluate the arguments commonly given in support of creating children as savior siblings.

Reproductive Freedom

First, it might be argued that having the second child as a savior sibling is a simple exercise of reproductive freedom on the parents' part. People are entitled to choose whether to have children, and creating a savior sibling is part of that entitlement.

I agree, at least in the sense that we should respect human beings' entitlement to decide when, where, and how they will have their biological children and how many. That is, as I argued in chapter 2, individuals have a *negative right* not to be interfered with in reproduction. I do not criticize savior siblings on these grounds. But the negative right to reproduce does not by itself vindicate the use of IVF, PGD, and tissue typing to create a child in order to be a savior sibling. And even if the creation of a savior sibling did not require expensive reproductive technologies, there are, as I show, moral arguments against it that make the exercise of reproductive freedom unjustified.

Illness-Free Existence

It might be argued that the savior sibling himself is benefited because the use of PGD that contributed to his existence increases the chance that he will not have the disease that is killing his older sibling (Spriggs 2005, 341). Sally Sheldon and Steven Wilkinson, however, point out that, strictly speaking, PGD does not benefit the child by *causing* him to be free of illness through curing him or removing a disorder. Rather, PGD merely lets medical personnel know which one(s) of the embryos created through IVF are free or likely to be free of disease or disorder. Hence, *if* PGD is a benefit at all to the savior sibling, it is a benefit only because it contributes to causing medical personnel to implant the embryo from which the child develops (2004, 535). It is not as if the child might have had an existence plagued by disease from which he was saved by medical science; it is this existence or none at all.

Sheldon and Wilkinson do not think that creating savior siblings is morally problematic, and they defend the practice. Nonetheless, their point serves to undermine the idea that savior siblings are benefited from the process of being produced as savior siblings. They are no more benefited than are any children that are created through IVF and PGD. And what is the benefit? Simple disease-free existence. Thus, if the defender of savior siblings wants to insist that disease-free existence is a benefit, then the defender is also committed to saying that all disease-free children are benefited by being caused to come into existence, whatever the cause. But that claim is unhelpful to the goal of defending savior siblings, for the argument then fails to pick out any *particular* benefit unique to savior siblings. (Whether children are in fact benefited from coming into existence is a topic that I turn to in chapter 6.)[5]

Saving a Life

The most important argument in support of creating savior siblings is that they end up producing an essential and hugely valuable effect: saving a human life. David Benatar suggests that children are always created to serve as means to some sort of end (2006, 129–130). Sheldon and Wilkinson agree. Among the "instrumental" uses of children they list "'completing a family,' being a playmate for an existing child, saving a marriage, delighting prospective grandparents, [and] providing an heir." They suggest that "having a child as a means . . . is not in itself objectionable," provided one does not "discard" the child once it has served its purpose (2004, 534). Robert Boyle and Julian Savulescu also agree: "Though we might aspire to a world where parents always dote on their children as unconditional ends, in reality many children are born for a purpose: to care for their parents, as a companion to a sibling, or to run the family business. . . . Provided that parents love their child, there is little problem with that child benefiting others" (2001, 1241). Perhaps, then, there is no better reason to have a child than to save another one (Benatar 2006, 130–131). Without savior siblings, some children will die who could otherwise have been saved. At the very least, as John Robertson, Jeffrey Kahn, and John Wagner point out, having a savior sibling "doubles the parents' chances of having surviving children" (2002, 36). Hence, the "onus of proof" is on those who condemn the creation of savior siblings to show why they should reject this means of saving a child's life (Sheldon and Wilkinson 2004, 533).

But there are several problems with this kind of argument. First, the argument depends on the assumption that it is morally unobjectionable to create a baby for the various purposes of completing a family, giving a playmate to an existing child, delighting grandparents, saving a marriage, providing an heir, and so on. As I hope the discussion so far in this chapter and in chapter 4 has shown, it is not self-evident that these reasons are unobjectionable. The fact that infants are treated as means for fulfilling adults' goals in other cases does not in itself make it acceptable to treat an infant as a means in the savior sibling case.

Second, the parents can't know in advance whether the processes of IVF and PGD will proceed without a hitch or whether the donation from the new baby will indeed prevent the existing sibling from dying. The sibling may die anyway, despite the donation from the new baby. The tissue match may not be close enough, or there may be an error in the PGD and tissue typing.

Despite this epistemic ambiguity, it may look as if creating a savior sibling is a risk worth taking; the parents must simply be informed in advance that their attempt to create a match may fail. If they are willing to take the chance and rear whatever child they get, then there is not a moral problem. But the difficulty is that the parents cannot be sure what their attitude will be if the ill child is not cured. They will then find themselves in a situation where they must continue both to care for the first child, whom they have not helped as they intended and whose death is now more certain than before, and to raise an additional child whom they would not otherwise have procreated and who has failed to serve the purpose for which she was created.[6] No one can be confident that this failure will not affect their attitudes toward the savior sibling.

The third problem with the "save a life" justification for creating savior siblings is that the parents are in a situation of conflict of interest. Their two children's interests do not coincide. The parents cannot be an unbiased advocate or surrogate decision maker for the new baby because they are acting on the basis of the first child's interests.

Nevertheless, it might be argued that once the second child is born, it *is* in his interests to contribute his blood or bone marrow: he is helping to cure his ill sibling so that he will continue to have that sibling in his life. (After all, if the younger sibling *already* existed, and an older sibling turned out to be very ill and needed the younger one's bone marrow, it would not seem inappropriate for the younger one to donate—although whether he can give informed consent will depend on his age.) Maybe the savior sibling will eventually even "derive pleasure from knowing that he has saved [the older child's] life" (Sheldon and Wilkinson 2004, 536). In addition, his parents will be so grateful and appreciative that they will love him even more.

But here is the odd feature of this case: the savior sibling's interests are inseparable from the reasons for his existence. That is, the savior sibling's interests in curing the older child and in pleasing his parents through his curative powers are the same as the reasons he was created. Now it's true that no child will have any interests whatsoever unless he exists. But the particular interests that most other children have are not so directly connected to the reasons for their creation. The savior sibling has certain interests (helping an older sibling, keeping the sibling alive, earning the gratitude of her parents) precisely *because* he was created to benefit already-living family members. The needs of others preexist and generate the child's interests. The fulfillment of the savior sibling's interests is dependent on his success in satisfying the other family members' needs.

The situation is made even more objectionable because of the *kinds* of benefits that are expected from the second child. For example, in order to obtain the maximum amount of umbilical cord blood to assist the ill older sibling, it is essential to clamp the new baby's cord promptly. But doing so deprives the baby himself of oxygenated blood that he would otherwise receive if clamping is not immediate. Receiving that blood during the time when the infant's respiration is first being established increases the baby's iron levels (Hutchon 2006, 1073). For preterm infants, the benefits of cord clamping delayed by one to three minutes may be even greater, "with reductions in anaemia, intraventricular haemorrhage, and the need for transfusion for hypovolaemia [decreased blood volume]" (Weeks 2007, 312).[7]

The extraction of bone marrow is even more problematic for the child from whom it is taken. The extraction usually occurs within the child's first two years and can cause pain. The marrow is extracted either from the hipbones or the sternum. Although the child is anaesthetized during the "harvest," the child may feel pain in the needle site(s) during his recovery (Children's Hospital Boston n.d.). A description of adults' recovery from bone marrow donation prescribes a week of recovery: "Common side effects of this type of bone marrow donation can include nausea, headache, and fatigue. These side effects are most often related to the anesthesia. Donors may also experience bruising or discomfort in the lower back" (American Society of Clinical Oncology n.d.).

Thus, savior siblings may be subjected to one or more debilitating and even painful medical procedures that they have not chosen, that are not warranted by their own medical condition, and to which they cannot give a meaningful informed consent. A medical procedure is ordinarily undertaken to provide a health benefit to the individual who undergoes it. But the savior sibling has nothing wrong with him. It is difficult, perhaps impossible, to think of any other situation in which an individual who is unable to give consent nevertheless undergoes medical procedures to benefit another person (Spriggs 2005, 341).

Of course, human beings frequently treat each other as means, though usually not *only* as means. And although the savior sibling functions as a means, he is not only a means. The child will not be treated as a mere commodity. Supporters of the creation of savior siblings make a distinction between why the child was created and how he is treated once he is here. Perhaps, as Sheldon and Wilkinson remark, "there is nothing objectionable about creating a baby as a 'means to an end' provided that it is also viewed and treated as a human being" (2004, 534).

After all, as already mentioned, the parents will very likely love the second child just as they love the first child. Thus, the child both is used as a means *and* is treated as an end. Robertson, Kahn, and Wagner suggest that the very fact that the parents are willing to create another child to protect and save the first one shows that they are "highly committed to the well-being of their children, and that they will value the second child for its own sake as well" (2002, 35).

If this is the case, then we can raise two questions. One is about the balance of the means and the end. The other is about whether the end justifies the means.

The Balance of Means and End

An important question here is whether the child is treated primarily as a means and secondarily as an end or whether he is treated secondarily as a means and primarily as an end (Chris Lowry, personal communication, March 2008). As an example of the first type of balance, I am reminded of a student who, after his course with me is over, is polite and considerate but needs me (and regards me) primarily as a provider of a graduate-school application reference. He uses me as a means to his own career goals, but he is respectful in so doing and in that respect also treats me as an end. I see nothing wrong with this use; the student is not my friend, and he is no longer even my student; if he was a good student, I feel responsible for providing some mentoring and academic career support. But surely that is not what a relationship with a child should be like. No child, even if respected and cared for, should be primarily a means to his parents' and sibling's ends. Such a treatment is inconsistent with a close, warm, loving familial relationship in which a child can thrive while developing his own talents and purposes.

As an example of the second type of balance, think of a friendship in which, in its beginnings perhaps, one person acquires certain benefits from another and that is the reason they first get to know each other. Writes Chris Lowry: "I'm finding it hard to think of a lot of examples where treating others as ends is the primary over-riding reason from the start. . . . In cases that involve freely doing something for someone or freely choosing to build a relation with someone, . . . benefit to self (widely construed) very often plays an initial role" (personal communication, March 2008).

Lowry may be correct that some friendships originate in that way. Eventually, however, one no longer sees the other person just as a means but instead comes to cherish the person as a valuable friend for her own sake. Thus, the balance gradually tips from mostly treating the person as a means to treating the person primarily as an end in herself. And when a savior sibling is created as a means and once born is used as a means, it is certainly better that his means-value gradually becomes secondary—when and if it does—to his value as an end in himself.

In fact, however, some friendships do not start out with the individuals seeing and treating each other primarily as means. In cases where *from the start* it is a true friendship that is sought, each person tries to value the other for her own sake, to recognize what is unique and interesting about her, and to treat her with friendly respect. The case of procreation is or at least ought to be much more like the second path to friendship, where the relationship is wanted not because it serves other purposes, but because the person is valued for herself.

It admittedly might be unusual and maybe even morally worrying for someone to have a child without wanting at least *some* benefits from doing so; in that sense, I suppose, the prospective parent prepares to use the child as a means. Similarly, one would probably not seek a friendship without wanting any benefits from the friend. But to be morally sound, both the motivation and the justification for forming the friendship or having the child need to be about much more than what the friend or the child can do for one. Moreover, just as in a friendship the benefits obtained from the friend are *derived from* valuing this particular friend for her own sake, so also in a parent–child relationship the benefits come precisely because the parents value this particular child for his own sake.

The child cannot be *created* for his own sake because he does not pre-exist his conception, but once born he can and should be *valued* for his own sake, and doing so precludes using him as a medical resource for another child. The parents, instead of wanting a child merely for the benefits the child may bring them, can seek to create a child whose unique value they will recognize and cherish and with whom they will have a parental relationship. There is a crucial moral difference between creating a child in order to benefit existing individuals and creating a child in order to value the child herself. Saying this does not mean that the child has value before he exists; it means that *when* he exists, he is valued for himself, not just used for others. In procreating, the parents should undertake to create a being whom they will value for his own sake.

In at least one important respect, of course, the developing relationship between parent and child is significantly different from a developing friendship. The difference in procreation is that the parent not only starts to build a relationship with the child but actually *creates* the person with whom she has the relationship. In choosing to become a parent, one sets out to create a relationship, and one also uniquely sets out to create the person with whom one has the relationship. One would think, then, that the moral responsibility to treat with respect and care the person who is created would be even greater than in a case where one has not created the other person in the relationship.

One would not start a relationship of any kind with a stranger by expecting—let alone demanding—the donation of blood or bone marrow. Yet that is exactly what happens in the case of savior siblings. The familial relationships—between parents and child as well as between the savior sibling and his ill sibling—*start out* with the new baby's being required to serve the rest of his family. If this requirement is not acceptable in a developing friendship with an adult, I cannot see how it can be acceptable in a developing relationship with a new baby.

Does the End Justify the Means?

The problem with the creation of the savior sibling, then, is that the new person who is created is created *to be used*. Perhaps, however, it might be retorted that the case of savior siblings is a situation in which the end justifies the means. The end or goal is an extremely good one: saving an existing child. At the point at which parents turn to the creation of a savior sibling, there is no other way in which to save the existing child. Indeed, Merle Spriggs goes so far as to say that the life of the ill older sibling *trumps* other moral conditions in this situation and in any other comparable one, even in the absence of informed consent from the donor (2005, 341 and 342).

To test whether this claim is as plausible as Spriggs assumes, let's consider some related cases. First, imagine that the parents whose child is ill are unable or even unwilling to have another child. Instead, they want to adopt an orphaned child who is an adequate genetic match for their own child. The adopted child will then be used as a source of blood and bone marrow in an effort to cure their sick child. If creating a savior sibling is morally acceptable, then shouldn't adopting one also be?

I suspect that many people would reject using an adopted child in that way. But if they see nothing wrong with a genetically related savior sibling, they should not have qualms about an adopted savior sibling. There are only two differences between the gestated savior sibling and the adopted savior sibling: in the adoption situation, the child already exists, and the child is not genetically related to the adopters (even though the adoptee would have to be a genetic match to the sick child). It is hard to see why these differences would make using the adopted child as a "savior" deeply morally different. In the twenty-first century, following the UN's recognition of the rights of children, the mere facts of having gestated a child and being genetically related to it do not give one ownership over it. Hence, a genetic relationship to a child does not make using the child more acceptable than using a genetically unrelated child would be. If anything, as I suggested earlier, the instrumental use of the expressly gestated savior sibling might in fact be more problematic because that child is created precisely in order to be used.

Of course, it might be pointed out that the adopted child is vulnerable; having lost its original parents, it is then transferred to new ones without being able to give consent. But the genetically related child is just as vulnerable and also cannot give consent to being used as a medical resource. I suggest that anyone who has moral qualms about using an adopted child as a savior sibling should also have misgivings about creating a genetically related child to use as a savior sibling.

If the savior sibling is used for what he was created or adopted for, then he *is* being used, even if he is otherwise loved and well cared for. And if using a savior sibling is morally justified, then many otherwise morally questionable treatments of children would also seem to be morally justified. Bone marrow is a renewable human substance. Consider what we might call nonrenewable resources, such as organs. Imagine choosing to have another child in order to provide a kidney for an existing child. In her novel *My Sister's Keeper* (2004), author Jodi Picoult depicts a savior sibling who is required throughout her young life to give repeated donations of blood and bone marrow and finally is asked for a kidney. My point here is not so much that having a child to provide bone marrow for an existing child will *inevitably result* in someone's having a child in order to provide nonrenewable bodily organs. This is not a "slippery slope" argument about the morally questionable behaviors that creating savior siblings may lead us to.[8] It is instead an argument about the scope and limits of moral justification and the significance of moral motivation in procreation. The Infertility Treatment Authority of Victoria, Australia, has opined that "the harvesting of organs such as kidneys [from savior siblings] is not acceptable" (Spriggs and Savulescu 2002, 289), but the reason is not clear. My point is that if having a child to provide bone marrow is considered morally acceptable, it becomes much harder to know whether or why there is anything wrong with having a child in order to provide a kidney.

Perhaps the defender of savior siblings would say that the answer is built into the question: bone marrow is renewable, whereas a kidney is not. But I'm not sure they are so very different. After all, the child has two kidneys. His life will be a little more difficult with only one, but he can accommodate himself to it. And his donated kidney will enable his sibling to live. Isn't the life of the older child worth the cost to the savior sibling of giving up a kidney? If saving the life of the older child is defined as the paramount value, then many possible uses for savior siblings will come to seem to be morally justified.

Suppose, for example, that it is not an older sibling who needs the donation from the "savior," but rather one of the child's parents, as has apparently happened in the Netherlands (Devolder 2005, 585).[9] Or imagine that a couple produces a savior offspring in order to sell the savior sibling's blood, bone marrow, or kidney to the parents of another child who is in desperate need of bodily substances or parts and will die without them. The savior's bodily substances and parts thereby benefit the other family's child and increase his own family's level of material well-being. Or, in case it is thought that it is the selling of bodily substances and organs that makes the situation morally wrong, imagine that the parents are more generous and simply *give away* their child's blood, bone marrow, or kidney to another couple's needy child, whose life is thereby preserved.

Such possibilities may provoke a visceral reaction of distaste and rejection. But if saving a human life trumps other considerations, as Spriggs and others appear to believe, then it is hard to know why these imagined cases are wrong. In none of them does the savior child consent—but in the standard cases with which I started out, savior siblings do not consent to donating their blood or bone marrow. So it can't be the absence of consent that makes it wrong to have a child in order to provide bodily substances or organs to his parent or wrong to give away his bodily substances or organs to someone else's child. It is difficult for me to see why the fact that one's existing child is terminally ill justifies the choice to have another child as a savior sibling, whereas the fact that a parent is terminally ill or someone else's child is terminally ill does not. I submit that neither the sibling relationship nor the genetic connection is enough to make choosing to have a savior sibling morally justified. That is, if it is not right to have a child to save a parent or to save someone else's child, then it is not right to have a child to save an older sibling. The end does not in this situation justify the means.

Psychological Damage to Savior Siblings?

In arguing against the creation of savior siblings, I have said nothing about the potential psychological impact of the role on the savior sibling himself, and this is for several reasons. First, the question of the psychological impact of being created as a savior sibling is an empirical issue, and I know of no studies so far that have examined these effects.[10] But, second, even if such studies are undertaken, the findings would, in my view, be irrelevant. Interestingly, Sheldon and Wilkinson take the same view. Indeed, they think that even if it can be shown that savior siblings are on average "*less* happy than other children," that fact (if it were a fact) would not be enough to count against the creation of savior siblings because, say Sheldon and Wilkinson, such children are unlikely to have lives that are worse than not being alive at all; their lives are likely to be worth living. If we think that the lives of persons with impairments are worth living despite their impairments, then we should also be willing to support the creation of savior siblings, who in all likelihood will have lives that are worth living (Sheldon and Wilkinson 2004, 536, my emphasis). Robertson, Kahn, and Wagner go so far as to say that because the child would not otherwise have existed, the child would not be harmed *even if* his parents gave him away if he was not a good match or if "they had obtained the umbilical cord blood and were not interested in rearing [him]" (2002, 36).

I suspect that these researchers are correct that savior siblings do have lives that are worth living. However, I do not share Sheldon and Wilkinson's sanguine attitude toward the possibility that such children might be less happy than others, and I reject the suggestion that the creation of a savior sibling would be justified even if he was given up for adoption. Such a view implies that mere existence can compensate for all manner of mistreatment and even abandonment of children. (In the next chapter, I discuss the question whether mere existence is a benefit.) Nonetheless, claims about the psychology of savior siblings are, I believe, unnecessary to my case. My objections rest not upon the potential psychological damage to the child (although for all we know there may be some), but rather upon a view of what parent–child relationships are and ought to be.

Advocates of the legitimacy of creating savior siblings might argue that every chosen child comes into existence because of the needs or desires of one or both parents. That fact does not mean that the child cannot be appreciated and loved. In that respect, savior siblings are not significantly morally different from other children.

By contrast, I suggest that the important moral question about any savior sibling is whether he would have been brought into existence at all if there was not a need for his cord blood or bone marrow. Even though the child cannot be brought into existence for his own sake—that is, to maximize his interests (because he does not preexist his own conception)—we can ask whether the child, once created, is *wanted by his parents for his own sake*—that is, whether he is valued for himself, not just valued for the benefits that he may bring to his parents and sibling(s). If the answer is no, then the child has been immorally made into a means, and, hence, choosing to have such a child is morally wrong.

It might be argued that this standard is too high. How many children are in fact wanted for their own sake rather than as means to an end? Perhaps not as many as we might hope. Nevertheless, the question here is not what our motives are, but what they should be—not what reasons people usually have for choosing to have offspring, but what reasons might justify the choice. Parents of savior siblings may complain that in no other circumstance are potential parents' motives "put under a microscope prior to conception" (Spriggs and Savulescu 2002, 289). My goal in this argument is not to police people's procreative motives but rather to show that procreative motives do matter and to encourage more careful ethical evaluation of one procreative motive that bioethicists have widely considered to be justifiable. In general, what is potentially problematic in the case of savior siblings is treating the child—in fact, any child—as a primary source of benefits to others, whether the parents or the existing siblings. Choosing to procreate is not or ought not to be a mere cost–benefit decision.

Conclusion

The consequentialist reasons that people advance to justify having a child are at least inadequate and unpersuasive and in some cases are downright foolhardy or immoral. These reasons can be condemned on both consequentialist *and* deontological grounds because they overlook women's and children's well-being and because they are potentially unjust to members of both groups. Given the paucity of very strong reasons to have children, it is safe to say that there is also no general obligation to have children.

Indeed, it is extraordinarily difficult to find reasons to have a child that stand up to three crucial moral tests: first, concern for women's and children's well-being; second, respect for women's autonomy; and third, refusal to use the child or the mother as a mere instrument for the accomplishment of some other goal.

6

Not "Better Never to Have Been"

In chapter 5, I noted in the discussion of savior siblings the obvious fact that children do not come into existence by choice. Indeed, "I didn't ask to be born!" is a reproach some children bring against their parents. Given that by the very nature of their situation it is impossible for children to consent to coming into existence, it is essential to ask whether human beings are benefited or harmed or neither by coming into existence. Answering that question is an important step in figuring out whether, when, and why procreation is morally justified or unjustified.

Such a question is not only of theoretical philosophical interest; it is also a pragmatic issue. In the United States, some lawsuits brought on behalf of seriously impaired children allege that the children suffer from "wrongful life." A claim of "wrongful life" is a civil suit "brought by a child (typically a congenitally disabled child) who seeks damages for burdens he suffers that result from his creation. Typically, the child charges that he has been born into an unwanted or miserable life" (Shiffrin 1999, 117). In other words, so serious is the child's suffering that it would have been better if he had not existed.

Some philosophers argue that bringing an individual into existence can benefit that individual (e.g., Parfit 1984, 487–490). Those of us who are parents probably take for granted, without further discussion, that the children whom we have brought or will bring into existence will on the whole be happy and that their lives will be worth living. Indeed, people often assume that their offspring should be grateful to their parents for giving them life. If they are correct, then the justification for having the child would be the child's own benefit. And the empirical evidence supports the belief that most people around the world are at least satisfied with and often very happy about their lives (Myers 2000).[1]

Yet children can also be harmed by coming into existence. As Seana Valentine Shiffrin points out,[2] procreation "ineliminably involves serious moral hazards. . . . [I]t faces difficult justificatory hurdles because it involves imposing serious harms and risks on someone who is not in danger of suffering greater harm if one does not act." In every case, voluntary procreation imposes an unconsented-to burden on a person, even though "the imposition is not necessitated by the need to avert greater harm" (Shiffrin 1999, 136, 139). Hence, there is a moral responsibility to ensure that there are very good reasons indeed for subjecting another person to the hazards of existence. The burden of proof, or at least the burden of *evidence*, is on the person who wants to have children.

But in a recent book chillingly titled *Better Never to Have Been: The Harm of Coming into Existence*, David Benatar argues vehemently that "coming into existence is *always* a serious harm" (2006, 1, emphasis added; subsequent citations to this work give page references only). The entire book is devoted to defending this claim, but as Benatar acknowledges, the main argument behind it is quite straightforward: "Although the good things in one's life make it go better than it otherwise would have gone, one could not have been deprived by their absence if one had not existed. Those who never exist cannot be deprived. However, by coming into existence one does suffer quite serious harms that could not have befallen one had one not come into existence" (1).

If Benatar is correct, then there is always a fundamental and irrevocable reason not to procreate. Not only does Benatar undermine the platitude that procreation is a prima facie good and that the decision to reproduce requires little moral reflection; he provides an argument that, if correct, means that procreation is never good and that moral reflection about reproducing should lead us to give it up[3] (Sue Donaldson, personal communication, February 17, 2008).

Someone encountering Benatar's argument for the first time might point out in response that those who come into existence, especially in the wealthy and privileged West, are also likely to experience benefits— material goods, pleasant experiences, family relationships, education, and accomplishments. It might be urged that those benefits in almost every case outweigh the harms (pain, illness, dashed hopes, unrequited love, and so on) that these people may also suffer.

Benatar's counterargument relies on what he thinks is a key "asymmetry" (30) between the absence of good and the absence of bad: "The

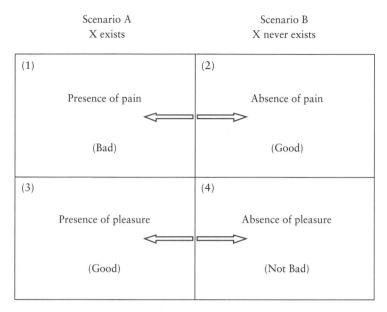

Figure 6.1

Source: David Benatar, Better Never to Have Been: *The Harm of Coming into Existence* (London: Oxford University Press, 2006), figure 2.1. Reprinted by permission of Oxford University Press.

absence of bad things, such as pain, is good even if there is nobody to enjoy that good, whereas the absence of good things, such as pleasure, is bad only if there is somebody who is deprived of these good things. The implication of this is that the avoidance of the bad by never existing is a real advantage over existence, whereas the loss of certain goods by not existing is not a real disadvantage over never existing" (14). Benatar uses the diagram given in figure 6.1 to illustrate his thesis (38).

I believe that Benatar's theory that it is better never to have existed is fatally flawed and that he therefore does not succeed in establishing a strong argument against all procreation. Three criticisms show why and one criticism demonstrates the potentially dangerous consequences of accepting Benatar's theory.

Criticism 1

Here I accept for the sake of argument Benatar's assumption that value is impersonal—that is, that it is legitimate to ascribe value to the absence or avoidance of good or bad, even without any sentient being to experience the absence. But the absence or avoidance of bad things and the absence of good things are not asymmetrical in the way that Benatar believes, for although the absence or avoidance of bad things is, as he says, good, the absence of good things is also at least sometimes bad, even if there is nobody who is deprived of those good things. That is, Benatar's claim that absent good things are not bad is false, and his asymmetry does not obtain.

There is an effective and an ineffective way of making this argument. The *in*effective way would proceed as follows. Think about an uninspiring, flat education—serviceable but boring. Or parents who do an adequate job of raising their children, but the experience for the children is joyless. Or a holiday where no disaster happens, but the weather is just poor enough that the vacationers miss out on most of the pleasures of the area they visit. In all those cases, we'd be inclined to say, the absence of pleasures is bad.

In response, Benatar stresses that his point is that pleasures that are absent because the individual who would have experienced them *does not exist* are different from pleasures that are absent in the life of an *existing* person. The absence of the former is not bad, although the absence of the latter may be bad. "We regret suffering but not the absent pleasures of those who could have existed [but never did]" (35), he says.

A refutation of Benatar's claim that the asymmetry of the absence of bad and the absence of good always holds begins with the following thought experiment. Imagine a nation of ten million people. Five million of them suffer from chronic illness and experience great and unremitting pain. The other five million are free of chronic illness and are able to experience happiness and fulfillment. One of God's angels appeals to God[4] and says, "Surely the suffering of five million of these people is too great. Can you not do something about it?" God agrees. "I will roll back time," says God, "and fix these five million people so that they do not suffer from chronic illness and pain." Time is rolled back, the unfortunate five million are re-created, but this time without their original vulnerability to chronic illness and pain. Like the originally happy 50 percent, they, too, are now capable of happiness and fulfillment, and the angel is pleased.

But after the angel appeals to God, God might alternatively say, "I see that these five million people are suffering. I will roll back time and change things so that this entire nation of individuals, all ten million of them, will not exist. That way, the suffering of five million does not exist." Time is rolled back, the nation of people no longer exists, and so a fortiori there is no chronic illness or pain and no suffering whatsoever.

I suggest that in this second scenario the angel would be justified in being appalled by God's actions. The nonexistence of the good of the happy and fulfilled five million is far too high a price to pay for the absence of bad of the suffering five million. What the thought experiment shows is that, contrary to Benatar's claim, the absence of good can be bad, *not* "not bad."[5] The angel is correct to regret God's failure to re-create the five million happy people; mere indifference on the angel's part would be inappropriate.

I think another important point can be made if we imagine that God responds to the angel's horror by trying another approach. Once again, then, God rolls back time, but this time he re-creates the nation with only the original happy five million in existence. The suffering five million do not exist. But once again the angel is, I predict, disappointed, for the angel believes correctly that with respect to most lives nonexistence is usually too high a price to pay for the avoidance of pain.

Benatar might protest that my thought experiments are unfair. He draws a useful and important distinction between asking whether a life is worth starting and asking whether a life is worth continuing (22–28). He says that the standards to be used in each case are quite different. The requirements are much higher for judging that a life is not worth continuing than for judging that a life is not worth starting.[6] Thus, although the amputation of an arm does not make the life of the amputee not worth living, "it is better not to bring into existence somebody who will lack a limb" (23). So Benatar might argue in response to the second version of the story, when God rolls back time and the nation of ten million no longer exists, that the existence of the hypothesized ten million people may be worth continuing even though it may not have been worthwhile for at least five million of them (indeed, in Benatar's view, all ten million of them) to be brought into existence in the first place. The reason, then, that the angel is appalled in the second and third versions of the story is that the angel sees that the standard for ending lives must be much higher than the standard for not creating them in the first place.

But in my thought experiment I am not comparing lives worth continuing with lives worth starting; I am, like Benatar, comparing existence and nonexistence. In both cases, the question for God is not whether to kill off the people, but rather whether to begin (or, more accurately, rebegin) the lives of the individuals in the example.

Perhaps Benatar would then argue that the nonexistence of the good people is bad, but only because it is bad *for God him/herself and for the angel*. Therefore, I have not shown that the nonexistence of good things is bad even when there is no one to experience their absence. But my thought experiment would still make my point even without God and the angel. Imagine that the original ten million people—five million happy, five million suffering—exist in a godless universe. Then, for no reason other than the mystery of the cosmos, there is a jump back in time. Time passes again, but in this case the ten million do not exist. Then there is another jump back in time, and now, after time passes, only the five million happy folk exist. God is unnecessary to the thought experiment except as an easily imaginable agent of change; the angel is merely the impetus that gets God to make the changes. But even in a Godless, angel-free world— provided we assume, with Benatar, that it is legitimate to ascribe value to the absence or avoidance of good or bad even without any sentient being to experience the absence or be deprived—the nonexistence of the happy people is bad.

The angel's first point (a reaction that I think most people would agree with) is that the absence of good can be bad, as in the case where we imagine that the five million happy and fulfilled people do not exist. The angel's second point is that in most cases nonexistence is (perhaps literally) an overkill solution to the problem of suffering, for it also prevents the good in people's lives. When we think about various people throughout the planet who experience misery of various kinds, we do not usually conclude that they would be better off never having existed. In a few cases, that may be true, where the suffering is severe, unremitting, and unavoidable. But in most cases we recognize that their nonexistence would be a loss to themselves as well as to others.[7] Most of the time we conclude that it would be best to deal with suffering by preventing it or ameliorating it. (Benatar recognizes this point at least once when he writes, "I have argued that our lives are very bad. There is no reason why we should not try to make them less so" [210].)

Consider another way to illustrate the latter point—that we ought to deal with potential harms by preventing them, not by preventing the existence of people who might or do suffer them. We can say correctly, "It would be bad if the person who holds job X experiences sexual harassment or racial bias." In saying this, we mean, first, that it is bad *for the person who fills job* X. We might also mean that it is bad for others who work with the incumbent in job X. Knowing that it would be bad, how do we deal with the situation? We ensure (as far as possible) that sexual harassment and racial bias do not occur to the person who eventually wins job X. We *don't* deal with the situation by refusing to fill the position or by abolishing the job altogether. That is, we do not decide to prevent the potential suffering by not bringing "the person who holds job X" into existence.

But Benatar's theory, if accepted, would imply that we should never bring into existence persons of any description. It would be bad if persons who live in City Y suffer from poverty. Benatar's theory would have us ensure that City Y never gets built or at least that no citizens are born or move there; in this way, we do not bring the persons who would live in City Y into existence and run the risk of their being poverty stricken. It would be bad if students who take Philosophy 204 go through the pain of failing the course. So we never offer Philosophy 204 to students. Since pain and suffering are possible in any role or position we might take on, by parity of reasoning Benatar's theory means that we should never create any new roles or positions or at least never fill them. Any theory with implications that broad is surely mistaken.

What Benatar advocates is fundamentally a small *c* conservative approach to existence. Imagine that each of us somehow had a choice about coming into existence on this earth. In effect, Benatar's advice to the would-be earthling is, "You're gonna get hurt, so don't risk it." "Of the pain of an existing person, [Benatar's judgment] says that the absence of this pain would have been good even if this could only have been achieved by the absence of the person who now suffers it" (31). An undergraduate student at Queen's University, Vishaal Patel, suggests the following analogy in a paper written for one of my courses: "Before you is a person with a bag full of jellybeans. The jellybeans come in two flavours: cherry-red, which you love; and black licorice, which you hate. . . . You are unaware of the proportion and size of the jellybeans because the bag is opaque. The person gives you the following choice: you may reach for a handful of jellybeans or not. If you choose to reach for the jellybeans, you must eat them. Would you be better or worse off having chosen to take a handful?" (2007, 4).

Patel suggests that each jellybean represents an experience, either harmful or beneficial, and that taking the handful represents coming into existence. Every handful will have at least one black jellybean in it, which represents one's death,[8] and most likely many more, representing all the various instances of suffering that we experience in a lifetime.

From Benatar's point of view, we should never take a handful because we will always be forced to eat at least one black one, which is bad, but if we refuse to take a handful at all, we will avoid the black ones altogether. Benatar's advice to a putative jellybean eater would be, "Do not reach for the jellybeans."

I find Patel's analogy helpful because it reveals that what Benatar presents is a highly risk-averse value system. Better to avoid jellybeans altogether in order to dodge the black ones. But a high degree of risk aversion is not the only plausible approach to human existence. Probably many people would say that life's handful of jellybeans is worthwhile provided at least that there are enough red ones and that the black ones are not too numerous or too big. My point here is that not only do many of us in retrospect say we are glad to be in existence; in addition, if we notice that Benatar's highly risk-averse outlook is not incontrovertible, then we might conclude that we would have chosen to come into existence ourselves if that option had, *per impossibile*, been offered to us. Such observations count against the claim that it is better never to have been.

Of course, in reality we do not make the decision whether to come into existence or not. Instead, others make that decision for us. It is risky. The question whether one is justified in imposing the risks of existence on *other* potential people is not the same as the question whether one should take on those risks oneself; that is, it is distinct from the question whether, for each of us, it is better never to have been. But surely Benatar cannot say that it is unacceptable to commit another person to risking any suffering at all (Davies 2008, 4). For one thing, adults commit their minor children to risks of suffering all the time. They have to. Every time a parent transports her child in a car, visits a park with the child, or signs the child up for sports, the child will run the risk of suffering if something

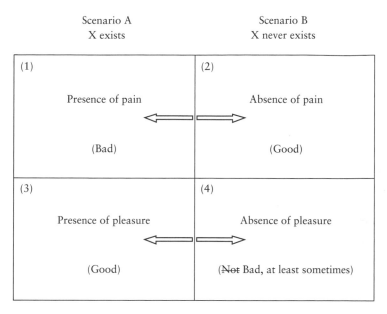

Figure 6.2

goes wrong. It would be bizarre to take the view that parents are wrong in presenting these opportunities to their children, for the correct assumption is that the likelihood of benefits far outweighs the risk of harms.

Therefore, in re-creating the people who would have suffered in such a way that they do not suffer very much, God would do far more good than by simply not re-creating them at all. If the absence of bad things is good, even without anyone to experience the absence, then the absence of good things can sometimes be bad, even without anyone who is deprived. Hence, in box 4 of Benatar's grid we should change "not bad" to "bad, at least sometimes," as indicated in figure 6.2.

Criticism 2

My first criticism assumed, along with Benatar, that it is meaningful to say that the absence or avoidance of bad things and the absence of good things can have value, whether positive or negative, even in the absence of anything that experiences the absence. I conceded Benatar's assumption that the absence of bad things is good, even without anyone to experience the absence, and I sought to show that the absence of good things can be bad, even without anyone who experiences the absence.

But this assumption is open to challenge. Let us consider now the possibility that Benatar misuses our usual moral language. Perhaps evaluative terms are inherently person referring—that is, they have meaning only by reference, at least indirectly, to persons.[9] If so, then it is neither meaningful nor plausible to speak of the absence or avoidance of good things or bad things as having value independent of entities to experience the absence or avoidance.

In standard usage, the phrase "the avoidance of the bad" implies the existence of a person, group, or institution that avoids the bad. Bad is avoided when some person, group, or institution avoids the bad. So we might say correctly that the avoidance of malaria is good. What we mean is that the avoidance of malaria is good for existing people (if we are talking historically, it was good for people who once existed, or if we are discussing the future, it will be good for people who will exist).

In Benatar's theory, the phrase "avoidance of the bad" *cannot* have a grammatical object because in the context of nonexistence there is no human subject, no individual (or group or institution, but Benatar is concerned with individuals) who has avoided the bad. In the absence of individuals who might suffer malaria, however, the idea of the avoidance of malaria is virtually empty. For example, Benatar might say, "The avoidance of malaria on Mars is good," but in so saying he has told us nothing about malaria, nothing about Mars, and nothing about what is good on Mars, for there are no persons (indeed, so far as we know, no sentient beings at all) on that planet.

In the cases that Benatar discusses, there is no being that actually "avoids" bad, and so his phrase "the avoidance of the bad by never existing is a real advantage" (14) is very odd indeed. For whom is it an advantage? Not for the nonexistent. Something can be an advantage only to those who exist—in the present, past, or future. As Benatar himself acknowledges, "Those who never exist cannot be deprived [or benefited]" (1). So if there is a genuine advantage, it can be an advantage only to those who exist in the past, present, or future.

Consider now another of Benatar's claims: "One harms somebody by bringing him into existence if his existence is such that never existing would have been preferable" (28). *Preferable* in this usage is an evaluative term, and it is therefore what I call a "person-referring" term. Some thing or condition cannot be "preferable" full stop. It has to be preferable by or to someone or several persons or a group of persons past, present, or future, real or hypothetical. If almost everyone does *not* prefer that they did not come into existence, and if for almost every person there is at least one other person and probably many who are glad they came into existence, there is no good sense in which it can be preferable that those persons did not come into existence. We cannot say that hypothetical people would prefer not to come into existence. We cannot consult people before they exist to find out whether they would prefer to come into existence or not come into existence. Hence, what it means to speak of the value of the avoidance of bad and the absence of good is necessarily tied to persons and does not have clear meaning on its own.

Now, Benatar says he makes the judgment that "the absence of pain is good, even if that good is not enjoyed by anyone" "with reference to the (potential) interests of a person who either does or does not exist" (30, emphasis in original removed). He recognizes that a critic might argue that because the judgment "is part of the scenario under which this person never exists, [the judgment] cannot say anything about an existing person." His response to this criticism is that the judgment does "say something about a counterfactual case in which a person who does actually exist never did exist." "Of the pain of an existing person, [the judgment] says that the absence of this pain would have been good even if this could only have been achieved by the absence of the person who now suffers it" (31).

This latter statement does nothing to advance Benatar's argument but merely restates it, for *good* in this situation is a person-referring term. So now we can ask, Good for whom? There is no one for whom the nonexistence of the person is good (unless, perhaps, the person has many enemies). A mere absence or avoidance is neither good nor bad unless it is good or bad *for someone*.

Benatar objects that if we cannot say that avoiding pains is good even when it is not good for anybody, then "we could not say that it would be good to avoid bringing suffering children into existence" (34). But rejecting as meaningless the claim that avoiding pains is good even when it is not good for anybody does not have this implication. We can still say it is good to avoid bringing suffering children into existence, the reason being that it is good *on the part of individuals who make the decision not to bring suffering children into existence*. In an article about Benatar's book,

Chris Kaposy suggests that Benatar's supposed asymmetry between the absence of bad and the absence of good appears plausible only because he conflates the *absence* of bad with the *prevention* of bad: "The duties and reactions that Benatar thinks are explained by the asymmetry (for example the duty to refrain from bringing a profoundly suffering child into the world) have more to do with the importance of avoiding being the cause of suffering, rather than with the goodness of absent suffering" (2009, 106). What is good is preventing bad and avoiding causing bad. It is wrong to create or even to permit suffering if we can avoid it; hence, it may be wrong to create individuals who will suffer. So it is correct to say, with Benatar, "Avoiding the pains of existence is more than merely 'not bad.' It is good" (39), but we can meaningfully say it only when there is some person or group of persons or institution that avoids causing a painful existence.

In criticism 1, I showed that *if* one assumes that it is meaningful and plausible to speak of the avoidance or absence of harm as bad, then, contrary to Benatar's key assumption, the absence of good can also be bad; it is not necessarily always "not bad," as Benatar claims. In criticism 2, however, I have called into question the idea that an absence can have any value at all in the absence of any sentient being to experience the absence. Hence, if we reject the initial assumption about the meaningfulness of ascribing values to absences, then both the absence of harm and the absence of benefit are neither good nor bad when there is no one for whom they are good or bad. On the basis of this criticism, then, we should change box 4 from "not bad" to "neither good nor bad" and box 2 from "good" to "neither good nor bad." See figure 6.3.

Criticisms 1 and 2 are alternatives to each other; each is built on an assumption that is the negation of the assumption that forms the basis for the other. So whether it is meaningful or not to say that the absence or avoidance of bad things and the absence of good things can have value in the absence of anything that experiences the absence, Benatar's theory is flawed. In criticism 3, I move to a different problem with Benatar's theory.

Criticism 3

Benatar treats coming into existence and not coming into existence as if they were ordinary properties of persons, like having brown hair, being

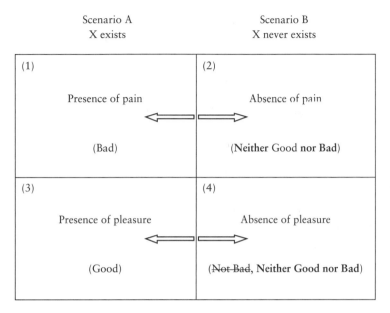

	Scenario A X exists	Scenario B X never exists
(1) / (2)	Presence of pain (Bad)	Absence of pain (Neither Good nor Bad)
(3) / (4)	Presence of pleasure (Good)	Absence of pleasure (~~Not Bad~~, Neither Good nor Bad)

Figure 6.3

good at sports, or lacking an arm.[10] In twenty-first-century North America, having brown hair is a neutral property, being good at sports is an advantageous property, and having no right arm is a disadvantageous property. But it does not make sense to say that existing is a disadvantageous property, any more than it would make sense to say that existing is an advantageous property. Instead, existing is a necessary condition of having or experiencing advantages or disadvantages. People are neither benefited nor harmed by coming into existence per se and independent of what happens to them during their lives because coming into existence is not a property like other properties. Existence is a condition of having any properties at all. Hence, whether being alive is a benefit or a harm *depends on the content of the life that is lived.*

A would-be critic of Benatar's argument might suggest that the fact that most people are reasonably happy to be alive counts as evidence against Benatar's views. But Benatar deprecates what he calls "the unduly rosy picture most people have about the quality of their own lives" (59) and points out that "I am glad I was born" is not equivalent to "It is better that I came into existence" (58).

There's something far-fetched about the idea that I and virtually everyone who says she or he is happy to be alive can be badly mistaken about the quality of our lives, yet Benatar insists that it is so (64). He cites psychological studies indicating that people usually remember positive rather than negative experiences and states, "We tend to have an exaggerated view of how good things will be." Moreover, "many studies have consistently shown that self-assessments of well-being are markedly skewed toward the positive end of the spectrum" (65). Indeed, says Benatar, human beings may be "engaged in a mass self-deception about how wonderful things are for us" (100).[11] This belief seems oddly inconsistent with his earlier distinction between asking whether a life is worth starting and asking whether a life is worth continuing (22–28). The requirements are much higher for judging that a life is not worth continuing than for judging that a life is not worth starting. But if so, then at least some credence must be placed on the individual's subjective experience that her life is worth living.

It seems unlikely that the vast majority of us is guilty of false consciousness. Benatar cannot possibly know this of every single human being who is happy to have been born. It is simply unfounded to deny the experience of literally millions of people who for the most part enjoy their lives and are happy to exist. Moreover, it is presumptuous for him to suppose that he (along with the few who may agree with him) is the only person who fully understands the human situation and has the appropriate response to it. Far from suggesting that our lives are very bad, people's positive outlooks and self-assessments tend to make their lives better. Research demonstrates that self-reported happiness is linked to other factors that promote well-being: "Compared with those who are depressed, happy people are less self-focused, less hostile and abusive, and less vulnerable to disease. They are also more loving, forgiving, trusting, energetic, decisive, creative, sociable, and helpful" (Myers 2000, 57–58). If in the present I do not remember most of my negative experiences, my life now is better than it would be if I did remember them. If I think that the future will be good, even if I overestimate its goodness, that fact too makes my current life more pleasant. And if I have a positive assessment of my well-being, this surely means that in at least one important way, my subjective self-assessment, I *am* doing well.[12]

Benatar concedes that "if one's life is very bad . . . , and one thinks that it is not, then in this one way it is actually better than it would be if one realized how bad it actually was. But to say that it is better in this one way is neither to say that it is better in every way, nor is it to say that it is so much better that it is as good as one thinks it is" (87). Benatar is correct. However, thinking that it is better than it is not only makes it better but also may *continue* to make it better by generating an ongoing positive outlook.

All of Benatar's psychological evidence in fact shows not that the quality of people's lives is necessarily worse than we think, but rather that people are happier than his theory allows. The point here is not, as he accuses another scholar of believing, that there is no difference between subjective and objective levels of well-being. Rather, the point is that the subjective level counts, and it counts for a lot. It cannot simply be disregarded just because some people's perceived well-being departs from their actual well-being. The fact that most people worldwide are at least satisfied with and often very happy about their lives is significant. It seems very implausible indeed to suppose that almost every one of them is mistaken.

Now it is true that the issue of whether people are happy or sad during their lives is different from the issue of whether they are benefited or harmed by being brought into existence. But Benatar recognizes this fact only in part. He stresses that person X can be happy at certain times without its being true that person X was benefited by being brought into existence. But I want to suggest likewise that person Y can be unhappy at certain times without its being true that Y was harmed by being brought into existence.

Benatar correctly identifies at least some of the genuine harms generated by the fact that we exist. Foremost among these harms is the fact that we all (apparently have to) die. I agree with Benatar that death is usually harmful and that it can be a harm at whatever age it happens (Benatar 2004b, 161–162). The inevitability of death means that life must end. Yet in other contexts we do not take the fact that something must end as a reason never to begin it. We do not avoid holidays on the grounds that we will have to go back to work. We do not eschew good movies because they always come to an end. Even though, ceteris paribus, death is bad and a long life is better than a short life, the fact of death is not sufficient to make coming into existence a harm.

If death is not sufficient, then what is? Is there any fact that is universal to all lives that suffices to make coming into existence always harmful? At the beginning of this chapter, I cited Shiffrin, who describes a number of ways in which one's life may be painful: "By being caused to exist as persons, children are forced to assume moral agency, to face various demanding and sometimes wrenching moral questions, and to discharge taxing moral duties. They must endure the fairly substantial amount of pain, suffering, difficulty, significant disappointment, distress, and significant loss that occur within the typical life. They must face and undergo the fear and harm of death. Finally, they must bear the results of imposed risks that their lives may go terribly wrong in a variety of ways" (1999, 137).

I agree that if these experiences are severe and especially if they are unremitting and unrelieved by any happiness, then coming into existence might be a harm. But not for all of us: pain, suffering, difficulty, disappointment, distress, and loss vary in their severity from one person to another. Yet in what starts to seem like a rather desperate attempt to show how bad our lives are, even for those with a prosperous existence, Benatar describes experiences such as the sensation of a full bladder (71), the feeling of being tired (72), and even the mere having of desires (75) as bad. But these experiences and others like them are not epistemic givens, not incorrigible sense data. As I suggested in chapter 1, feelings and sensations do not wear their meanings and values on their faces but are always subject to interpretation and therefore can have varying valences. So, for example, the sensation of a full bladder can be merely neutral, giving the signal to urinate. Feeling tired can be pleasurable, not necessarily painful, perhaps after a day of fulfilling work or a long hike. Even the pain of childbirth, although sometimes excruciating, can be interpreted as the powerful working of the woman's body to impel the infant into the world.

And, contra Benatar, having desires is not only not necessarily painful but is possibly a condition of being human, giving us always something to aim toward and look forward to.[13] We can see this if we try to imagine a life without desires at all. It is hard to see how we would even be persons in the absence of any desires (Horrobin 2007). If alternatively we imagine a life in which, to supposedly minimize suffering, we have desires, but they are fulfilled within minutes, such a life seems virtually emptied of meaning. Hence, having desires is hardly the inevitable harm that Benatar claims it is. In general and perhaps for most people, Benatar greatly exaggerates the suffering of human existence.

Maybe the problem is that Benatar's calculus of pain and pleasure is mistaken. Matthew Kersten points out that, according to Benatar, it is simply a fact that *no* amount of pleasure outweighs the suffering of our existence.[14] Now, even if that claim were true, it would be a merely contingent fact about our existence. It would therefore be open to us, as human beings, to attempt to improve our lives and our living conditions so that in the future the pleasure might outweigh the suffering. But in any case it seems just false that there is *no* human being for whom the pleasure of life already genuinely outweighs the suffering.

Perhaps, then, Benatar's belief that no amount of pleasure can ever outweigh the suffering of existence is an a priori assumption, an assumption independent of the facts that arises from the very concepts of pleasure and pain that he holds.

To see this, imagine World 1, in which two people, Jack and Jill, exist.[15] Jack experiences a great deal of pain in his life (very bad) and only a little bit of pleasure (good, but not very good). Jill, by contrast, experiences only minimal pain (bad, but not very bad) and a tremendous amount of pleasure (very good). In World 2, neither Jack nor Jill exists, and the absence of their pain is good, whereas the absence of their pleasure is not bad. (Here, I am accepting for the sake of argument Benatar's views about the value of the absence of pain and the absence of pleasure). According to Benatar, World 2 is always and clearly better not only for Jack but also for Jill because it is always "better never to have been." But surely we can concede that nonexistence is better for Jack *without* conceding that it is better for Jill; in World 1, Jill's pleasure does outweigh her suffering. And so in Jill's case we are making the comparison shown in figure 6.4.

For Jill, World 2 merely offers "good" and "not bad." But World 1 offers her "not too bad" and "very good." Hence, World 1, in which she exists, is still better for her, and it is *not* better that she never exist.

Of course, not every life will be like Jill's. But some will. And Jill's life shows that at least sometimes it is *not* better never to have been. If Benatar denies this latter possibility, it must be because he has an odd view of bad or of good or perhaps of both. Perhaps his view is that any bad whatsoever, no matter how little, can always outweigh any good, no matter how much, that may be present. But if so, that assumption is surely

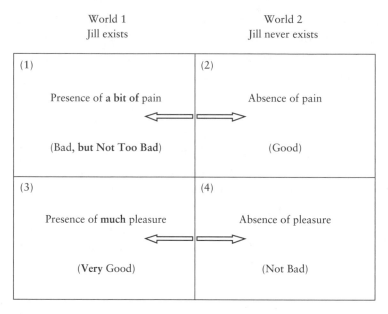

World 1
Jill exists

World 2
Jill never exists

(1)

Presence of **a bit of** pain

(**Bad, but Not Too Bad**)

(2)

Absence of pain

(Good)

(3)

Presence of **much** pleasure

(**Very** Good)

(4)

Absence of pleasure

(Not Bad)

Figure 6.4

false. We often undergo certain kinds of pain (bad) precisely because of the greater happiness (good) that we will thereby gain. As Kersten puts it, there are goods that "not only *undo* pains but in fact *compensate* for them" (personal communication, November 16, 2009, his emphasis). This process is evident whenever we human beings expend great physical, psychological, or intellectual effort, sometimes to the point of suffering, in order to attain an outcome that we strongly value—an athletic achievement, for example, or a spiritual insight, moral growth, creative product, or scientific or philosophical finding. The fact that the process was uncomfortable or even painful, perhaps very painful, does not in any way cancel out the good of what we have achieved. Most of us would not say it would be better that we had not existed, despite whatever suffering and pain as well as the joys, pleasures, and rewards our lives have included. Instead, most of us would say that the joys, pleasures, and rewards (and perhaps also the challenges) compensate for the suffering and pain and make us glad to be alive.

Perhaps, however, Benatar has an odd view of good—the view that good is merely the absence of or the recovery from bad. We can see this view in an example that Benatar himself uses elsewhere (Benatar 2004b,

160). Person A gets sick (bad) but has the power to recover quickly (good). Person B never gets sick (good) but lacks the power to recover quickly (not bad). Person A is supposed to be like all of us in that we exist; Person B represents nonexistence. But the analogy fails. The ability to recover quickly is merely a kind of antidote to being ill. But pleasure is more than just a recovery from suffering or the absence of suffering. Pleasure is a real experience in its own right, and because it can vary in quantity and quality, its presence in our lives is capable not merely of counteracting our suffering, but even, with sufficient quantity and quality, of outweighing it. For example, for many and perhaps most women, giving birth to a baby is not merely a kind of antidote to or recovery from the difficulties of pregnancy and labor. The baby is a joy, perhaps an unquantifiable joy, but nonetheless a positive and valuable good in itself, who more than outweighs the pain and problems of pregnancy and labor. (If it were not so, then almost no women with access to contraception would ever have a second child.)

Thus, it is only if Benatar makes an implausible assumption about good, about bad, or about both that his calculus of good and bad can support his conclusion. He is not justified in assuming either that pain always outweighs pleasure or that pleasure is merely the recovery from or the absence of pain.

Criticism 4

My final criticism is not intended to show that Benatar's theory is mistaken; I assume that the previous three criticisms have done that. I intend here to show the possible negative effects on and implications for women in particular if Benatar's theory is accepted and widely adopted.

To begin, recall that I opened chapter 5 with the observation that in general we think making *people happy* is a good thing; so why then should we not recognize an obligation to make *happy people*? Benatar thinks his supposed asymmetry between the absence of bad and the absence of good explains the common view "that while there is a duty to avoid bringing suffering people into existence, there is no duty to bring happy people into being" (32).[16]

Benatar is right to believe that this view is common (at least among those who actually think about their procreative potential) and that it is likely correct. However, as I explained at length in chapter 5, we can account for the absence of any duty to bring happy people into being quite easily by reference to the importance of women's bodily autonomy and the moral necessity of respect for women's well-being and reproductive rights; we don't need Benatar's dubious asymmetry to explain it. That is, women are entitled to control their bodies and protect their own well-being, and that right militates against any supposed duty to reproduce, even if happy people would be the result.

Now, Benatar momentarily appears to recognize some of these points. He writes, "It is usually thought that our positive duties cannot include a duty to create lots of people if that would require significant sacrifice on our part. Given that having children involves considerable sacrifice (at least to the pregnant woman), this, and not asymmetry, is the best explanation for why there is no duty to bring happy people into existence" (32–33). According to Benatar, however, the weakness of this protofeminist response is that it implies that "in the absence of this sacrifice we *would* have a duty to bring happy people into existence. In other words, it would be wrong not to create such people if we could create them without great cost to ourselves" (33, his emphasis).

There are several things wrong with this counterargument. First, who are "we"? It seems unlikely that he means women because there is no indication that he counts himself among the group of people who are capable of pregnancy. So the "we" must be men or society at large. Benatar is claiming that women's right not to reproduce has a rather precarious status. The implication seems to be that if we do not assume that the absence of good is not bad, and if women found pregnancy relatively easy, then individual men or perhaps society might have at least a moral duty to require women, whether willing or not, to procreate for the purpose of creating happy people.

But even a pregnancy in which the woman is vitally healthy is not something she has no right to refuse. I'm reminded of Judith Jarvis Thomson's thought experiments in her classic article about abortion. Thomson imagines a situation in which "pregnancy lasted only an hour, and constituted no threat to life or health." Nonetheless, she says, although in such a case it might be "morally indecent" to abort the pregnancy, it is not the case that the fetus acquires a right to the use of the woman's body (1975, 100, 102). Nor, I suggest, does the woman lose the entitlement to choose not to undergo the pregnancy in the first place; it is, after all, her body and nobody else's.

Second, can it ever really be the case that procreation requires no sacrifice or cost? In reality, pregnancy lasts about nine months and is followed by a delivery that is seldom a breeze. And that is not all. Someone must feed the children who are born; someone must care for them and support their development; someone must provide the resources to maintain them; someone must provide their education, health care, and housing. For these reasons, procreation is never undemanding and low cost. It always requires effort, caring, concern, material resources, and intelligent thought and planning. Procreation is never a no-sacrifice process.

In other words, even if, as I am urging in this chapter, Benatar's asymmetry thesis is mistaken, there would still be no moral duty to make babies. Even if pregnancy and birth were easy for all women (a highly unlikely scenario), many other costs are incurred by procreation, costs that often fall primarily on women but may also be incurred by men and by society generally. As a result, an appeal to the right not to reproduce, founded as it is on protecting women's (and men's) reproductive freedom and protecting women's (and men's) well-being, is a more than adequate alternative to Benatar's dubious asymmetry hypothesis as a bulwark against a moral obligation to procreate.

In general, Benatar is surprisingly oblivious to the implications of his theory for women's rights and well-being.[17] Most of his discussion of procreation is curiously gender neutral.[18] At the same time, his theory implies that women's reproductive labor produces bad consequences.[19] That is, the idea that it is better in every case never to have been implies that women's reproductive labor in pregnancy, birth, breastfeeding, and even rearing children contributes to the accumulation of net harm on this planet.

It's unlikely that downgrading procreation in this way would do much for the status of women, particularly in societies where women's status is dependent primarily on their role as childbearers. If Benatar's theory were to gain credence (unlikely though that may be), then one of women's primary social contributions, recognized even (or especially) in the most misogynist societies, would be seen as a liability. Might this view lead to an increase in the infanticide of girls or to assaults on pregnant women?

If these outcomes seem unlikely, then notice that the theory can be interpreted to mean that both contraception and abortion should be mandatory. Benatar himself imagines a society aimed at ensuring nonprocreation. He suggests the administration of a "safe, highly effective contraceptive" via drinking water or "aerial spray" without the population's knowledge or individual people's consent. He describes this approach as "unobtrusive and gentle" because it avoids "invasions of privacy and bodily intrusions." He acknowledges that such measures would violate personal autonomy, but he never recognizes the serious costs for women (as well as men) of compulsory contraception (107).

Conclusion

I have shown that David Benatar is deeply mistaken in claiming that "it is better never to have been." My approach has not been to offer evidence that it is better to exist. It isn't always. Instead, I have offered three criticisms showing that the theory is false and one criticism showing that its adoption would be dangerous, especially to women. People are not harmed by the mere fact of coming into existence, but, I suggest, people are not benefited either. Mere existence is not a benefit-conferring or harm-conferring property. Prior to conception, there is no being who can be benefited or harmed by coming into existence. We can see, however, that in many and perhaps most cases individuals, once in existence, do have good lives and are glad to exist. Hence, we must always "look and see" whether persons are benefited or harmed throughout their lives. Whether they are benefited or harmed depends on a host of factors, including the material circumstances of their lives, their health, their happiness and suffering, their education, their opportunities, and their possible experiences of oppression.

Even if Benatar were right that the absence of pain is good and the absence of pleasure is not bad, it would not follow that it is better not to exist. Whether it is better not to exist would then depend on how we add up the goods and bads—that is, whether the good constituted by the absence of pain in the case of nonexistence is greater than the good that might be created if the individual were to live her life. It is not self-evident that in every case nonexistence is better.

Hence, Benatar's thesis that it is better never to have been does not generate a moral reason not to procreate. At the same time, as I argued in chapter 5, even if someone will be benefited by having a good life, there is no obligation to any such hypothetical nonexistent person to bring him or her into existence.

7

An Obligation Not to Procreate?

If David Benatar were correct that for every single person it is better never to come into existence, then there would be a strong reason for believing that we always have an obligation not to procreate. I have shown that Benatar's theory does not stand up against a variety of criticisms. Nonetheless, other important moral reasons may count against having children. In investigating these reasons, I consider whether and when a case can be made that there is an obligation not to have children.

James Lenman writes, "We might well believe that in every generation very many people will lead lives of at best highly compromised happiness and some people will lead quite terrible lives. Nonetheless our interest in having children is such that we may find the risk acceptable" (2004b, 147). The question is whether we are morally justified in finding that risk "acceptable" and to whom it ought to be acceptable. It's not clear whether Lenman's "we" means—or should mean—individual prospective parents, society at large, or even the children themselves. Perhaps no one should blithely endorse creating serious risks that others will have to run.

It might be thought that my defense of the right to reproduce in the negative sense—that is, the entitlement not to be interfered with in reproduction—means there cannot be an obligation not to procreate. But that would be a mistake. We sometimes have a moral responsibility not to exercise a right. For example, the right to free speech does not give us a moral entitlement to say whatever we want whenever we want, for we sometimes have a moral obligation to keep our mouths shut. If I have promised to honor a secret you have told me, my right to free speech does not obliterate my moral obligation not to gossip about you. Similarly, although we have a right not to be interfered with in procreation—not to have others intervene in our sexual lives, not to be coerced to use contraception, not to be compelled to undergo forced sterilization or abortion—it does not follow that all our decisions to procreate are necessarily morally justified. It is possible that sometimes at least it is morally wrong to procreate, and we may sometimes have an obligation not to.

Before examining the various reasons that might be given to support an obligation not to procreate, let's consider what such an obligation would and would not mean in practice. In speaking of a possible obligation not to have children, I am saying nothing about what the state should or should not do to curtail procreation. That is a matter of social policy, which I am setting aside in this book. Instead, what I'm interested in here is the possibility of a moral responsibility to limit one's own reproductive activities and outcomes. If there is ever an obligation not to procreate, it is plausible to suppose that it would mean in practice a moral responsibility to use safe and highly effective contraception when engaged in activities with a chance of resulting in pregnancy. It might also mean a responsibility on a woman's part to obtain an abortion if she becomes pregnant.

But it is less plausible to say that an obligation not to procreate requires behavior so onerous as to make one's life miserable. For example, because almost all people enjoy sexual activity, and because sexuality is a crucial aspect of a good human life for most people, it seems unjust to say that an individual's obligation not to procreate might mean in practice a blanket prohibition on (hetero)sexual activity for all the years that the individual is fertile. For the most part, people (of whatever sexual identity) cannot be expected to give up sex. But there are, of course, many ways of being sexually active, and some run no risk of pregnancy. Thus, if no effective and safe methods of contraception were available, then an individual who has an obligation not procreate would be morally required to avoid heterosexual activities likely to result in pregnancy. In addition, it may be too much to say that an obligation not to procreate requires sterilization at the beginning of one's reproductive life. Giving up one's fertility forever is too high a cost, unless the harms to the children who would otherwise be created are so horrific as to make their lives not worth living, the risks of such harms are extremely high, and the risks will never disappear over the course of the individual's lifetime. There are, then, some limits to the behavior we can reasonably expect people to undertake in order to honor an obligation not to procreate.

But what circumstances or conditions might possibly generate a moral obligation not to have a child? To begin exploring the answers to this question, I want to introduce two distinctions.

First, just as there can be bad reasons to choose to have a child, so also there can be bad reasons for thinking one should not have a child. The fact that choosing to have a child may at times be the right decision does not make all possible reasons for choosing to have a child good ones. In a similar way, the fact that choosing not to have a child may at times be the right decision does not make all possible reasons for choosing not to have a child good ones. Not all reasons for choosing not to have children are morally equal. For example, perhaps a person chooses not to have children simply because she wants to spite her parents, who desperately want grandchildren. Her reasoning is not morally admirable. In addition, to say, as I did in chapter 1, that choosing not to have children is easier to justify than choosing to have children is not to deny that some reasons for choosing not to have a *particular* child might be morally dubious. An example would be aborting a fetus because the fetus has been tested and shown to lack, let's say, the genes for blond hair or blue eyes. The woman who wants an abortion for those reasons should not be denied the service because she should not be compelled to undergo pregnancy against her will; forced procreation is a great evil. Nonetheless, her justification for the abortion is less than morally impressive.

Second, we should distinguish between a general, life-long obligation not to procreate and an obligation not to procreate *at a particular time* in one's life or *with a particular person*. It is possible that some people might have a lifelong moral obligation not to procreate, whereas others might have such an obligation at one point in their lives and not at others or in some particular circumstances and not in others or with a particular partner but not with others.

Having made these distinctions, I now turn to the examination of a series of possible reasons that have been offered to justify an obligation not to have children.

Might There Be a Moral Responsibility to Oneself Not to Have Children?

As long ago as 1916, sociologist Leta Hollingworth described childbearing as "in many respects analogous to the work of soldiers: it is necessary for tribal or national existence; it means great sacrifice of personal advantage; it involves danger and suffering, and, in a certain percentage of cases, the actual loss of life" (1916, 19). For women in developed nations, the risk of death in childbirth has diminished, yet the choice whether to procreate or not remains life changing for women.

Radical feminist Shulamith Firestone famously argued that "the heart of woman's oppression is her childbearing and childrearing roles," and she believed that this oppression is inevitable because "the sexual imbalance is biologically based" (1970, 72, 9). Hence, women will be freed from the oppression of motherhood only if the child-rearing role is spread over all adults of both sexes and technology is used to free women "from the tyranny of their reproductive biology by every means available" (1970, 206).

But to see, like Firestone, women's biology as inherently oppressive is to engage in a form of misogyny. Other feminist philosophers and theorists do not subscribe to this rather simplistic biological reductionism; they recognize that in some contexts women's capacity to create new life is a strength, an advantage men do not possess. They endorse the idea that motherhood can be oppressive but believe that its oppressive characteristics are culturally produced. What is problematic about motherhood is not the biological capacities themselves, but the social interpretation of the meaning of motherhood and the conditions under which women engage in mothering. Thus, Claudia Card claims that motherhood is still "so deeply flawed that [it seems] to me unworthy of emulation and reproduction" (1996, 2). Jeffner Allen agrees. In her view, motherhood is "dangerous to women" "because it denies to females the creation of a subjectivity and world that is open and free." Motherhood is "men's appropriation of women's bodies as a resource to reproduce patriarchy." Allen advocates "evacuation" from motherhood by deciding not to have children, thereby giving priority "to that which is already given, [one's own] life and [one's own] world in their actual presence to [oneself]" (1983, 315, 317, 326, 325).

French writer Corinne Maier (2007) has more recently published an uncompromising polemic, directed at men as well as women, advocating that one should choose not to procreate and offering forty reasons in support of her recommendation, some of which pertain to the alleged bad effects of parenthood on parents themselves. I won't list here every one of her reasons individually. Some of them are criticisms of the culture of childhood, not of the experience of having children—for example, the expectation that children must be perfect (2007, 111–114). Some reasons are simply repetitive and can be grouped together.

First, procreation is physically unpleasant for women because "labour is torture" (Maier 2007, 20; subsequent citations to this work give page numbers only), and "breastfeeding is slavery" (24).

Second, the child comes to be "the focal point of the family" (44); the parents become the pawns of experts (71) and the toadies and victims of their children's schools (91–95).

Third, children themselves are detestable. Writes Maier: "Children are like dogs: if they were two or three times bigger, they would be ferocious beasts, your very worst enemies" (45). Children are "conformists" (47); indeed, "childhood is a long neurosis" (48). Children use (and require their parents to use) "idiot language" (32). Children must also be entertained (54–57).

Fourth, children are an economic liability. "Children cost a fortune. They are among the most expensive purchases the average consumer can make in a lifetime. In monetary terms alone, they cost more than a high-end luxury car, or a world cruise, or a two-room apartment in Paris. Even worse, the cost goes up as time goes by" (49). And children are dedicated consumers (51–54) who have a powerful influence even on adults' tastes (78–81).

Fifth, having children ruins the parents' adult lives. The parents no longer have fun (24), and "kids signal the end of your youthful dreams" (84–88). "Life with kids is trivialized," and "your kid will be your ankle shackles" (26). Parents can't express their real feelings (99–104). Because of their children, parents experience "death by boredom" (88), but at the same time it's very difficult to obtain childcare and other activities for children (89–90). Having children means parents lose their friends (28), and the family wins out over other social relationships (82). Children cause the loss of a sex life (37, 41) and the loss of "lust" (39) and bring about "the death knell of the couple" (41). Your children may even take you into conflict with the law by complaining that you sexually abused them (114–117).

Sixth, parenthood is especially bad for women: "For all mothers' multidimensional flexibility, it's astonishing how little market value they have. Have you ever seen a company going out of its way to hire mothers who are more than forty-five years old?" (51). The mother becomes a "merdeuf" (65), a woman consumed by motherhood and incapable of anything else, yet also a person who feels guilty about failing to live up to the ideal of motherhood (69). The work of child rearing still falls on women (105), and mothers are excluded from interesting work and professional advancement (106–108).

Finally, parents do not try to change the world; they are too busy changing diapers (87).

All of these authors—from Hollingworth right up to Maier—make bold and disturbing claims about parenthood, especially about motherhood. If you *perceive* parenthood to be this bad, this dangerous, this compromising of the self, then regardless of the truth of these various claims, you *do* have a responsibility not to procreate because your perception of parenthood does not bode well for the quality of your parenting. You are likely to loathe child rearing and to be, at the very best, ambivalent about your children. But to attribute such a responsibility may be otiose because choosing to have children is unlikely to be a live option for you anyway.[1]

The question is whether these arguments create an *objective* case for a responsibility to oneself not to reproduce, whether parenthood *is* so bad—not just *seems* to be bad—that no one should have children.

The evaluation of some aspects of parenthood may simply be a matter of individual preference. For example, some women (and I include myself) deeply enjoy the breastfeeding relationship with their infant and, contrary to Maier, do not find it "slavery" at all; indeed, it can be far less restrictive and more satisfying than bottle feeding. No doubt some people find parts of child rearing boring. Yet many aspects can be both satisfying and fun—rediscovering with one's children the poems, books, songs, and films from one's own childhood and discovering new ones; taking one's children to parks, pools, museums, libraries, and playgrounds; talking with one's children; playing games and sports with one's children; helping one's children develop their abilities, interests, and skills; and so on.

There is little doubt that parenthood can be hard even in the best of circumstances. Being a parent does require making sacrifices. Moreover, in Western society children *are* expensive, and both childhood and parenting are easily co-opted in capitalist societies to facilitate and extend retail consumption. Maier, however, arguably overstates the difficulties, expenses, and sacrifices. She writes as if it is unreasonable for any adult to be anything but carefree at all points in his or her life. Indeed, Maier's irresponsible outlook is reflected in the final chapter of her book, where she concludes, "I would prefer . . . not to have children. *Not to work*" (125, ellipsis in original, my emphasis). If that is her goal, she needs to be independently wealthy as well as childless.

Many of Maier's arguments about the alleged bad effects of parenting on parents themselves amount to little more than vicious child hating and include statements about an entire category of human being that she would never dare to utter about members of more protected categories such as adult men. Children are no more essentially "ferocious beasts" than men are. Insofar as some children are difficult and unruly, much of the blame must be laid either on the parents themselves, who have failed to teach these children how to become what Sarah Ruddick calls "acceptable" persons (1993, 373–375), or on the social conditions in which many children grow up (poor nutrition, shelter, education, and health care; racism; sexual and physical abuse; poverty; war; and so on), which may make them aggressive, uncooperative, and antisocial. Maier herself admits that children can be conformists; to the degree that they cause problems, they may well be imitating the models they find in their environment or at least reflecting the absence of good role models.

The far more serious argument is what Maier and Allen say about the political effects of parenthood, especially on women. Unlike them, I will not generalize about all of motherhood; the causes, conditions, and consequences of being a parent are much too variable. Yet women still do the bulk of the reproductive labor from the moment of conception and are responsible for the majority of child rearing; most women still earn less than men; many women still sacrifice jobs and personal development to be with their kids; their reward is often to receive less respect than if they had devoted all their time to being successful in paid work. Many women are made vulnerable to abuse when they are pregnant or caring for small children; many women are seen as lesser beings because they are mothers; many women are valued for little more than their sexuality and their capacity to procreate. In such conditions, refusing to procreate may be seen as a political act. Sue Donaldson writes, "My decision to forgo children is an act of rebellion—a rebellion against the social pressures to procreate and the stereotypes that say giving birth, and caring for dependents, [are] a defining feature of womanhood; against the current societal environment in which we are expected to raise children; against the view that forgoing an experience somehow diminishes one's life; and finally, against the view that we should happily embrace our biological destiny" (2000, 8–9).

A woman may indeed have a responsibility to herself not to procreate in contexts where motherhood can be negotiated only under oppressive, burdensome, dangerous, and unjust conditions. Such conditions may not even permit free procreative decisions. To the extent that people do have a choice, they have a responsibility to resist the entrenchment of their own oppression. In conditions of oppression, then, unless there are very strong reasons to procreate, reasons that do not further undermine the woman's dignity, freedom, and capacity to flourish, women may have a responsibility to themselves not to procreate.

I do not believe that every mother is tyrannized as a mother; such a view sees mothers only as victims, the dupes of patriarchy. But some are. The question, then, would be whether there are other reasons for procreating that in an oppressive environment override the prima facie obligation not to. To suppose that there is none is to imagine that every such mother is guilty of false consciousness, failing to recognize and resist the conditions of her own oppression. Instead, I believe that for some and perhaps many women, mothering is a decision not to deepen their oppression but to enrich their lives. For some women, having a child might be one of the few bright spots in an otherwise dreary life.

Might There Be a Responsibility Not to Have Children Because One Cannot Achieve "Procreative Beneficence"?

Most parents would say it is the offspring themselves who put the lie to the idea that motherhood is nothing but oppressive and self-compromising. But even though the children in themselves are sufficient for many women to undermine across-the-board criticisms of motherhood, children's very personhood nonetheless requires that we consider *their* well-being. Perhaps in some cases a concern for the potential child's well-being grounds an obligation not to have children.

According to philosopher Julian Savulescu, human beings who procreate should adhere to a moral "Principle of Procreative Beneficence"

(PPB) (2001, 2007). This principle is "the moral obligation to have the best children": "Couples (or single reproducers) should select the child, of the possible children they could have, who is expected to have the best life, or at least as good a life as the others, based on the relevant, available information," says Savulescu (2001, 415). In effect, if you procreate, then you must produce the best available child. It is "morally required" (2001, 425).

Savulescu's aim is to place a particular moral requirement on procreation. In another paper, Savulescu and Guy Kahane claim that the PPB is "neutral on the question of what reasons we have to *have* children" (2009, 275, fn. 3, their emphasis). Savulescu simply argues that if one is going to reproduce, one should create the best possible child, according to his concept of best, which involves selecting from among the possible children one might have the one who can be expected to have the best life.

If one fails to make this selection of the best, one is then presumably doing something wrong. Hence, we might interpret the inability or unwillingness to abide by the PPB as providing the basis for an obligation *not* to procreate. If achieving procreative beneficence is a necessary condition for justifying procreation, then if you cannot or will not adhere to it, you ought not to procreate.

To decide whether the failure to achieve procreative beneficence plausibly creates an obligation not to procreate, it is necessary to evaluate the principle itself. Some philosophers are critical of the PPB (e.g., Parker 2007[2]), but their criticisms fail to take much notice of the effects on women of following the principle other than to express some concerns about women's reproductive autonomy or liberty. But the principle does have additional worrying implications for women, and they are the basis for my criticisms of it.

In his discussions of the PPB, Savulescu shockingly does not even refer to women; he writes almost exclusively of "couples" and occasionally of "single reproducers." But the PPB, if adopted, would weigh far more heavily on women than on men, for, as Savulescu points out, achieving procreative beneficence in his sense necessitates the use of preimplantation genetic diagnosis after IVF.[3] His ideal is that every potential mother would be required to undergo this process: "Procreative Beneficence implies couples should employ genetic tests for non-disease traits in selecting which child to bring into existence and that we should allow selection for non-disease genes in some cases even if this maintains or increases social inequality" (2001, 415). Who are "we"? Savulescu never tells us. Savulescu and Kahane say that the "[P]PB *instructs* women to seriously consider IVF if natural reproduction is likely to lead to a child with a condition that is expected to reduce well-being significantly, *even if that condition is not a disease*" (2009, 281, my emphasis). Possible nondisease traits that might be deliberately selected against include clinical depression, autism, "negative affect," Asperger's syndrome, "cognitive and physical abilities, personality traits, propensity to addiction, sexual orientation, etc." (Savulescu and Kahane 2009, 276). Once couples have decided to use IVF, "PGD has few 'costs' to couples (Savulescu 2001, 413). He also claims that IVF and PGD have "fewer psychological sequelae" than prenatal testing followed by abortion (Savulescu 2001, 416). He provides no empirical evidence for these claims.

Although Savulescu and Kahane assert that the PPB is compatible with several moral theories (2009, 277), it is an expression of utilitarianism. As I suggested in chapter 5, we seldom have a moral requirement to conform to the principle of utility because maximizing good is supererogatory, not morally required; it places unacceptable demands on individuals and would lead to self-stultifying perfectionism, the inability to complete tasks, or martyrdom and running oneself ragged. A requirement to maximize good would be ineffective and demoralizing; it would make morally justified behavior unachievable and create moral failures out of us all.[4]

In the particular case of the PPB, it is simply unreasonable to require that all women who want to have a child should use IVF to maximize (supposedly) the well-being of their future offspring. IVF is extremely expensive;[5] in many jurisdictions, it is available only to the wealthy. IVF also requires the use of drugs to stimulate the production of multiple ova, following which the ova are removed from the woman's body, fertilized, and inserted into her uterus. This process is far more complex and potentially harmful than sexual intercourse or even simple insemination. Women who abide by the PPB would be engaging in a massive medical experiment on their own bodies and those of their prospective children. In addition, the chances of success are low, particularly when IVF is used for women with infertility problems; they are likely to be better if used by women without such problems, but IVF is unlikely to come close to the success rates for ordinary heterosexual intercourse. Because fertility declines with age, older women who want to follow the principle will have to undergo multiple IVF attempts before succeeding—if they ever do.

In addition, if multiple embryos are transferred to the woman's uterus, perhaps to increase the possibility of success, the chances of multiples (twins, triplets, quadruplets, etc.) are high. The gestation of multiples is dangerous both for the woman and for the infants. For the woman, the risks include "hypertensive disorders, thromboembolism, premature labor and delivery, urinary tract infection, anemia and vaginal-uterine hemorrhage (placental abruption, placenta previa), fluid overload and pulmonary edema in association with parenteral tocolysis [inhibition of labor]. Women with multiple pregnancies [i.e., pregnant with multiple fetuses] are at increased risk of requiring long periods of bed rest, hospitalization, administration of medication to prevent preterm labor and increased risk of surgical procedures (Cesarean section, cerclage)" (Wennerholm 2004, 26). Moreover, "risks to the fetus[es] increase several-fold in multiple pregnancies. . . . [P]reterm birth and very preterm birth are the major cause of neonatal mortality and morbidity. Even if the children are healthy, the consequences for the family are severe; among them, long-term stress and depression are well-documented, especially in the case of raising triplets" (Wennerholm 2004, 23). Thus, acting on procreative beneficence turns out not to be beneficent at all, either for prospective mothers or for their future children.[6]

Now, Savulescu might say in response to this objection that *if* none of these costs were incurred in order to choose the best embryo, *then* we would have to adhere to the PPB. Indeed, he and Kahane state that the PPB's strength can be most clearly seen "when there are no opposing reasons" (2009, 281). But there are almost never "no opposing reasons" when we undertake a morally complex human project involving human bodies. In another paper, Savulescu concedes that the interests of "parents or reproducers" are also reasons for action and that "couples should not undergo IVF and its risks if the harms are significant and the additional benefits small" (2007, 286). However, it is inaccurate to say that *couples* undergo the risks of IVF; it is *women* who go through it. And it is impossible even to imagine a viable way of producing and then choosing among possible embryos that does not involve time, technology, expense, medical expertise, and serious interventions into women's bodies.

Nevertheless, if *per impossibile* there were a magic way of selecting embryos (and magic seems to be what it would take)—if, that is, embryo selection were to cost a woman little or nothing (in terms of money, time, bodily invasion, uncertainty, anxiety, low success rate, and the dangers of pregnancy with HOMs)—then the objection about the immediate costs to women would disappear. But the PPB would not thereby be vindicated. After all, women might still want to conceive through ordinary sexual intercourse. For many women and men, there is a special significance to conceiving a much-wanted child by making love; it is a significant part of their relationship and their first steps to parenthood. Using another method would be a heavy price to pay.

Perhaps Savulescu would reject such delicacy of feeling. But there is still another reason to criticize the PPB. Recall that, according to Savulescu, women and their partners are morally required to use PGD to detect not only disease-causing genes but also non-disease-causing genes in order thereby to select the best possible genetic combination in their future children. If we accept a moral obligation to improve embryos by means of characteristics that will be deemed advantageous in future offspring, we are in effect endorsing a project of creating enhanced offspring. Hence, the adoption of the PPB would send society down a very slippery slope, a slope that would be especially problematic for women. The concept of procreative beneficence gives us no reason to believe that beneficence should end at the embryonic stage. Indeed, Savulescu and Kahane specifically link their principle to the "moral reasons parents have to care about the potential for well-being of their future children. . . . Couples often wait years to build financial, emotional and other resources, in order to provide a better environment for their future child to grow. In waiting to have a family, they are selecting a child who will have a better life" (2009, 276). They also link their principle to choices about children's "educational environment" (2009, 284); that is, they are clearly interested in a "beneficence" that goes well beyond embryo selection.

Thus, adhering to the PPB might generate a variety of additional requirements, primarily but not exclusively for women, to ensure the existence of a child "who is expected to have the best life." Any woman planning to have a child would likely have a moral obligation (perhaps along with her partner and her society) to create the best possible circumstances for any conception, pregnancy, and childbirth that she undergoes.

For example, excellent nutrition would become not just a wise choice but a moral obligation, along with complete abstention from alcohol, caffeine, and even many prescription medications for her own physical and psychological well-being, because all of these things can harm the fetus. Perhaps a woman would have a moral obligation to quit her job or move to an area with a better climate or one that provides the best possible prenatal care.

Maybe it would not stop there. To ensure the best possible life for a child, the parents would have to consider whether to sacrifice enough to provide music lessons, computer classes, swimming instruction, or hockey practice. Or maybe all of them. The parents would have to choose, whatever their costs, the best possible education for their children, the best possible health care, and the best possible neighborhood in which to live. Perhaps they ought to move to a larger home, immigrate to another country, or provide three siblings if those actions are in the child's best interests. Perhaps they should even give up the child to other parents; even if the original parents can provide a satisfactory upbringing, there are likely others who can do better. We would need to have a national or international registry of excellent parents to whom children could be transferred once their original parents failed to maximize their well-being.

Although some of these measures *might* potentially contribute to producing the best possible life for future children, it is highly implausible to say that they all are moral obligations because most are far beyond what can be expected of any human being and require psychological and material sacrifices so stringent that people are likely to reject procreation altogether.

Savulescu and Kahane say that the PPB is not an "absolute obligation"; it can be overridden by other concerns, including "the welfare of the parents, [and] of existing children" (2009, 278). So Savulescu might say that none of the extraordinary measures I cited earlier would be morally required if there are reasons not to do them—namely, the harm that they cause to "reproducers." Moreover, procreative beneficence "is an essentially *private* enterprise," he says, aimed at generating "the best child, of the possible children, a couple could have" (Savulescu 2001, 424, my emphasis). "[The] [P]PB is not the view that reproducers should be coerced into selecting the most advantaged child, or punished if they don't" (Savulescu and Kahane 2009, 279). Hence, the PPB does not allow a government or social agencies to police pregnant women's behavior or to make IVF and PGD compulsory. Savulescu adds, "For the purposes of public policy, there should be a presumption in favour of liberty in liberal democracies. So, ultimately, we should allow couples to make their own decisions about which child to have" (2001, 425). (Notice that there is still no indication of who "we" are.)

But adopting the PPB sets the stage for at least some of the potential harms to parents described here to be considered morally acceptable in the interests of producing children who have the best life possible, up to the point where the harm to "reproducers" overrides the benefits to children. Moreover, implementing the PPB on a wide scale *would*—despite Savulescu's disclaimer—affect public policy, for it would require a massive redeployment of medical resources and health-care personnel. It is just false to assume that a widely adopted moral principle respecting human reproduction is neutral with respect to social action or that it will not have effects—in this case, negative effects—on women's well-being and freedom. I therefore conclude that there are no good reasons to adopt the PPB. Women do not have an obligation to use IVF and PGD to produce the supposedly best possible child.

At the beginning of this section, I said that Savulescu's PPB might be regarded as a possible basis for an obligation not to reproduce: that is, if one could not achieve procreative beneficence, then one would have a responsibility not to procreate. However, I have argued that the PPB itself is not morally acceptable. Hence, the failure to abide by the PPB cannot provide a morally compelling reason not to have children.

It is noteworthy that the debates about whether to conform to the PPB, like the debates about the Repugnant Conclusion (described in chapter 5), are conducted with complete disregard for the fact that human persons—women—are necessary to produce children. They ignore the basic feminist principle of concern for women's well-being and reproductive rights. It is odd that the utilitarians who discuss these concepts separate from each other never see their negative relationship. The goal of having the best possible child undermines the goal of maximizing the number of children produced because large numbers of children—whether in a family or in a society—are likely to have less material well-being, less parental attention, and possibly greater risk of serious illnesses. That is, to the extent that the PPB is adopted, it undermines the Repugnant Conclusion, and to the extent that the Repugnant Conclusion is adopted, it undermines the PPB. It is surely philosophically significant that these utility-based principles are not simultaneously viable.

Both the Repugnant Conclusion and the PPB require that women maximize certain reproductive outcomes. In discussing procreation, however, proponents of the Repugnant Conclusion and the PPB do not require maximization from other persons, the state, or institutions—even though there are other methods, far less costly to women, of attaining at least some of the procreative goods that the Repugnant Conclusion and the PPB allegedly offer. The goal of procreative beneficence, for example, would be assisted by excellent prenatal, maternal, and neonatal care; the development of effective contraception and readily accessible abortion services; universally available childcare and outstanding education; universally available health care; and the reduction of socioeconomic inequalities.

Might There be a Responsibility Not to Have Children in Order to Avoid Causing Harm?

Critic Michael Parker rejects Savulescu's PPB. He nonetheless thinks that people have an obligation to "consider carefully whether it is reasonable to expect that the child they are thinking of conceiving is going to be born under conditions conducive to the possibility of a 'good life.'" But he adds, "What counts as the good in a particular case, will be meaningful and reasonable only within the context of discursive rules, including rules of justification, of the communities within which it is being used as a justification" (2007, 282).

Unfortunately, if that is how "what counts as the good" is determined, his statement may well imply that in a male-dominant and patriarchal society, it is "good" for every woman to be uneducated and married young, to be subject all her life to her husband, and to bear as many babies as possible. Although such customs would reflect that community's practices and values, its "discursive rules" would doom all women to lives that in many and perhaps most cases are demonstrably not all that good in terms of the women's talents, potential, and life happiness. The concept of the good life that we should seek for our offspring is surely not entirely dependent on the particular community within which we are rearing children.

Nonetheless, Parker's suggestion about the relevance to procreation of "conditions conducive to the possibility of a 'good life'" for the possible child is well taken. Parker allows the possibility, on grounds of beneficence itself, that there may be "objective conditions required for the possibility of flourishing of any human life" (2007, 282). We need to investigate whether any general conditions are required for human flourishing such that their absence creates an obligation not to procreate. In the following sections, I consider some possibilities.

1. A Responsibility Not to Procreate Because of Being Too Young or Too Old

If children flourish when their parents are an appropriate age to rear them, perhaps individuals have a responsibility not to have children if they themselves (the prospective parents) are too young. Derek Parfit invents a now-classic example of a fourteen-year-old girl who chooses to have a child: "Because she is so young, she gives her child a bad start in life. . . . If this girl had waited for several years, she would have had a different child, to whom she would have given a better start in life" (1984, 358). Should we say that this girl, a child herself, had a moral obligation not to procreate at that particular time?

Parfit has other philosophical goals in mind, and he never mentions the kinds of worries that feminists or concerned parents might raise about the circumstances under which a fourteen-year-old becomes pregnant. Some of us would wonder who made this child pregnant and whether she was the victim of sexual assault; what the father's capacities and moral responsibilities might be; whether others can help with rearing the baby; and the degree to which a fourteen-year-old is capable of making fully informed decisions about the continuation of her pregnancy and the rearing of a child.

Parfit would no doubt claim that these worries are irrelevant to the case itself, which he uses to raise questions about the identity of the baby. (I say more about what he calls the "Non-Identity Problem" in chapter 8.) Yet their complete omission is connected to the problems with the Repugnant Conclusion that I cited in chapter 5. It is one more indication of the ways in which Parfit and other philosophers (such as Savulescu) who explore abstract issues related to population are oblivious to the fact that it is women (or in this case girls) who become pregnant and bear children and that it is their lives that are made better or in some cases unutterably worse by the conditions and circumstances in which they procreate. The failure to take into account the lived experience of procreation and child rearing for women and for men not only makes these discussions highly "theoretical" and unrealistic but also introduces errors into moral reasoning about the justification of procreation.

A fourteen-year-old is unlikely to choose parenthood freely and autonomously. Her capacity to make such a major decision would be compromised by her age and perhaps by other factors such as poverty, sexual violence, inadequate and incomplete education, and drug and alcohol use. Kenneth DeVille cites evidence that pregnant adolescents in the United States, "when compared to their non-pregnant peers, are poor problem solvers and frequently cognitively deficient." He also mentions studies that show that "as a group, pregnant adolescents possess fewer social skills, poorer self images, and fewer familial and social contacts than other adolescents their own age" (1997, 263). Hence, these girls cannot be considered morally culpable for their childbearing "choices." If "ought" implies "can"—if, that is, the ascription of a moral obligation requires the existence of the ability to carry out the obligation—then it is otiose to say that young girls, including Parfit's fourteen-year-old, ought not to choose to have children.

In general, pubescent and early-teen girls—as well as their male peers—are too young to become parents. This claim is not an argument for enforced celibacy for young people, nor is it a case for compulsory contraception or compulsory abortion. It is simply the recognition that the younger the parent, the more difficult it is to take on the parenting role and the greater the likelihood of worrisome outcomes not only for the child but also for the teen parent. Yet the minimum age for good parenting is in part culture dependent. Although an eighteen-year-old in one social context can be a satisfactory parent, in another she might not be, regardless of her own personal characteristics.

In general, the more inadequate the society's social safety net, the harder it will be for a young person to be a successful parent. In addition, the more complex and "developed" the society, the longer young people must spend in education and the more they must postpone paid work and independent life—along with parenthood. Indeed, young women in the West can be forgiven for noticing that there seems to be no good time for a woman in the twenty-first century to have a baby, given the cultural message that she must fit in getting educated, hunting for a job, finding a life partner, and developing some financial security before becoming pregnant.

The issue of when one is too young for motherhood is complicated by the fact that women's fertility gradually declines through their late twenties and early thirties; hence, there may be good reasons for having a baby earlier rather than later. Indeed, some argue that "Western society's stigmatization of teen motherhood [is] profoundly hypocritical and misogynistic. Young women's instincts to procreate . . . 'are suppressed in the interests of society's timetable'" (Hilary Mantel, quoted in McLaren 2010, L3). As I suggested in chapter 1, we should be suspicious of the deployment of the concept of "instinct" in the context of childbearing. Nonetheless, the contemporary tendency toward later and later procreation does not mean that a pregnant woman of twenty or twenty-one is necessarily making a mistake, provided the pregnancy is the result of well-considered choice, she has the necessary social support, and she is prepared for motherhood.

The other side of the age issue is the question whether some people ought not to have children because they are too old. The idea of being "too old" for parenthood is strongly gendered. Women older than thirty-four having their first child are sometimes referred to as "elderly primigravidas." In contrast, men, because their fertility lasts longer, often father children when they are well past the age of sixty, seventy, or even eighty. Their offspring are regarded as tributes to their continuing virility, and these older fathers are seldom subjected to criticism. But a woman who has a child in her midforties is likely to be subjected to stern moral scrutiny.

Such criticisms are unjustified. If men are not too old in their midforties to be parents, it is unfair to declare women too old and to say that women have a moral obligation not to procreate after a certain age. It is both ageist and sexist. Older women can do a fine job of nurturing children, as is evidenced by grandmothers who sometimes end up raising their grandchildren when the children's own parents are unavailable, unable, or unwilling. Critics sometimes express the worry that older women will not live to raise their children to adulthood. Children supposedly have a "right" not to be orphaned (Parks 1999, 84). Yet there is at least an equal danger with respect to older men; in fact, the danger is greater because men's life expectancy is on average lower than women's.

Indeed, we cannot predict who will live and who will die. A young mother of twenty-five might be killed in a car accident. A woman who gives birth at forty-five may live for another thirty-five years. If critics were genuinely worried about the supposed fate of orphans, they would be urging men as well as women not to become parents if they work in dangerous industries, fail to care for their health, or engage in risky leisure pursuits.

Moreover, as Jennifer Parks points out, we can't necessarily assume that the forty-five-year-old first-time mother could simply have chosen motherhood at an earlier age: "Due to a lack of equal opportunity in the workforce many women established their careers at the expense of motherhood. The time, energy, and dedication that their careers demanded compromised their option to be mothers during their career building, reproductive years. The years during which women are most fertile are the years during which their careers are most demanding: to take time off for maternity leave, for sick days for one's children, and for other maternal duties is to put one's entire career at risk" (1999, 80). Thus, I don't think we should say that some women ought not to reproduce just because they are too old.

Nonetheless, I am not endorsing the use of reproductive technologies to even out the biological differences between women and men by enabling women to gestate and give birth well into their sixties. Although men are able to become biological parents later in life, egalitarian ideals do not require that society automatically provide the technology and resources for women to become pregnant after their reproductive years have ended.

Although there have been cases, thanks to IVF using other women's eggs, of successful pregnancy in women who are sixty or older, such choices are not necessarily morally justifiable. What is morally problematic about them is not the simple fact that the woman is well past the usual reproductive age; much more problematic are the facts that such pregnancies are so difficult to achieve and sustain and that the infants and mother are subsequently at greater risk. Postmenopausal procreation is an experiment. No one knows the long-term effects on the women or their offspring. Moreover, such women do not produce their own eggs;

they need one or more eggs donated by or bought from another woman. They need IVF to fertilize the donated or purchased egg(s), using their male partner's sperm or that of another man. Then the fertilized egg(s) must be inserted into the uterus. Postmenopausal women do not produce adequate hormones to initiate and sustain a pregnancy; so they need many drugs. The use of IVF increases their chance of carrying multiple pregnancies; the result is a high-risk pregnancy, with health dangers for both the women and their babies.

Another problem of technologically induced pregnancies in older women is the costs they incur for health-care personnel, facilities, and resources. Doctors are arguably not justified in using their expertise for postmenopausal pregnancies because when resources are used to support a sixty-year-old woman who wants a baby, they are less available for other gynecological, obstetric, and perinatal needs, including preventing infertility, treating infertility in younger women, prenatal care, and care for neonates, especially premature babies.

Finally, one can ask about the legitimacy of providing children for postmenopausal women in the context of overpopulation (I discuss the issue of overpopulation at length in chapter 9). It is highly unlikely that the babies of postmenopausal women contribute in any significant way to problems of overpopulation, but some philosophers argue that even one extra child incurs a serious cost to the planet.

I conclude that the moral question about older women having babies is not a matter of their stage of life. Sheer chronological age is not sufficient to make it morally unjustified for a woman to seek motherhood, and she does not have an obligation not to procreate simply because of her relatively advanced age. The issue rather has to do with the extent of the costs to the health-care system, the risks to herself and her infant(s), and the requirement of other women's gametes in order to meet her desire.

2. A Responsibility Based on the Potential Parent's Sexuality or Marital Status

Those who highly value the so-called traditional family, consisting of a married heterosexual couple and their biological offspring, sometimes argue that it is harmful to children for them to be born to a single woman or to a woman who has a lesbian partner. In chapter 1, I suggested that the burden of providing justification should rest not on those who desire not to have children, but on those who choose to have them. But those who choose procreation who happen to be single or in a same-sex relationship have no higher burden of justification, I argue, than do those who are married and in a heterosexual relationship.

In fact, in my view the burden of evidence ought to be on those critics who regard procreation by single persons or by same-sex couples as morally wrong. They do not provide empirical evidence for such a claim. Instead, the bases of the claim are a belief (often bolstered by scriptural references) in the intrinsic rightness of heterosexual married unions and perhaps a repugnance for any woman who is not sexually and romantically tied to a man. Although there is not space to make a full and complete argument here, I reject biases based on relationship status or sexual orientation. Whether parents harm or benefit children depends on how the children are raised, the parents' maturity and psychological development, and the material and social conditions in which they live, not the status of the parents' relationship or the nature of the parents' sexuality. Given that there are growing numbers of families in which parents are single or of the same sex, I know of no evidence showing that children are harmed by the mere fact that their parents are not together or are of the same sex. In fact, the most recent evidence indicates that offspring of lesbian mothers do very well (Gartrell and Bos 2010).

If critics are worried in particular about the influence of lesbian parents' sexuality on the child, I would make two points. First, the concern about the influence of the parents' sexuality *assumes* without argument precisely what is at issue: that there is something problematic about same-sex sexual orientation. No one worries about what children learn about sexuality from heterosexual parents. The bias against same-sex sexuality is an unfounded a priori assumption whose correctness we have no reason to accept. In effect, the critics assume what they should be trying to prove. Second, there is no particular evidence that children acquire their sexual identity by learning from their parents. If they did, then it would be impossible for so many gay, lesbian, and bisexual offspring to come from heterosexual parents and for heterosexual offspring to come from gay, lesbian, or bisexual parents. For these reasons, I deny that same-sex sexual orientation is the basis for an obligation not to have children.

The one complicating factor that *appears* to be connected to the potential parents' sexuality arises in the case of two men who are in a relationship and want to have a child biologically related to one of them. They will, of course, have to invite a woman to conceive and gestate the offspring. This situation potentially raises issues about adoption (if the nonbiologically related man wants to be the child's legal parent). More important, however, it also introduces various moral problems related either to so-called contract motherhood or paid surrogacy (if the men hire a woman to be the gestator) or to a woman's willingness to engage without pay in the biological labor and make no claim on the child she bears (so-called altruistic surrogacy). These problems are complex moral, social, and practical issues, which I have chosen to exclude from this book. However, it is noteworthy that the potential problems here are not connected to the men's sexuality per se; the problems are connected to the biological fact that men cannot gestate and bear children.

What about a woman who is without a partner? Does she have an obligation not to have a child? Surely this is a case where it is impossible to generalize, but her single status is not in itself a factor that morally precludes motherhood. Every single woman who wants a child must make the decision based not just on the longing for a child, but on a clear assessment of her personal and material resources and her network of social support. (In that respect, her situation is not different from the kind of assessment that couples need to make.) Pragmatically speaking, it tends to be better for a parent to have help in raising a child. Child rearing is both a psychological and a physical challenge. It may not literally "take a village," but no human being can function twenty-four hours a day, and everyone can benefit from other individuals' assistance, advice, and experience. That help can come from the child's other parent, or it can come from other relatives, friends, neighbors, colleagues, babysitters, and childcare centers. Hence, the mere fact that a parent is without a partner does not mean that the parent is alone, that she cannot be a good mother, or that her child will have a bad life.

However, if a prospective parent is truly alone, without any reliable family or friends, then she would have good reason to reconsider parenthood. If such a person is alone because of an inability to sustain good relationships, then it seems unlikely that she can be a good or even an adequate parent. The child certainly will not fill the void in her life or heal her psychological wounds. Hence, in that case, any obligation on the part of a single woman not to have children would occur by virtue of her inability to sustain connections to other human beings, not by virtue of her single status. (We can imagine that some married persons might have the same problem and therefore also ought not to have children.)

3. A Responsibility Based on the Potential Parent's Material Situation

The potential parent's or parents' material situation might make child-bearing morally unjustified if the parents are so poor as not to be able to support the child. Ironically, of course, it is precisely the poorest prospective parents who are unlikely to have access to reliable and safe contraception or to safe and legal abortion services; hence, they are less likely to have a *choice* about whether to have children. Within developing nations, they may also be more likely to want to have children because in very poor environments children are one of the few assets that one can produce oneself; they are a source of labor and of household and personal care. In the wealthier West, however, children are less likely to be or to be needed to be a labor and care resource. Indeed, they are much more likely to be a financial liability; so of course it makes sense for prospective Western parents to think seriously and carefully about their financial capacity to support their offspring.

Yet there is altogether too much media handwringing about the supposed fecklessness and even manipulativeness of poor people, who allegedly have more children than they can "afford" and who therefore end up taking advantage of whatever paltry support the state may offer. Before such persons are condemned, it would be necessary to know a great deal about their intentions, motives, social networks, and material situations. It would also be necessary to know whether and to what extent they have choices about how many children to have.

Most important of all, it is unjust to require that childbearing and rearing be a privilege available only to the wealthy. Those who are poor relative to the mainstream suffer enough without being told that they ought to be childless. If we simply say that "the poor" ought not to have children, we are falsely generalizing across a large number of varied individuals in varied circumstances and heartlessly condemning individuals who are not wealthy or middle class to missing the pleasures and rewards of child rearing.

The crucial point here is the minimum standard that should be used. It is not completely clear what constitutes being able to "afford" children and what is the financial line below which no one should reproduce. People's circumstances change throughout their lives. At a point when women are most fertile, an individual's or couple's resources may be minimal because they are still relatively young. Their financial and material prospects may grow as their child grows.

Moreover, good child rearing is just not a function of the number of toys, clothes, or computer games the parents can provide. The minimal desiderata for providing a decent life for one's children are too often defined by reference to what the wealthy and well educated regard as important. Such a culture-bound definition of "not too poor" would be too high. The middle- and owning-class standards of abundance set by contemporary "helicopter" parents cannot be taken to constitute an appropriate minimum for the morality of procreation. Setting the standard too high makes luxuries such as private schooling, the latest technology, and designer clothing seem essential. The consumer culture of twenty-first-century Western life may make a child without a room to herself or access to a cell phone seem pitiable.

That's clearly a mistake. Although in the West each generation wants more than its predecessors, the "hedonic treadmill" is such that people become accustomed to more and more luxury and are no happier as a result. Yet during the Great Depression millions of parents succeeded in rearing healthy, functioning, and flourishing children with very few resources. Some basics are obviously essential: nutritious food, secure shelter, competent health care, and sufficient education. But no parent can be expected to provide even these basics entirely on her own; it makes sense to insist that parents be assisted at the very least through the provision of public education and publicly funded medical care.

Thus, although one's material resources (or lack of them) are certainly relevant to the morality of the decision whether to have children or not, it is unjustified and even impossible to make blanket statements about the supposed level of financial eligibility and material well-being necessary for child rearing. At the same time, it seems obvious that if one has no prospects and truly cannot even feed or clothe oneself, then one ought not to have children at all. Inadequate material assets may likewise generate an obligation not to have more than one child so that one can direct one's minimal resources to caring for that child. Of course, if an adult is compelled to live in abject poverty, her situation is not just an argument against child rearing. It is evidence of the injustice, incompetence, and indifference of the society within which she lives. Such a person certainly ought not to have a child, but that moral responsibility may be as much or more the result of her society's failure, indifference, and neglect as it is of her own unsuitability to be a parent.

4. A Responsibility Based on the Likelihood That the Child Will Be Harmed by Living in the Society

Conscientious parents sometimes have the thought that the world is too dangerous a place for children. My own mother grew up hearing stories from her father, who survived the trenches of World War I. She herself lived through the Great Depression and World War II. She told me, her firstborn, that as a young adult she wondered if she was doing the right thing in choosing to have children. I had similar qualms before conceiving my own first child, although my concerns were based at that time on fears of nuclear devastation, environmental degradation, and overpopulation.

How dangerous is too dangerous to justify the choice to have a child? The question is similar to the earlier one, about how poor is too poor to justify the choice to have a child, and probably just as difficult to answer. Yet in circumstances where prospective parents have a real choice about procreation, it seems that there must be a threshold of hazard or oppression below which individuals have a responsibility to choose not to procreate.

Historically, prospective parents must have relied a great deal on faith (in their ability to protect their offspring), hope (that the times would change and improve), and even a selective inattention to the risks. Otherwise, a concern for dangers to their offspring would often have made them fear for their offspring's life and would have led some—those who truly had a choice—not to have children at all.

Sue Donaldson suggests that we need to distinguish between "necessary human suffering" (death, incurable illness, psychological and mental pain from the inevitable exigencies of human life) and "contingent human suffering" (resulting from poverty, violence, and avoidable disease) (personal communication, February 17, 2009). What's in the first category is unavoidable just by virtue of being human. For David Benatar, it will be recalled, these facts of human life are always enough to make coming into existence a harm. I have argued that there are ample reasons to disagree with him. No one can ensure their child a pain-free existence or a life with no suffering, yet life is usually well worth living nonetheless.

There is a real question, however, about whether and to what extent the likelihood of contingent human suffering should count against the morality of procreation. Consider the harms arising from violent or harsh environments, famine and widespread malnourishment, war, and environmental threats. Consider also the existence of oppression, as a result of which one's prospective child may be badly and unfairly treated because of her sex, race, sexuality, impairment, or ethnicity. One might argue that to choose not to have a child because of the dangers from sexism, racism, or other forms of oppression is to acquiesce in the continuation of those oppressions. One might even argue that one's future child *might* be the special person who helps to resolve planetary threats such as starvation and war. But such responses take a genuine risk on behalf of one's child, who has no choice whether to come into existence. And no child should be expected to function as an instrument for diminishing social conflict.

As with the condition of poverty, it seems almost impossible to make useful generalizations about which social environments are too dangerous to justify procreation. Yet I think that conscientious prospective parents who wonder whether the world is too dangerous for procreation are not mistaken in giving the question serious consideration. In addition, where the risks are extreme and unrelenting, children's suffering highly likely, and the probability of improvement quite small, the dangers of procreation may become so dire as to raise questions about whether it is even worthwhile to continue the human species (a topic I discuss in chapter 9).

5. A Responsibility Based on the Likelihood That One Will Not Be a Good Parent

Onora O'Neill remarks that it is "hard to know exactly what the minimal requirements for child rearing in a given society are; hard to foresee one's own capacities and situation over a long stretch of life; and impossible to tell what difficulties a particular child may bring" (1979, 29). These factors are the great unknowns of choosing to have children, especially the first child, although some of the unknowns apply to subsequent children as well. Nonetheless, before making such a decision, we surely have a responsibility to be aware of our potential strengths and weaknesses vis-à-vis childcare—what Lisa Cassidy calls our "parenting competence" (2006, 44)—and to decide accordingly.

Cassidy argues, "Those people who anticipate being incompetent parents should not parent" (2006, 46). I take this claim as obviously true, even though there may well be epistemological questions about how to determine *whether* one will be incompetent (Cassidy 2006, 49). Parenting is the kind of activity in the West that one probably learns as one goes along, and it is affected by the kind of child(ren) one has. One might be an excellent parent to one child, but not as good with another who has a different temperament, set of abilities, or psychological development. Perhaps we cannot know in advance how well we will do. But Cassidy gives the example of a friend who attempted to care for a puppy and in so doing realized that her abusive behavior toward the animal made her not a good candidate for parenthood (2006, 45). That would be important evidence to consider. People who abuse their children or who fail to provide even the necessities for existence are obviously bad parents; anyone who suspects herself of being likely to engage in such behavior should choose not to procreate. We have a fundamental duty of nonmaleficence, refraining from doing harm, and that duty extends to the well-being of children who might come into existence as a result of our choices.

There are also evaluative questions about how to determine what constitutes competence. Cassidy argues that "those people who anticipate being *averagely* competent parents should not parent"; hence, individuals who anticipate that they will be less than excellent parents should choose not to have children. "Parenting is just too important to do in a way that is just good enough. . . . [A]ll things considered, excellent parenting is markedly preferable to average parenting" (2006, 46, 47, my emphasis). Cassidy thereby generates an explicit standard for the justification of procreation: individuals who choose to have a child must be the sort of person who will be an excellent parent.

At first sight, that standard appears very high, and it seems unlikely that many current parents would meet it. In fact, we do not require "excellence" in teachers, coaches, or babysitters, all of whom spend a great deal of time working with children. Excellence is certainly laudable, but if everyone were required to be excellent, very few adults would even be allowed near children.

Of course, the ability to meet the standard depends on what is meant by "excellent parenting" and "average parenting." According to Cassidy, excellent parents are "patient, giving, accessible, calm, fun, compassionate,

[and] strong." By contrast, her description of merely competent parents is chilling. Such parents "do not regularly beat their children, though perhaps they lose their tempers and spank them. Competent parents do not psychologically torment their children, but they may be smothering, or selfish, or cold, or overly demanding, or uninterested, or have any other of those utterly mundane qualities that would make someone a less than ideal parent" (2006, 49, 48).

Given these descriptions, Cassidy's rejection of merely adequate parenting is easier to accept. Indeed, one wonders why people who are merely competent in Cassidy's terms would even want to have children. Perhaps they are ignorant about children's needs. Perhaps they are self-deceived about their own personalities and suitability to be parents. Perhaps they are simply selfish and don't care what the costs of their behavior might be to their vulnerable and dependent offspring. We certainly cannot say that life as the child of merely competent parents would not be worth living; it is quite likely to be worthwhile. But if we hope to do what is right, we ought to aim to give our children a good life, and such a life may well be precluded if we are capable of only average parenting in Cassidy's sense. Hence, we have a responsibility not to reproduce if we cannot meet a high standard of parenting capacity. Despite the normative and epistemological difficulties of that statement, it is safe to say that it is correct.

6. A Responsibility Based on the Dangers of Multiples

Earlier in this chapter, I talked briefly about the serious dangers of gestating multiples to both women and their future children. I suggest that women have a responsibility not to deliberately seek to have triplets, quadruplets, and other HOMs. If the only way that they can procreate is by having HOMs, then they have a responsibility to avoid procreation. Of course, it is unlikely that very many women are faced with the choice between HOMs and no child at all. Nonetheless, the immorality of deliberately choosing multiples should not be underestimated.

Women who give birth to twins, triplets, or quadruplets cannot be said to have acted irresponsibly if their multiples are conceived by chance and not as the result of any type of deliberate intervention. However, the situation becomes morally more complex the more that technologies such as IVF are introduced into the reproductive process. To increase the odds of a pregnancy in IVF (and sometimes to speed up a woman's family completion plans), several embryos may be inserted into her uterus at once. The woman who, through her doctor's agency, carried this procedure to its biological extreme is Nadya Suleman, the (in)famous and cruelly named "Octomom," already a single mother of six children under the age of seven who then gestated and gave birth to eight more, all of whom survived. Having that many children all at once is simply wrong,[7] and it was even more wrong of her physician to transfer so many embryos to her uterus.

The transfer of a large number of embryos is often defended on several grounds. First, the very high costs of IVF and embryo transfer lead physicians and parents to want to increase the chances of success by transferring more than one or two. But reducing the personal costs of reproductive technology is not an adequate reason for putting infant lives at risk. Second, the embryos are considered to be the property of the woman (and her male partner, if any), and the assumption is that the owners may do what they like with their possessions. But ownership of property does not give one the right to do anything whatsoever with that property. (Ownership of a baseball bat does not entitle one to swing it in the vicinity of someone else's head.) Moreover, because the embryos may one day grow into persons, they belong to the prospective mother not so much in the way that inanimate objects such as books and dishes are property, but in the sense that the prospective mother has authority over their disposition. She can, for example, decide (subject to medical suitability) whether to donate the embryos to other women or to offer them for medical research. But there are limits on that authority. Because of the dangers to the future children and the difficulty of competently raising so many simultaneously, procreation via the implantation of a large number of embryos is not morally justified. The responsibility for safe and appropriate transfer lies with the physician; Suleman's physician failed in that responsibility—indeed, failed drastically. Physicians have no obligation to acquiesce in a prospective mother's request to transfer a large number of embryos. Indeed, for all the reasons I have listed, they have a moral obligation to reject such demands.

Suleman's behavior cannot be justified as the exercise of her reproductive rights because the choices she made go far beyond the right to reproduce in the negative sense—that is, the right not to be interfered with. Instead, she chose and required extensive medical interventions (including the donation of sperm) in order to create and then sustain the pregnancy and then to care for the tiny infants and herself after the birth. The moral problem is not that she is a single mother; I have already argued that marital status by itself is irrelevant to fitness as a parent. But several other problems can be noted. First, there are the risks she took in gestating eight fetuses at once as well as the drain on medical services that her pregnancy, delivery, and care of her premature newborns required. No one knows, at this point, what kinds of developmental needs her children may have in the future and the specialized care they may require as they grow up. Second, how will she care for all these infants, even with her own parents' help and even with the quarter-million dollars she has received for allowing her family to be filmed (Bowe 2009)? Unless one is (at least) a millionaire who can afford to hire excellent help, caring warmly and attentively for so many young children all at once is impossible. Third, the chances that the children will have a close relationship with their mother are, by virtue of the competition for her attention, very small. And fourth, as I discuss in the next chapter, it is unconscionable for one lone woman to place such a large burden on the planet's resources.

None of these comments casts or is intended to cast any aspersions on the children themselves. As J. David Velleman puts it in another context,

> Suppose we judge that people should not have more children than they can adequately care for. Have we implied that there are children who should not have been born? Yes, of course, if that statement means just that some children are born after their parents should have stopped having children. Yes, too, if it means that the birth of a child destined to be neglected is a regrettable kind of event. But we have not implied, of any particular child, that his existence should be regretted or that his birthday should not be celebrated. Loving an individual child and rejoicing in his existence is perfectly consistent with thinking it wrong for parents like his to have had so many children. (2005, 364)

Conclusion

The discussion in this chapter has necessarily been a mixed bag. Recall that in the first chapter I suggested that the burden of proof or, more accurately, the burden of justification should rest upon those who choose to have children, not on those who choose not to. Simply not wanting to have children, it seems to me, is a very good reason not to have them; no vulnerable lives are thereby in danger of being harmed by one's indifference or dislike. The person who believes it would be bad for herself to have children is similarly justified, perhaps even obligated, not to have them.

In addition, the likelihood that one will be a bad parent or even a merely competent parent in Cassidy's rather chilling sense surely makes one responsible for not becoming a parent. Extreme poverty and the dangers in one's world—violence, war, famine, racism, and so on—should at least make any responsible person hesitate to procreate. And I believe that the proven dangers of HOMs in pregnancy demonstrate that it is morally wrong to make choices that will result in the gestation of quadruplets, quintuplets, and so on.

By contrast, most of the complaints that are made about some prospective parents' sexual identity or relationship status are simply irrelevant: the claim that a person ought not to procreate because she is single or nonheterosexual is not based on any evidence that marriage and heterosexuality improve parenting or are better for children. The relevance of parental age, however, is complex: extremes are undesirable (no one is advocating fifteen-year-old mothers or ninety-year-old fathers), but what matters is not the potential parent's chronological age per se, but rather her or his capacity to be a genuinely good mother or father.

Finally, Julian Savulescu's PPB sets a standard for reproduction that is outrageous: adhering to it would generate risks and costs for women, dangers for their babies (especially if multiple embryos are transferred), and a great deal of extra expense for health-care systems. Rejecting the principle does not, however, mean that the risk of illness or impairment in one's offspring is irrelevant to the decision whether to procreate or not. In the next chapter, I look at the implications of potential illness or impairment in the fetus for deciding whether to reproduce. I also briefly discuss the significance of impairments possessed by potential parents.

8

Illness, Impairment, and the Procreation Decision

In chapter 7, I argued that there is no obligation to achieve procreative beneficence in Savulescu's sense of the term, largely because of its costs to women. But that is not to say there is no responsibility at all to consider the future child's health. It ought to be obvious and not in need of argument that the aim in procreating should not be merely to produce a child whose life is minimally tolerable. One should aim much higher, and I think the vast majority of women and men do. In this chapter, I consider the moral implications of illness and impairment with respect to the procreation decision.

The question whether adults with impairments should be "allowed" to become parents has a long and mostly unsavory history. The issue was raised in eugenics debates during the nineteenth and twentieth centuries about the supposed need to improve the human species by discouraging and preventing procreation by individuals with certain mental or physical characteristics. And the question of whether and when abortion may be morally justified on the grounds of fetal impairment is a familiar one to both philosophers and the public. In jurisdictions that place legal restrictions on abortion services, access is often permitted on the basis of the fetus's characteristics.

I examine the first question, whether illness or impairment in the potential parents morally precludes their procreating, later in this chapter. The second question, whether and when fetal impairment or illness can morally justify abortion, is not the main part of my focus here. Instead, I am interested in a problem that appears more extreme: Are there cases where fetal impairment or illness makes abortion not merely permissible, but the morally obligatory choice? In other words, are there cases where the obligation not to procreate is so strong that *failure to abort* because of the fetus's condition would be a moral wrong? And because the choice of abortion is at best the decision of last resort to prevent procreation, it is also necessary to ask whether there are potential conditions of the fetus (and the child it would otherwise become) that merit the prevention of conception altogether. These questions about the conception of impaired or ill fetuses and the failure to abort them are where I shall begin.

A responsibility to use contraception does not appear morally equivalent to a responsibility to have an abortion. For several reasons, a responsibility to have an abortion seems more demanding. For example, having an abortion may often require a higher degree of intervention into the woman's body than contraception. But not always. The comparative degree of intrusion depends in part on the kind of contraception used: hormonal methods might have a very powerful effect on the woman's body, whereas the use by her male partner of condoms likely will not. The degree of intrusion also depends on the kind of abortion and the stage of pregnancy at which it takes place: a very early abortion will involve less upheaval to the woman's body than a very late one.

At the same time, the responsibility to abort appears to be a more demanding duty than the responsibility to use contraception because, whatever one's metaphysical views of the fetus's status, it is indubitably a living thing whose existence ends when an abortion is performed, whereas the practice of contraception simply prevents a being from coming into existence. In addition, for some women, having an abortion can be like the end of a relationship, a relationship that the woman may have chosen to initiate and value very highly: the relationship to her fetus and to the child that it may become. "If the child is wanted, parents often view their fetus as their already existing child, a distinct person" (Vehmas 2002, 49).

For these reasons—that abortion can require major intervention into the woman's body; that it can be like the end of a relationship; and that it ends the life of the fetus—a moral requirement to abort will usually require a stronger argument in support of it than will a moral requirement to use contraception.

The Non-Identity Problem

To begin, consider some thought experiments—cases proposed by Derek Parfit and James Lenman. In the classic Parfitian case (Parfit 1984,

367–71), we are asked to imagine that a woman may give birth to an impaired or ill infant by conceiving this month or alternatively give birth to a healthy and nonimpaired infant, necessarily a different ("non-identical") one, by conceiving at a later month or year. Parfit also gives us the case of Jane: "Jane has a congenital disease, that will kill her painlessly at about the age of 40. This disease has no effects before it kills. Jane knows that, if she has a child, it will have this same disease. . . . Knowing these facts, Jane chooses to have a child" (1984, 375). Lenman presents the case of Agnes, who knows she carries a gene that will make any child of hers suffer a painful and unpleasant life, but she has intense maternal instincts and goes ahead and has it anyway (2004b, 146).

The first characteristic of these thought experiments to notice is that they all presuppose (and yet do not even recognize, let alone comment on) an odd view of women. In fact, they're arguably misogynist. The thought experiments proceed as if women are as likely as not to make procreative decisions that will disadvantage, perhaps severely, their offspring. In real life, as opposed to in male philosophers' minds, it is unlikely that women would make deliberate and informed decisions with such results for their future children. On the contrary, although some women may be feckless, negligent, or ignorant, most are highly concerned about their children's well-being and do their utmost to protect it. A woman who is indifferent to her future child's health is likely to be dealing with serious problems of her own—abuse, lack of education, extreme poverty, deep depression, or addiction. Hence, examples of women who happily or at least indifferently contemplate giving birth to suffering children are scarcely believable.

I have little doubt that Parfit and Lenman would say that these qualms are irrelevant. Regardless of whether women routinely make procreative decisions in full knowledge that the decisions will harm their children, Parfit and Lenman would urge us to consider what these hypothetical cases indicate. And, indeed, their thought experiments do what they are intended to do: vividly raise the question of whether there is sometimes an obligation not to have a child in order to avoid harm to the child. I have already argued that Benatar is mistaken in claiming that it is *always* better never to have been. At the same time, it is evident that not existing is *sometimes* better, at least when the circumstances of life are intolerable and unlivable. Is there an obligation not to procreate when one's potential child will be ill or impaired? Are the women in Lenman and Parfit's thought experiments engaged in wrongdoing?

Parfit points out that the kinds of procreative choices we make now affect not only the circumstances but the actual identities of the persons who will exist in the future (1984, 362–363). According to what Parfit calls the "Non-Identity Problem," *when* we procreate determines *whom* we procreate. Most people probably think there is something wrong with creating an impaired or ill infant if a small postponement in conception would create another child who will be healthy. But Parfit thinks it is difficult, in light of the fact of non-identity, to show why it is wrong, for if we make seemingly bad choices, choices that result in harm to our children, we nonetheless bring into existence persons who, without those choices having been made, would not exist at all, persons whose lives are in most cases at least minimally worth living and often much more than that. (People with impairments are, after all, usually glad to be alive.) So it would seem that we have not harmed *them*. It therefore appears difficult, Parfit suggests, to see what is wrong with any procreative decision, provided it creates someone whose life is worth living.

Indeed, although Parfit does not mention it, the Non-Identity Problem seems to justify a variety of ill-advised and morally dubious procreative behaviors. For example, suppose a man insists that his wife must give him a son; as a result, he repeatedly makes her pregnant and demands that she abort when prenatal tests show that the fetus is female. But the son who is born after her fifth attempt would not otherwise have existed, and he has a life that is worth living, so his existence justifies the serious of pregnancies and abortions. Does it?

Or imagine a heterosexual couple who decide they want to become famous and wealthy by raising a family of sextuplets or septuplets. The woman undergoes repeated hormonal priming to produce multiple eggs; they are fertilized and inserted into her uterus, and she becomes pregnant. She gives birth to seven infants, all of them premature. One dies and several of the rest have serious physical and mental impairments. They require a lifetime of medical care, and some of them experience great pain. But they would not otherwise have existed, and their lives are not so bad as not to be worth living. So those six surviving lives, even with impairments, justify the process that produced them. Do they?

The Parfitian puzzle of non-identity is even broader than these imaginary cases, for many different kinds of changes in both our individual and our collective behavior will have an effect on which children are born. These changes include the building of factories, the placement of roads, the amount of trade, and the nature of communication (Harman 2004, 89). A society that produces nuclear armaments, widespread contamination of water, rapid industrialization, and military conflict will generate different children than if it had not engaged in these dangerous practices. Children are harmed by nuclear proliferation, environmental degradation, the spread of factories, and militarization. Yet the fact of non-identity seems to mean that a wide range of repellent collective behavior cannot be condemned on the basis of its damaging effects on children because the children produced would not otherwise have existed at all, and they presumably have lives that are at least minimally worth living.

There must be something wrong with a concept that provides a rationalization for such immoral behavior. And, indeed, there is another way of looking at the identity of offspring, a way that does not justify morally repellent behavior.

In the genetic sense certainly, a child's identity will be changed if the child is conceived at a different time, for a different egg and sperm will produce a genetically heterogeneous infant. This is the type of identity that is presupposed by the Non-Identity Problem. In that sense, the slightest difference (not to mention the big differences) in behavior is likely to change the potential identity of one's offspring. In another sense, however, and from the point of view of the parent or parents, the child's identity will be the same no matter when she or he is conceived, for it is also possible to identify one's child in terms of its social place in the family. Prospective parents are ordinarily not especially interested in having the specific child that will result from the union of one particular egg and one particular sperm. Simo Vehmas argues that from parents' point of view the exact moment of conception does not produce a different child (2002, 52). During a pregnancy, the child the couple is anticipating is their *first child*, for example, or their *second child*. We can say that from their point of view the identity of the child is simply "our first child" or "our next child." They want the child to be biologically related to them, of course, but they do not care about the specific gametes from each parent. Nor should they. Rather, they are simply interested in having their child, a child who is expected at a particular point in their lives. This latter form of identity is the kind they care about and not the kind quibbled about in the context of the Non-Identity Problem.

Thus, much of the contemporary debate about the Non-Identity Problem and the permissibility of having an impaired child has little connection to real-world parents because the child's identity means something quite different to prospective parents than it does to these philosophers. As a result, the fact that our procreative choices (as well as other sorts of choices) determine the unique genetic identity of the children who will exist in the future (and who would not otherwise exist apart from these choices) does not in itself constitute a justification for particular procreative choices we make. Even if on the whole we produce children whose lives are at least minimally worth living, our choices can harm the people who will be our children—our first child, our second child, and so on. Whatever egg and whatever sperm a child is made from, parents want that child to be in good physical and mental condition. They want that child, *the child who will have a particular place in their family*, to have as many advantages (and avoid as many disadvantages) as possible. When a woman has her first (or second or third) child, she wants that child to be as healthy and happy as it can be.

Nonmaleficence

Clearly, then, and contrary to what the Non-Identity Problem appears to show, it is genuinely *possible* for prospective parents to do wrong by deliberately creating children with impairments or severe illnesses, even though the children with those genetic identities would not have existed if they were created at another time. And governments can sometimes do wrong by taking steps that endanger nations and harm the environment, even if the entire generation of people now in existence would not have existed without those harmful actions.

It therefore makes sense to say that where one can avoid causing impairment in the fetus (for example, as a result of exposure to diseases such as measles) by not conceiving now but instead waiting a month or even a year to conceive, then the parents have an obligation not to conceive now. The harm of conceiving now is the injury that might result to their first child or to their next child. In that version of identity, harm to their child *can* be avoided while *preserving* the child's identity (as first, second, or next child), and it is usually not asking much to say that such persons should postpone conception until the danger of causing the impairment is at an end.[1] Hence, the woman in Parfit's example whose child will be born impaired if conceived this month should wait a month or more in order to create a healthy child.

As Laura Purdy puts it, where we can be certain about the "degree and inevitability of the suffering" our child will endure, "there is at least a *prima facie* case against reproduction. . . . If we want to reproduce in a situation of this sort, we need to ask ourselves whether we truly have the welfare of our possible offspring at heart, or are we merely gratifying a desire of our own" (2000, 318). By procreating under such circumstances, one may not violate obligations to a genetically specific future child, but one might violate obligations one has "concerning the having of children," as Vehmas puts it (2002, 56)—the children who will be one's own biological children, one's first child or second child, regardless of which particular parental gametes produce those children.

In general, we can say that the prospective parents have a responsibility of nonmaleficence (avoidance or prevention of harm) to their future first, second, and so on (if necessary) children. The responsibility of nonmaleficence toward future offspring has, I suggest, two components. The first component is the responsibility of care toward any being that one brings into existence. Vehmas, for example, writes, "Future parents assume (or at least ought to assume) a strong responsibility towards the well-being of their prospective child *the minute they decide to reproduce*" (2002, 48, his emphasis). He presumably means that the pregnant woman should eat well, get good prenatal care, protect her health, avoid toxic environments and violence, and so on. There is also little doubt that during pregnancy the woman should eschew excessive alcohol consumption (which can result in fetal alcohol syndrome) and the use of illegal drugs, which can be teratogenic.[2]

Although all of these behaviors are also good for the pregnant woman herself, her capacity to engage in them may be mitigated by a variety of factors, including addiction, poverty, an abusive or addicted partner, lack of education, the necessity of living or working in a dangerous or contaminated environment in order to survive, and oppression. In such cases where her free choice with respect to the health of her pregnancy is severely compromised, she cannot be held morally responsible for damage to the fetus. A society genuinely concerned about child health would endeavor to reduce the incidence of alcoholism, drug addiction, and "domestic" abuse through education, prevention programs, psychological support, health care, and poverty reduction, in order to diminish the potential harms sustained by fetuses. Moreover, a woman who in good faith takes drugs prescribed to her by a physician can hardly be held morally accountable if they harm her fetus (as the sad cases of Thalidomide and Diethylstilbestrol demonstrate). In such a situation, the fault (if any) lies with authorities—governments, policymakers, researchers, granting bodies, and health-care workers—that fail to adequately test, monitor, and regulate the use of the drug. So although pregnant women have a prima facie responsibility of nonmaleficence toward their future children, the failure to abide by this responsibility can sometimes be due to factors beyond their control.

Thus, the responsibility of care for future offspring begins even before conception, and it falls not only on future mothers but on future fathers and the societies in which they live. According to the Barker Theory (so named by its creator, scientist David Barker), "a woman's diet at the time of conception and during pregnancy have [*sic*] important effects on the subsequent health of her offspring" not only during infancy and childhood, but throughout adulthood (Barker n.d.). Given that the future child's health depends largely on its health as a fetus, and given that the fetus's health depends on the health of the individuals who create it, prospective parents ought to be in good physical condition at the time they conceive. Meeting that condition requires that they already be taking care of their health even before choosing to have children. Thus, the moral responsibility for children's well-being begins substantially before individuals decide to reproduce; it begins with the education of, health care for, and flourishing of future parents throughout society.

The second component of nonmaleficence toward one's future offspring is the responsibility not to deliberately create offspring who will endure serious suffering. Some illnesses and impairments unfortunately cannot be avoided altogether. Like Jane in Parfit's example and Agnes in Lenman's example, persons with heritable impairments (such as Huntington's chorea) or diseases (such as HIV) are in a different situation from those who can simply postpone conception. It doesn't matter when they conceive; there will be the same likelihood that infection or impairment will be passed on. Similar risks may occur in cases where there is only a small window of opportunity in which to procreate—for example, for a woman who has only recently become free of other responsibilities (such as caring for siblings or aged relatives), is close to menopause, and has only a year or two left in which to become pregnant. Because she is at an advanced stage in her fertile years, her chance of creating a child with an impairment is higher than it would have been when she was in her twenties. Her choice is to (try to) conceive now or not to conceive at all. That is, she has no way (setting aside the hiring of a contract mother or the use of a "donor" ovum, both of which raise moral problems of their own) of avoiding the risks to the fetus. What is the moral responsibility of persons in these situations?

Purdy is uncompromising: "It is morally wrong to reproduce when we know there is a high risk of transmitting a serious disease or defect. This thesis holds that some reproductive acts are wrong, and my argument puts the burden of proof on those who disagree with it to show why its conclusions can be overridden" (2004, 144).

It's plausible enough to say that *deliberately* conceiving and then sustaining the gestation of a child who will *certainly* suffer is not morally justified. The best example is the one Purdy herself uses: Tay-Sachs disease, which involves painful deterioration and early death (2004, 144). Where there is no way of minimizing the risk of suffering from serious illness, I agree that it is prima facie wrong for a woman who has control over her conceptive decisions to conceive biologically related children, wrong for a man to cause her to conceive, and wrong for the woman to continue the pregnancy if she has the opportunity to abort it. However, procreative situations may not always be as morally clear-cut as the Tay-Sachs case.

Epistemic Issues

In order to decide whether procreation is morally wrong in a particular case, it is first necessary to recognize potential epistemic uncertainties. Unlike Jane's and Agnes's hypothetical situations, one cannot always know that one carries an illness or the gene for an impairment or know the likelihood of passing it on. Given this uncertainty, it is more difficult to generalize about the responsibility not to procreate. Vehmas, however, goes even further: "The argument of parental responsibility . . . does not require an obligation to know one's genetic disorders. Parents have a prima facie right to remain in ignorance concerning their genetic make-up, especially if they are willing to assume the responsibilities and care for *any* kind of child" (2002, 59, his emphasis).

Vehmas's claim is dubious. First, it is at least questionable that our rights include an entitlement to ignorance. Our ignorance may at times be understandable or excusable; that is, ignorance can be explained, and it is sometimes, though certainly not always, morally pardonable. And genetic tests ought not to be forced on individuals; perhaps that is what Vehmas means. But for ignorance of one's genetic makeup to be a matter of moral entitlement would require that others have a duty to protect one from knowledge about one's genetic inheritance, perhaps by not presenting information when it is already available, perhaps by not arguing for the value and importance of genetic testing (when it is relevant), and perhaps by not even offering the opportunity for genetic tests. Yet it is just implausible to suppose that family members and health-care providers have an *obligation* to protect their relatives or patients from access to knowledge about their own bodies. Indeed, the reverse is more plausible: that those who possess genetic knowledge or the means of acquiring it have an obligation to make that knowledge or the means to it available to the individuals to whom it is relevant.

Moreover, even if, as Vehmas says, prospective parents stand ready to "assume the responsibilities and care for *any* kind of child," that readiness may not be morally sufficient to counterbalance the suffering that a child may experience if she or he is born with a serious illness or impairment as a result of the parents' willful ignorance. The question for prospective parents should not merely be "Am I ready to care for a child with a serious illness or impairment if I ignore information about my own genetic liabilities?" but also "What price will my child pay for my ignorance by being born with a serious illness or impairment?" Thus, contrary to what Vehmas claims, prospective parents do have, generally speaking, a moral responsibility to inform themselves, where the health-care services and medical technologies are available, about their own health and about the likelihood that they might pass on serious illnesses or impairments. Ignorance is not always a morally acceptable excuse.

There is, however, a second epistemic factor that complicates Purdy's uncompromising statement that "it is morally wrong to reproduce when we know there is a high risk of transmitting a serious disease or defect." That factor is the difficulty of predicting the kind of life a future child may have. Bonnie Steinbock and Ron McClamrock propose that prospective parents "should ask themselves, 'What kind of life is my child likely to have?'" Even if "the child's life, while miserable, is not so awful that he or she will long for death," no loving parent can or should want that for their offspring (1994, 17, 18). Even if a person prefers life over non-existence, she or he may still have been wronged by being brought into existence (Steinbock and McClamrock 1994, 19). A truly good parent, a virtuous parent, wants her or his child to flourish.

Yet in many cases the child's potential quality of life is difficult to predict. We cannot always say in advance what the likelihood of suffering is; indeed, many of the problems children experience may be entirely unanticipated and even unpreventable (as, for example, with the kinds of problems that babies who are unexpectedly premature can experience). Moreover, we cannot always quantify the amount of pain and suffering an individual will have in her life, nor can we know in advance how much happiness and fulfillment she will have and whether that happiness and fulfillment will, from her perspective, be sufficient to compensate for the pain and suffering. "Prospective parents will have to base their decision on such factors as the risk of transmission, the nature and seriousness of the disease, the availability of ameliorative therapies, the possibility of a cure, and their ability to provide the child with a good life" (Steinbock and McClamrock 1994, 21).

Impairments

The very nature of impairment is a further complicating factor in figuring out whether there is a responsibility not to procreate when there is a risk of fetal impairment. Following the World Health Organization (WHO), I define "impairment" as "a problem in body function or structure." Impairment is not the same as disability. The WHO defines "disability" as "a complex phenomenon, reflecting an interaction between features of a person's body and features of the society in which he or she lives" (2010). Based on these definitions, an impairment appears to be a condition that is "biological" in origin, whereas a disability results from the social conditions in which an individual finds herself. If there is no accommodation for the impairment—a typical example is the absence of ramps and curb cuts for persons who use wheelchairs—then the person is in effect rendered disabled: she may not be able to use sidewalks without curb cuts or to enter buildings that lack an entrance ramp.

However, the concept of impairment is in fact more complex than this simple description suggests. Impairments are not simply biological and physical in nature because not every variation in "body function or structure" is a problem, and those that are problems may be problematic not in themselves but because of attitudes toward or stigmatization or treatment of them (Tremain 2001). Hence, what constitutes an impairment is in part socially defined. Bodily variations are in part constituted as impairments (1) by the numbers who have them, so that a variation that is rare is more likely to be interpreted as an impairment, and (2) by the specific values of the culture in which they occur, which will make some characteristics a problem and others not.

Without too much difficulty, we can imagine a situation where a characteristic that belongs to a small minority and that is currently considered an impairment in our present culture is instead regarded as just another human difference. Sophia Isako Wong, for example, envisions a world in which half the people have Down syndrome and persuasively suggests that in it "there would be integrated households, educational resources, public facilities, and political structures." In this world, "the interaction between people with [Down syndrome] and those without it would . . . be seen as essential to the flourishing of the human species" (2002, 102). Down syndrome as a specific genetic condition is an impairment only within a particular social environment, the environment in which we happen to live, where people with Down syndrome are a small minority. The same might well be true of impairments such as dwarfism and conjoinment: if half of all people had these conditions, the conditions would not be considered "problems" of function or structure, any more than being male or being female is. In this alternate world, the built environment and the culture would treat little people and conjoined twins as normal—for example, by having public buildings, transportation, and open spaces that are purposely constructed for persons who are very short or who are conjoined in various ways.

Susan Wendell provides an illustration of the way in which some impairments are socially constituted through a society's particular values. Some people simply live their lives at a slower, perhaps more placid, perhaps more reflective tempo than others. But "keeping up" is a normative requirement of our fast-paced, technologically driven society, and anyone who has trouble keeping up is effectively rendered impaired, even though their life tempo would be quite ordinary and acceptable in other cultures. Wendell points out that as the pace of life increases, "everyone who cannot keep up is urged to take steps (or medications) to increase their energy, and bodies that were once considered normal are pathologized" (1996, 90).

Thus, to suppose that impairments are straightforwardly biologically given and that some infants are simply born with them (or acquire them through injury later in life) fails to take into account the ways in which what constitutes an impairment depends on the society in which it exists and the numbers who share the particular characteristic. What an impairment is can change over time.[3] The social nature of many impairments exacerbates the epistemic problems concerning knowledge of whether one's child will have an impairment and, if so, what kind of life she will have.

Moreover, an impairment is not necessarily an outright misfortune. Consider the following example. My uncle, nicknamed "Jack," who was my mother's younger brother and the only boy in a family of four children, was born with profound cognitive impairments. Whether the impairments were caused at birth, during gestation, or at conception, no one knows. After his birth in 1928, my grandmother did something almost unheard of for the time: she kept her impaired baby at home instead of following all the doctors' advice and putting him in an institution, where he would soon die. As a result, Jack lived a long life, not dying until he was in his late seventies. During this time, he never learned to speak ordinary English, although he communicated with gestures and sounds. He could never read or write, though he enjoyed making marks on paper. He was never independent of other adults, though he could feed himself and take care of his own toileting. He was sharply observant and could keep track of household items and locate them when they were lost. He disliked balloons but enjoyed comic books, magazines, television, stuffed animals, sweet desserts, and being with his parents and sisters. He was happy, and he often smiled and laughed.

Many people regard impairments as inevitable misfortunes insofar as such impairments make it difficult or impossible to engage in the kinds of activities that they would want the option of choosing or of being available for their children to choose. From that point of view, even if an impaired person has a very happy life, he is nonetheless thought to be less fortunate than people who enjoy more diverse opportunities for fulfillment.

But I want to insist that Jack's life was not a misfortune. It was not even unfortunate relative to the lives of nonimpaired people. Despite Jack's extensive impairments, I cannot think of his life as a tragedy. My reason for making this claim has to do with our ideas about "major life activities" and "opportunities." I want to say that Jack did not miss out on opportunities. It makes no sense to speak of missing an opportunity to do x when one is congenitally unable to do x. It makes no sense to speak of not being able to engage in life activities if those life activities are far beyond one's capacity, one's desire, or even one's imagination. I think Jack was a fulfilled individual. His life was not rich in the way that we might want our lives to be rich, but it was rich in terms of using his abilities and talents, such as they were.

Of course, I can imagine counterfactual situations in which Jack's life would have been a misfortune. If, for example, he had suffered great physical or psychological pain, then his life would have been a misfortune. But he did not. Or if he had been institutionalized, as the doctors advised my grandparents, for then he would not have been loved, read to, talked to, given his favorite foods, or provided with books, magazines, and television programs. My point is not that impaired people like my uncle cannot suffer and cannot be disadvantaged and disabled; of course they can if their environment is bad, their social support weak, or their health care inadequate. I am not presenting a Pollyannaish view that impairments are never a problem and never cause suffering. My point is simply that impaired people are not necessarily unfortunate if, for example, within the scope of what they can do, they are given all the opportunities that they can take up.[4]

The situation is quite different if one has the capacity to do x but misses out on doing it either because of lack of resources in one's environment or because of outright oppression or obstacles. Nonimpaired people in the developing world definitely miss out on opportunities for fulfillment—for example, through the acquisition of literacy skills—because they lack the resources, not the capacities, to engage in many life activities. We tend not to think of such persons as disabled because they are not impaired. Yet they are disabled, I would argue, in the sense that their society does not provide them with the means to do what they are capable of. That is, one can be disabled without being impaired, just as one can be impaired without being disabled.

Thus, having an impairment does not *inevitably* make one's life less fulfilling. My uncle probably had less unhappiness, much less frustration, and more fulfillment than his older sister, my mother, whose frustrations came from growing up in a social context where girls were not expected to go to university or have a career but instead were expected to become wives and mothers. My mother had no impairments, yet she was, relative to her high innate capacities, more disabled than my uncle. In that respect, she was like millions, perhaps billions, of nonimpaired people all over the world whose opportunities are foreclosed not by their own embodiment, but by the world in which they find themselves.

The import of these autobiographical observations is this: a fetus with an impairment is not inevitably doomed to become a person who suffers, who has an unfulfilling life, or who cannot flourish within society. Whether an impairment has that effect depends both on the impairment itself (some impairments may cause pain that is ongoing whatever the circumstances and cannot be fully relieved) and on the society into which the child is born. The first-person anthology *Defiant Birth: Women Who Resist Medical Eugenics* (Reist 2006) documents the individual experiences of women who were pressured to abort their pregnancies. They were made to feel guilty for gestating and birthing their infants who had Down syndrome (Schiltz 2006, 189) or dwarfism (Whitaker 2006, 214). Given what I have said about impairments and illustrated with the case of Jack, I cannot state categorically that these women ought not to have procreated, for, as it turned out, those children's impairments were not misfortunes either for the children themselves or for their families.

There is, then, a significant moral difference between (1) the imaginary cases of Jane and Agnes, who deliberately or negligently conceive a being that has impairments, and (2) refusing to abort a being that turns out after diagnosis to have impairments that were not deliberately or negligently created. The actions of Jane and Agnes, unusual and implausible as they may be, are clearly morally unjustified. They know what they are doing, they know the risks to the fetus of illness, suffering, or early death, and they go ahead and conceive anyway. For several reasons, however, I am reluctant to say that a woman carrying an impaired fetus is *always* morally required to abort or that she is *always* morally wrong not to abort. First, as my previous arguments have shown, a person who has an impairment will not necessarily suffer or experience an unfortunate life because of it. The greater the evidence that the person will suffer, the greater the responsibility to abort; the less the evidence that the person will suffer, then the lower is the responsibility to abort. Whether he does suffer or become disabled will depend in part on the nature of the impairment, but also in part on the society in which he lives and the persons who care for him; the woman is entitled—indeed, obligated—to take both of these factors into account when determining whether to continue the pregnancy. Second, when a woman knows or has strong evidence to believe that her future infant will have an impairment, is educating herself about and preparing herself for what that impairment might entail, and wants to birth the infant, then she arguably has made a moral commitment to the future infant. She is embarking upon a relationship with her future child.[5] In such a case (and assuming that the child will not suffer), the moral requirement to abort is lower. Hence, women do not always have a moral obligation to abort fetuses with impairments.[6]

Attitudes toward Persons with Impairments

People sometimes express eugenic concerns about the collective effects on the human gene pool of the procreation of individuals with illnesses or impairments. Others worry about the alleged costs "to society" in terms of greater expenses for health care, education, accommodation, and long-term care if individuals who are chronically ill or impaired continue to be born. For these reasons, some might argue that there is a responsibility not to procreate when the future child will be ill or impaired.

Both these worries are in part about empirical matters and cannot merely be assumed to be true. Will there possibly be a distinct effect on the genetic heritage of humankind if people procreate individuals with chronic illness or impairments? Will social costs be significantly increased if people with illnesses and impairments continue to be born? Where is the evidence? But it is also striking that Western society has not collectively worried about the effects on the gene pool or the potential social costs that are incurred by reducing maternal and infant mortality or combating severe disease via vaccinations, antibiotics, and improved medical care. All of these latter measures are highly desirable and progressive, yet they arguably affect the human gene pool by enabling many people to survive who would otherwise have died and thus perhaps permitting the perpetuation of genes that might have "died out." And those measures also increase social costs by requiring better and better care for more and more people who now survive instead of dying. Thus, eugenic worries and concerns about social costs appear to be highly selective, and that selectivity is morally dubious.

No one is advocating that human beings deliberately perpetuate genes that cause inevitable suffering or that prospective parents intentionally create fetuses with impairments. That is precisely why the cases of Agnes and Jane are so improbable. But unless we are prepared to abandon many of the most important medical advances of the past two centuries, we should not agonize about the supposed costs of caring for and supporting people who are born with chronic illnesses or impairments but instead help to create the resources necessary for caring for them as well as for disease prevention and cures. And rather than fretting about the supposed future of the human gene pool, we should be concerned about promoting healthy, flourishing lives for all.

Indeed, in that regard a legitimate problem arises in the debate about the moral justification of creating children with diseases or impairments. We arguably have a responsibility not to act in such a way as to disparage the lives of people with impairments or diseases or to assume that the lives of persons with impairments or diseases are not worth living. The so-called expressivist argument articulates the worry that the more common the practice becomes of preventing the births of persons with impairments (especially prevention that involves prenatal diagnosis and abortion), the more likely it will be that prejudice against and oppression of persons with impairments will increase. The idea is that material measures to reduce the birth of people with impairments will *give the message* that persons with impairments should not exist: their existence should have been prevented.

Rebecca Bennett, for example, raises the question of how it is possible to justify the apparent belief that there should be fewer people with impairments. Given that this claim is "not usually couched in terms of resource allocation (i.e. that the impaired will be more expensive to cater for)" (2008, 267), and assuming that persons with impairments find their lives worthwhile, then, she says, the claim appears to assume that impaired people simply have lower moral value than those without impairments (271) and that a world without impaired people would be better than a world with them. We wouldn't be justified in making such a claim about any other group of people; it seems morally unjustified to apply it to people with impairments.

The objection involves in part an empirical claim about the possibility that the mistreatment of persons with impairments will grow as a result of the supposed message sent by the prevention of the birth of persons with impairments. However, in the past, when contraception was rather ineffective and abortion mostly unavailable in North America, persons with impairments were often treated as shameful, hidden from society, and provided with little care and almost no education. Today, in societies where abortion for fetal impairment is widely available, there is no evidence that the situation of persons with impairments is getting worse. Indeed, there are growing efforts in the West to respond helpfully and supportively to people with impairments, improve their health care, provide appropriate and stimulating education, and create social environments and practices that are inclusive of them. This is not to say that the situation for persons with impairments is without problems or that no improvement is possible. Much more work certainly can and must be done, not just to "accommodate" but to welcome persons with impairments in all aspects of human life. Nevertheless, it appears that increasing methods and tolerance for avoiding or preventing the birth of persons with impairments is not correlated with increasing *in*tolerance for persons with impairments. The objection is not borne out by the evidence.

Norvin Richards gives a related argument about the alleged moral problems in choosing not to procreate children with chronic illness or impairments. In a paper entitled, with deliberate irony, "Lives No One Should Have to Live," he argues that when prospective parents consider whether to create a child or not, they should ponder the "authority" a potential child would have over his life if he were to exist (2010, 466):

Prospective parents go wrong . . . when they pay no attention to the fact that their child would be someone who would come to have the ability to make her own decisions about her life, and decide not to create her because her life would not be worth living, based on their sense of what that life would be like. . . . That is to act as if the experiences were all there would be to her life, as if she would not also be someone who would come to lead that life but only someone who would suffer it, and thus as if they were contemplating a creature whose life would not be hers to judge. (469)

Richards's argument manifests respect for persons with impairments, who often say, "The fact that *you* think you would not want our lives does not mean that *we* do not want our lives; nor does it mean that we are wrong to do so." There is, however, a problem with Richards's approach. His argument implies that a concern for quality of life can very seldom be a legitimate reason for not having a child, provided that the child will someday reach a state in which he will be able to evaluate the value of his life—unless there were "some other form of concern for him [that] was more important than paying him this respect [of being allowed to judge the quality of his own life]" (2010, 473).

However, the concern for what the child's life will be like is not just a consideration of that life in some implausibly atomistic way, as if the child's existence can be considered in isolation from his social environment. Instead, it is a concern for the child's life in the context of his relationships to his parent or parents and to other members of the family and the broader society of which they all are a part. Much depends on whether the woman and her partner, if any, have both the ability and the commitment to care well and appropriately for a child that may be born with the impairment. The moral justification of choosing not to create a child with illness or impairment is not in every case a simple function of the condition of the child's body only; it is also a function of the potential parent's own capacities and limitations and the social context that the parents and child must inhabit. The potential parents, especially the potential mother, are entitled to decide how much they are capable of handling and whether and to what extent they can properly care for and raise a child with congenital illness or impairment. Hence, a decision not to procreate such a child does not necessarily reflect disrespect for the prospective child's future judgment that his life is worthwhile; instead, the decision is at least in part an expression of the parents' judgment about their own material, physical, and psychological capacities.

Moreover, to say that someone should not have been born with impairments is not to malign that person, to regret his existence, or to say that his life is not worth living. Recall Velleman's distinction, described in chapter 7, between assessing a person, assessing the event of his coming into existence, and assessing the act of creating him. We can consistently say that it *may* have been a mistake for parents to have a particular child while still "rejoicing in his [the child's] existence" (2005, 364). As an analogy, think of the situation when someone is seriously injured, perhaps in a fire or an earthquake, and sustains long-term injuries. Our reaction usually has at least two facets: sorrow and empathy for the person's suffering as well as regret (sometimes even anger) that he has been subjected to a painful and harmful event. What we don't feel is a desire for the person not to exist; nor do we make that judgment. We may well wish that steps could have been taken to protect the person from the injurious event or to prevent its occurrence, but we don't—unless his suffering is severe and unremitting—think the person is without value or his life not worth living.

My conclusion is that human beings have a general moral responsibility of nonmaleficence to avoid deliberately creating offspring who they know will experience severe suffering. We ought not to harm deliberately or negligently (for example, through serious drug or alcohol use) a fetus that will be brought to term. Ignorance of the likelihood that a fetus will be impaired or have a congenital disease is not always a mitigating factor in one's responsibility of nonmaleficence. However, there are genuine epistemic barriers to knowing whether a fetus will have a particular condition and how that condition will affect the life of the person whom the fetus will become. An impairment may cause suffering and be a misfortune, but in some cases it does not and is not. Hence, women do not always have an obligation to abort fetuses with impairments, especially when they have developed a relationship with and a commitment to the fetus and the person it will come and have taken steps to prepare for the future child's life. At the same time, the choice to abort because of fetal impairment or disease is morally defensible.

Thus, there is no easy, one-size-fits-all answer to the question whether the prospect of fetal impairment or illness creates an obligation not to procreate. Sometimes it does, as I have shown, and sometimes it does not. Whether there is a responsibility not to procreate when there is a risk of illness or impairment in the offspring is not just a function of the physical condition of the fetus. It is also strongly affected by the characteristics of the parents and of the culture in which they live.

Prospective Parents with Impairments

Some people believe that individuals with impairments of their own have a moral obligation not to procreate. As Rosaleen Moriarty-Simmonds points out, "Even in this day and age there are still people, particularly in the medical profession, who actually believe that disabled people should not have children" (2006, 249). Someone might hold such a position, first, because she or he believes that the person with impairments will pass on the impairment. I already discussed the moral significance of potential fetal impairment in the previous section. Not all offspring with impairments are born to parents with impairments, and not all parents with impairments give birth to offspring with impairments. The mere fact that a potential parent has an impairment does not necessarily tell us much, if anything, about what the health of her infant will be. Moreover, the mere fact that an infant has an impairment does not always tell us much, if anything, about what the child's life will be like because not all impairments are misfortunes. The real issue has to do with the parents' wellness, in particular the potential mother's capacity to sustain a healthy pregnancy.

Second, someone might hold that impaired persons should not procreate on the grounds that they are supposedly not able to care for the child. But impairments are not inevitably incapacitating. A person with an impairment may well be quite healthy and is likely to have worked out ways of living her life that enable her to compensate for, learn from, and flourish with her impairment. Persons with impairments live independent lives, hold jobs, have warm personal relationships, and care for children. Moriarty-Simmonds herself is Thalidomide impaired, and her limbs are radically incomplete. She is successfully raising the child whom she gestated and birthed. She has to make adjustments in how she handles the child, but her son is thriving.

The question of impaired prospective parents might seem more urgent when the impairments are cognitive or psychological in nature. Surely, someone might say, we do not want people with cognitive limitations or serious psychological problems raising children. But there are always risks in generalizing across an entire group of people based simply on their possession of a particular characteristic. After all, there are people without impairments who do an execrable job of raising children. The issue is not simply whether a potential parent has an impairment. The issue, as I said in chapter 7, is potential parents' ability to nurture and care for children: we have a responsibility not to reproduce if we cannot meet a high standard of parenting capacity.

Impairments come in a range of severity. Some are so severe as to compromise or eliminate an individual's capacity to care even for herself. Persons with such impairments obviously should not have children, but they are unlikely to be able to make autonomous choices about their own procreative behavior. Other impairments, such as Wendell's example of individuals who have trouble keeping up with the accelerating pace of life, are not problems at all until the social environment makes them into problems; even then, though, a social network can help to compensate. A person with a minor cognitive impairment, for example, might not be able to function in a highly technological, fast-paced, overwhelming environment, but she might be fine in an environment where she is part of a network of social support and is not confronted with demands and tasks that are beyond her capacities.

Some individuals with impairments decide of their own accord not to have children. Their reasons are sometimes like those of childless persons without impairments: they have other interests and goals. In other cases their illness or impairment makes them disinclined to have children; given that living with their particular condition may take up much of their attention and energy, they are aware that they do not have the physical stamina or the emotional strength necessary for good child rearing. In some cases they may be aware that pregnancy will require them to stop taking a prescription medication that is crucial to their well-being (Casey 2006, 68). People with chronic illness or impairments are—like persons without impairments—usually in the best position to know what they can handle and what they are capable of.

At the same time, it is important to be aware of the extent to which "what one is capable of" can be in part a function of one's material resources and socioeconomic status. We ought not to condemn impaired persons who are not wealthy to a moral obligation to childlessness or to put the burden of refraining from procreation on those who lack the material resources to care for a child. But it is obviously easier to raise a child if one is not impoverished. If one has an impairment, it is easier to raise a child if one has the appropriate social supports.

Thus, the moral question about procreation by persons with impairments is not a matter of the impairment itself, but rather a matter of what the prospective parent(s) are capable of doing or not doing and of the social support—from other family members and friends, health-care resources, the educational system, and accessible housing, shopping, and employment—that is available. A necessary condition for justified procreation is that persons with impairments, like persons without impairments, must be more than merely adequate parents. They must have the ability to care for and raise the children they may create—and not just at a minimal level, so that the children basically stay alive, but at a level at which the children will develop and flourish. The decision whether to procreate or not is an individual choice for women and men, but it is inevitably made within a social framework. Whether there is a moral obligation not to procreate is contextual: it is not a straightforward derivative of one's physical, psychological, or cognitive condition, but rather a complex function of one's place in a particular society at a particular time.

9

Overpopulation and Extinction

The discussion in previous chapters has demonstrated and defended several ethical principles for procreative choices. First, it is essential to recognize and respect the reproductive rights described in chapter 2. Human beings have a right *not* to reproduce; hence, there is no general obligation to procreate. Human beings also have a right to reproduce in the negative or liberty sense—that is, a right not to be interfered with in their procreative behavior and a limited right to reproduce in the positive or welfare sense. Second, as the discussion in chapter 3 demonstrated, we must keep in mind the gendered nature of reproduction: procreation requires much more of women than of men, and this will remain the case *even if* a safe and successful form of ectogenesis is developed. One must consider the material contexts in which people make decisions about procreation and the social environments in which they will raise their children, not just hypothetical thought experiments with no connection to the challenges real people face. Third, as I showed in chapters 4 and 5, most of the traditional reasons that have been given for having children are weak and easily defeated. Nonetheless, justified decision making about procreation must be based at least on a consideration of the consequences of our procreative decisions and in particular of their effects on existing children and on women. There is no obligation to produce as many children as possible, even if doing so will maximize the amount of good in a particular society. Fourth, it is always wrong to use any person primarily as a means to an end, and infants, children, and women are particularly vulnerable to being so used in procreative decisions.

Fifth, as chapter 6 showed, children are neither benefited nor harmed by coming into existence. Mere existence is not in itself a beneficial or harmful property. Instead, we must always "look and see" whether persons are benefited or harmed throughout their existence in order to know whether it is good or not that they came into existence. Even if a possible person is likely to have a good life, there is no obligation to any such hypothetical nonexistent person to bring him or her into existence.

We can distinguish between future people and possible people, the set of all future people being a subset of the set of all possible people. Future people are the set of all people who *will* definitely exist at some point after the present as a result of our actions and choices. Possible people are those who might or might not exist, depending on which choices we make. We are not in a position to know which ones, among all the possible people, will actually be future people, although we can presumably make predictions about at least some of them, those who will be our very near descendants—our grandchildren, perhaps. But possible people do not have a *right* to come into existence, and no one is wronged if he or she is not created. As James Lenman remarks, "No matter what happens, we can always suppose there to be an infinity of possible individuals who never get to exist. But it is hard to make much sense of the thought that this is a bad thing—either for the individuals themselves or otherwise" (2004b, 139).

Sixth, as chapters 7 and 8 showed, many of the reasons typically proffered to support an obligation *not* to procreate are not very strong. There is, for example, no obligation not to reproduce because of failure to follow Julian Savulescu's Principle of Procreative Beneficence (PPB). Yet it is easier to justify a decision not to procreate than to justify a decision to procreate because in the latter case the child's potential well-being will be affected. There is a strong moral responsibility to undertake procreation only if one is very likely to be the kind of parent who will enable a child to flourish. But sexuality, relationship status, age, and impairment have no necessary relationship to parental ability. Whether there is a responsibility not to procreate is strongly dependent on the prospective parent's or parents' environment and social context.

Philosopher Michael Bayles assumes that people always make decisions about whether to have a(nother) child "in isolation" from consideration of the decisions made by other families (1979, 19). In a way, he is right; an individual or couple planning a family does not ask what the individual or couple next door will do. But choosing whether to have children nonetheless is and must be a deeply social decision; it is related to laws, cultural customs, national policy, employment patterns, and the environment, both human and nonhuman. How one makes a procreative decision can be significantly affected by the material conditions in which one is making the choice, and those material conditions include the social policies of the state in which one lives. The connection between individual procreative decisions and social context is most clearly apparent with respect to a society's health-care system and the medical and social services and resources that are or are not provided—services and resources for contraception, abortion, sterilizations, prenatal care, birthing, and infant and mother care, as well as reproductive technologies and treatments for infertility. You can't choose to use contraception or to have a hospital birth if neither is available.

In previous chapters, I examined a variety of different conditions—of the parents, the siblings, the home environment, and the immediate social network—that arguably ought to be taken into account in procreative decisions. In this chapter, I investigate the broadest possible context of procreative decision making: the significance of planetwide changes in population size. Procreation is in this respect a global issue. There are two possibilities, both extremes, that we need to consider: acute overpopulation on the one hand and the threat of the extinction of the human species on the other. What might our procreative responsibilities be in situations of overpopulation or impending human extinction?

It might seem that concerns about overpopulation or extinction are much too big for individuals or couples to take into account in making their procreative decisions; hence, prospective parents cannot be morally required to consider them. But what I am trying to do in this book is to reveal the wide-ranging nature of the moral decision whether to have a child or not. The decision is not a matter of mere individual preference, for all procreative decisions affect other people, and many individual choices collectively have sweeping social implications. It is no longer possible for human beings, especially in the West, to pretend we all are not related: international travel, environmental changes, and global resource extraction, manufacturing, and trade demonstrate that national boundaries count for much less than they once did. We cannot legitimately believe that our decisions have no consequences or even that our decisions have only modest consequences. Most people do care about the well-being of their nation or at least of their town or their neighborhood. Supplied with information about the effects of unlimited population growth (or, however unlikely it may seem at this point, the effects of significant population decline) and with arguments about the importance of making justified decisions about procreation, people may be less likely to make such decisions "in isolation" and more likely to consider the social context in which they procreate. And so, I argue, they should.

Extreme Overpopulation

In the past in the West, large numbers of children in a single family were not uncommon, occasionally even as many as 25 (Worth 2002, 127–143, 281–290). These children were presumably not the result of choice but rather of necessity and inevitability in an environment where reliable contraception was unknown, agriculture required many workers, and moral and religious beliefs supported being fruitful and multiplying.

Today, reality shows depict procreative carelessness in shows such as *I Didn't Know I Was Pregnant* and give reason to worry about the possibility that the citizens of some developed nations, including especially the most powerful one, are indifferent to population overgrowth. Consider the media attention given to large families. It includes both families that are large because of the birth of multiple children at once (such as the Gosselin family in *Jon and Kate Plus Eight* and its successor *Kate Plus Eight*, which are about a family with twins and sextuplets, and the Hayes family in *Table for Twelve*, about a family with two sets of twins and a set of sextuplets) and families that are large because of the birth of many children serially (the most notorious of which is *Nineteen Kids and Counting*, about the Duggar family, the parents of which have set no limits on the number of children they will "welcome"). We can refer in the former case to the production of large families synchronically and in the latter case to the production of large families diachronically. Today, many people would say that it is morally acceptable to have such large numbers of children provided the family can sustain them all and do a reasonably good job of rearing them. I argue that this view is profoundly mistaken.

Worries about global overpopulation and the extreme stress on the planet's carrying capacity are familiar news. Jennifer Wise writes, "On a global level we produce millions more babies each year than we can possibly care for. According to UNESCO, we allow over 10 million children to die of poverty, war, malaria, and other preventable diseases—every year" (2006, 128). Indeed, there are more and more human beings on this planet, but the fertility rate varies from nation to nation, and some areas are growing much faster than others.

According to the *2008 Revision* of the official United Nations population estimates and projections, the world population is projected to . . . surpass 9 billion people by 2050. . . . Most of the additional 2.3 billion people will enlarge the population of developing countries, which is projected to rise from 5.6 billion in 2009 to 7.9 billion in 2050, and will be distributed among the population aged 15–59 (1.2 billion) and 60 or over (1.1 billion) because the number of children under age 15 in developing countries will decrease.

In contrast, the population of the more developed regions is expected to change minimally, passing from 1.23 billion to 1.28 billion, and would have declined to 1.15 billion were it not for the projected net migration from developing to developed countries, which is projected to average 2.4 million persons annually from 2009 to 2050. (United Nations 2008, 9)

One reason for the difference in fertility rate between developing and developed nations is simply that women in developed nations tend to have more education, and the more education a woman has, the less likely she is to have children. "Why this is happening is the subject of much theorizing: educated women delay childbearing until it's no longer an option; they refuse to pay what economists call the 'motherhood premium' in which the salaries of university-educated women plateau after childbirth and then drop, while fathers' incomes are unaffected; they recognize that raising children is a sacrifice of time, money and freedom they're not willing to make; or they simply don't want to have children and are able to say no" (Kingston 2009, 39–40). Some researchers point to later marriage, access to better contraception, and reduced poverty as causes of Western women's lower fertility rates (Vallely 2008). Moreover, delaying childbearing stretches out the generations and results in the birth of fewer people (Dawkins 1989,[1] 110–111).

It is not controversial that humanity's long-term goal must be, at the very least, to achieve a population size compatible with our continued existence on this planet. But that compatibility must surely be such that human beings do not merely survive but also thrive—and not just some of us, but all of us. Given the facts about population size, I leave open what precisely the immediate population goal should be—whether it is to bring the population down to a particular size, to reduce the rate of population growth, or to even out variations in population growth either geographically or temporally (see O'Neill 1979, 32–33). But what do the facts about population growth indicate about the ethics of childbearing, especially within the developed world, the focus of this book? There is an interesting division of opinion. On the one hand, some express concern about the relatively low rates of birth in Western nations. For example, consider the views of Margaret Wente, a Canadian journalist. Writing about Patricia Rashbrook, the Briton who gave birth at 63 to a baby created with a donor egg, Wente writes hyperbolically: "We should kiss this mother's feet for making her own contribution to the future of Western civilization—this is her fourth child—because the demographic curve of Western civ is not promising, to say the least" (Wente and Eddie 2006, F7). The Infertility Awareness Association of Canada similarly supports a demand for public funding of IVF by stating, "Canada needs more babies" (quoted in Hanck 2009, C2).

On this view, overpopulation is not a problem for the developed countries; the problem lies in the developing countries. But comments such as Wente's are at least incipiently xenophobic because they are posited on fears about the possibility that North Americans and Europeans are being outnumbered by those who are not part of "Western civ" (Rashbrook, a white woman, gave birth to a white child). But if the future of Western civilization seems threatened by its "demographic curve," Western countries can always increase their rates of immigration. Civilization can just as well be preserved by nonwhites as by whites and by immigrants as by the native born.

In contrast to Wente, Corinne Maier writes, "It's not that there are too many people on the planet—there are just too many *rich* people. We are the planet's freeloaders, and we keep increasing our consumption. . . . If you live in Europe or America, then having kids is immoral" (2007, 121, her emphasis). Two physicians, John Guillebaud and Pip Hayes, agree:

Should we now explain to UK couples who plan a family that stopping at two children, or at least having one less child than first intended, is the simplest and biggest contribution anyone can make to leaving a habitable planet for our grandchildren? We must not put pressure on people, but by providing information on the population and the environment, and appropriate contraception for everyone (and by their own example), doctors should help to bring family size into the arena of environmental ethics, analogous to avoiding patio heaters and high carbon cars. (2008, a576)

They are correct: in general, children in developing countries generate less net cost to the environment than children in developed countries. Guillebaud and Hayes recognize that planetary capacity is not merely a matter of how many human beings there are, but how those human beings live their lives. From that point of view, overpopulation is not (just) a problem for the developing countries; the currently bigger problem lies in the developed nations.

Guillebaud and Hayes appear to be exhorting physicians to take some responsibility for fixing that problem, but it's evident that they also think their patients—indeed, anyone who is fertile—have a responsibility to limit their procreative behavior. Children are persons, not consumer goods. But *having* children and being able to afford them are a luxury—both for the parent and also for the planet. Because of the dangers of planetary overload, the responsibility to limit the number of one's offspring falls on people living in the developed world.[2] It may also fall upon people in the developing world; I don't want to rule that out. However, at the very least it's a responsibility of people in the West, for several reasons. First, most of us living in the global West are on average well educated. As a result, we know (or should know) about the dangers of overpopulation. We collectively are also sufficiently informed to know how to curb our numbers. Second, we in the West consume far out of proportion to our numbers. Most of us, based on nothing but the accident of where we were born, have the privilege of living in what is probably the most comfortable and luxurious society that has ever existed in human history. Those luxuries are not free; at the very least, we need to help pay for them by curbing our fertility. Third, we in the West have the ability—the research, resources, and technologies—to limit the number of children we have. Fourth, we in the West do not have the same economic needs for many children that people elsewhere have (or think they have). Finally, if prosperous westerners make a concerted attempt to limit their numbers, then arguments to citizens of developing nations that they should consider using effective contraception likewise to limit the numbers of their children will be far more credible. Hence, whatever citizens of the developing world may decide to do (or may have decided for them by their leaders), we in the developed world have a moral responsibility to limit our numbers, given the current threats to planetary carrying capacity posed by overpopulation.

Individuals in the West might wonder why this burden should fall on them—that is, why a global problem should become theirs to solve. Surely, they might say, problems of overpopulation must be resolved at the level of cultures, societies, and states. I agree, but this issue is not a matter of either/or. Entire societies must take responsibility for curbing population growth; decisions must be made and policies enacted on a national level. Nonetheless, population will not stabilize, let alone decline, without active decisions being made by individuals. Societies do not have fewer babies; individuals do.

A Proposal for Procreative Limitation

By how much should individuals and couples limit their procreation? American philosopher Thomas Young says that the motives behind both reproduction and overconsumption are "often identical: cultural expectations, improved status, elevated self-esteem, increased happiness, or an altruistic desire to share with others" (2001, 185). Hence, Young argues, if we regard having children as morally permissible, let alone desirable, then we must say the same thing about "ecogluttony"—that is, increasing one's own consumption to a level equal to adding to the American population another human being who will live to eighty (2001, 185–186). Doing so is clearly wrong. He concludes that because "having even just one child in an affluent household usually produces environmental impacts comparable to an intuitively unacceptable level of consumption, resource depletion, and waste," human procreation is morally wrong in most cases (2001, 183).[3] His arguments are aimed at Americans in particular rather than at persons in the developing world, whose consumption is a tiny fraction of that of U.S. citizens. Even if one American has just two children, those children will use huge amounts of resources during their lives, and they will then probably go on to have children of their own, compounding the problem. "Two more children . . . in a world with over six billion people is insignificant; yet most agree that the cumulative effect of a number of people acting that way is, and will continue to be, disastrous for species diversity, ecosystem preservation, and future generations," says Young. The implication is that having any children at all is likely to be morally wrong: "Since having even just one child in an affluent household usually produces environmental impacts comparable to what mainstream environmentalists consider to be an intuitively unacceptable level of consumption, resource depletion, and waste, they should also oppose human reproduction (in most cases)" (2001, 185, 182).

I have argued throughout this book that citizens of developed nations have a responsibility to see procreation as a moral issue and to evaluate their reasons for reproducing. I agree with Young that environmental degradation and overpopulation behoove all of us to limit the numbers of offspring we create.[4] However, I disagree with Young's idea that westerners (at least those who care about our outsize environmental impact) should give up procreation altogether.

Given the centrality of childbearing and child rearing to human existence, an obligation not to have any children at all would be a huge sacrifice, one that is too much to expect of anyone who wants to have children. Moreover, people are not likely to adhere to such an obligation, not only because it would be so difficult in the first place (given how much some people value procreation), but because it would most likely be violated in some instances, thereby lowering their own motivation and drastically increasing resentment. It would also be hard to undertake such an obligation knowing that once the population was sufficiently reduced, people in the future would no longer have to adhere to it. In addition, unlikely as it is, if large numbers of people did not have children at all, then a sizable gap in the population would develop that might create serious problems within a few decades as a result of lack of workers (unless adoption from the developing world were undertaken on a massive scale). For all these reasons, I suggest both that people cannot be expected to accept an obligation to have no children and that there is no such obligation.

Perhaps, however, in the spirit of Young's proposal we should consider a moral obligation to have only one child per couple (the legally mandated requirement for most couples in China). Although such an obligation would not face the insuperable difficulties of an obligation to have none, it would still create major problems, some of which would be similar to the problems of an obligation to have none. Once again, limiting procreation to such a degree might be a major hardship for many. People are not likely to adhere to such an obligation; some would likely violate it, thereby reducing potentially compliant individuals' motivation. It would also be hard to undertake such an obligation knowing that, if it is successful, then in the future people would not have to make such sacrifices.

In addition, I suggest that a further problem with the one-child-per-couple obligation is that it implicitly negates one person in the couple. If a couple has two children, however, there is a child for each one—not in the sense that each raises only one child, but in the sense that each individual has replaced himself or herself. By contrast, a moral rule of only one child per couple says, in effect, "You ought not to replace yourself." (Perhaps it would also carry the message "You do not deserve to be replaced.") Such an obligation would also incur hardships for single people seeking to procreate, who would violate the obligation unless they were in some way paired with another person who does not have a child.

There are also important questions about the likely results of raising a nation of children who have no sibling relationships at all. Not all sibling relationships are positive, but there is plenty to be learned from such relationships. In China, the one-child policy is in effect a long-term social experiment on a grand scale. Although it is good not to have families so large that the children are overlooked or taken for granted, it is also good not to have so few offspring around at any given time that most of the next generation lacks familial peers and cannot learn from experience and observation how to relate to and care for babies and other children in the family.

Even more worrying, in nations where there are strong preferences for children of one sex/gender (usually boys) rather than the other, the one-child policy leads to high rates of abortion for sex selection and tragically high frequencies of neglect, abandonment, and infanticide of females. In China, since the introduction of the one-child policy in 1979, substantial numbers of girls and women are simply "missing" (Ebenstein 2010), and the proportion of males to females is very high. We cannot assume that Western nations are so free of sexism as not to be motivated by preferences for children of one sex over children of the other; the preference for the sex of offspring might be exacerbated by an obligation to have only one child per couple. And unless the nation's social safety net is highly developed, a one-child-per-couple arrangement puts elderly people into a potentially precarious position because almost every adult will eventually have to care for two aging parents. Even when eldercare is socialized, there may not be enough young workers to support very elderly citizens (MacKinnon 2009, A12). For all of these reasons, then, an obligation to have only one child is at most supererogatory and unlikely to be sustainable.

It instead makes more sense to say that every individual adult has a moral responsibility to limit himself or herself to procreative replacement only. The idea of the two-child family is not, of course, a new one; it was advocated at many times during the twentieth century. What may be somewhat novel, however, is to think of procreation limits in terms of one child per adult person, whether the person is single, in a heterosexual relationship, or in a same-sex relationship.[5] I am of course not saying that people *must* replace themselves; if they choose not to have a child at all, they have done nothing morally wrong and in fact are contributing to population reduction. Nor, given what I said in chapter 2 on reproductive rights, am I suggesting that anyone is somehow owed a child or that anyone has a moral right to a baby. Nor am I advocating the violation of people's liberty right to reproduce: I am not arguing for social constraints on or interference in people's procreative behavior or for sanctions against those who produce a large number of children. I am simply saying that we should consider it morally justifiable for every individual, whether in a relationship or not, to have one biologically related child; it would then be permissible for a couple to have two. (However, they could presumably increase the size of their family by adoption, fostering, or the formation of blended or communal families—that is, any approach that involves the inclusion in the familial group of children who already exist.)

This responsibility to have no more than one child each is easily justified. All persons get to (try to) have a child of "their own," if they want one, and the value of every adult is implicitly endorsed through the fact that each one is allowed to reproduce herself or himself. Such a responsibility implies that every person is sufficiently valuable as to be worth replacing (even though a one-child-per-person morality will eventually result in population decline, given that some people will have no children and some couples will choose to have only one). Because one child each is already close to the reproductive norm in many developed countries, it is more likely to be accepted and acted upon. In addition, for those couples for whom the sex/gender of the offspring matters (whether such a preference is rational or fair or not), there would be two opportunities to have the kind of child they want.[6] Finally, "one child per person" is not the same as "two children per couple." "One child per person" is preferable because it is not based on a sexist and heterosexist notion that women must necessarily be in a couple and that every couple must consist of a male and a female. "One child per person" recognizes the possibility that a single woman might procreate, as might two women in a committed relationship.

Criticisms of the One-Child-Per-Person Responsibility

Proposing a moral responsibility to have no more than one child each is likely to provoke many objections. Bear in mind that I am *not* suggesting that this reproductive limit be *legally* required or enforceable or that its violation be legally punishable. I am also doubtful that social policies should be put in place to enforce it—for example, by providing baby bonuses only for the first two children or by offering no more maternity leaves after the second child. Such policies would simply make children— in particular, those born third and later—and their mothers suffer. Such a consequence is insupportable. So my proposal is not to embed the "one adult/one offspring" suggestion in state laws or policies but simply to argue that it is a matter of individual moral responsibility. I'm saying that having children ought to be undertaken within a commitment to self-limitation and to the moral justification of one's choices. Individuals should be thinking about why they want children and about their reasons for the number that they want to have.

A citizen of the West might protest that of course she can have three or four children because so many others in her society have only one or even none. But such an argument may not be sustainable. Unless extensive state regulation of procreation is introduced—regulation that would infringe on people's reproductive rights and violate their privacy—there is no way of ensuring against the possibility that others might reason likewise. That is, if one couple may have four children because another has none, or a second couple may have three children because another has only one, we would then have a series of procreative choices that are perilously dependent on very specific decisions by other couples. And although I do believe that we need to take others into consideration when we make procreative decisions, we cannot count on others' reduced fertility as a way of exempting ourselves from a responsibility to limit our own. If everyone reasoned similarly, then no one would adopt the one-child-each responsibility; in effect, all persons would be handing procreative limits on to others while exempting themselves.

I can imagine that once the global population stabilizes at a level that is compatible with the planet's carrying capacity and flourishing by all, individuals might be able to justify somewhat larger families, both because the dangers of overpopulation would no longer be so imminent or overwhelming and because by then human society would have evinced a long-term pattern of reduced fertility on which individuals might plausibly depend for planning a larger number of children. We are nowhere near that point yet, and although fertility levels are declining in most of the developed world, they are declining at varying rates. I would argue that they have not been low for long enough to justify one's having more children simply on the supposed grounds that others can be counted on to have fewer.

In response to arguments like mine, Clifford Orwin, a Canadian political scientist, is skeptical. He writes of a study that calculates that the environmental impact of each new child "is almost 20 times greater than whatever energy the parent could save by all other righteous choices combined." In response, he says, "I'm sorry, learned researchers, but my calculus is different from yours. Looking at my own two children, now young adults, I find myself completely unrepentant. . . . I wish I could have had more." He adds to those who are trying to decide whether to have children, "Go ahead, have kids, the more the merrier. God has commanded it, and nature's cool with it" (2009, A11). Obviously no one expects Orwin to regret the births of his two children or even to reevaluate the choice to have them, but his failure to acknowledge any environmental responsibility is reprehensible.

Though Scott Wisor takes the problems more seriously, he nonetheless argues that people in the West have no particular obligation to reduce the size of their family for the sake of environmental concerns. He agrees that "affluent individuals" have obligations to prevent environmental destruction and even, where possible, to reverse past environmental harms. But he thinks that limiting family size in order to prevent environmental harm is a form of "consumer-driven activism" that will not be successful in changing the world by changing individual behavior. The reasons, according to Wisor, are that consumers lack adequate knowledge about their environmental impact; they therefore make irresponsible choices. Some simply choose not to make environmentally responsible decisions because they don't care. In addition, consumer activism inappropriately "relieves pressure" on states and institutions to lead the end to environmental degradation (2009, 26, 27, 28). Environmental activism requires changing institutions, not changing individual actions.

I agree with most of Wisor's claims, but they are not sufficient to obviate an obligation to confine procreation to one child per person.[7] Even if dealing with environmental destruction is a state responsibility, it is also an individual responsibility: a person who lives in a nation that is taking active steps to conserve resources does not thereby have the right to be profligate with those resources. If some individuals are ignorant about what steps to take to reduce their environmental impact, then the state has a responsibility to educate them, and they may have a responsibility to educate themselves.

Wisor also claims that "in some cases increased population sizes have actually led to increases in environmental stewardship and preservation of natural resources" (2009, 28). Even if there were some truth to this factual claim, it would be a risky foundation for allowing populations to increase and for not recognizing a responsibility to limit one's procreative behavior. He acknowledges that one U.S. citizen consumes as much energy as 900 Nepalis: all the more reason, then, for North Americans to acknowledge a responsibility to limit the number of new citizens they create.

Wisor thinks that even though it is practically and morally justified to consider whether one can care and provide for additional children, one should not make procreative decisions based on the children's potential impact "on their community and world" (2009, 29). He's right insofar as it would be problematic to *have* a child for the sake of the child's effects on society and the environment. In chapter 5, I argued against making purely consequentialist assessments of children's value. But those who are deeply concerned about the effects of population growth, especially in the wasteful West, are arguing instead that people should choose *not* to have many children in order to avoid those children's potential effects on society and the environment. There is a difference. The former would be a case of creating and using children for ends that are neither chosen by the children nor necessarily tied to the children's own interests and goals;

it would be wrong. The latter is a case of choosing to limit one's behavior and have fewer offspring in order not only to protect environmental resources in general but also to try to produce a world that will be far better for the offspring one does have. Whereas Wisor thinks it is morally appropriate for reproduction to be motivated by "the desire to have a *large*, fun, supportive family" (2009, 29, his emphasis), I am arguing that there is something morally problematic, perhaps morally wrong, about having a large family in the wasteful, consumerist West. Although there may be ways by which one can reduce a family's environmental footprint, every additional child nonetheless produces a substantial additional cost to planetary resources—a cost that is likely to persist for eighty or more years.

Some people would reject any moral limit on numbers of offspring on the basis of the deontological arguments discussed in chapter 4. These arguments include passing on one's name or property, having a genetic link to children, keeping a promise, and fulfilling duties to other family members. As I argued there, those reasons for having children are for the most part weak and uncompelling. But even if they seem compelling to some people and hence appear to provide urgent reasons for procreation, the opportunity to have one child or two with a partner can and should satisfy people's desires to "do their duty" in the way that deontologists understand it.

The one deontological reason that might not be satisfied by the responsibility to have no more than one child per person arises from the teachings of some fundamentalist religions that expect women to treat the production of lots of babies as a woman's purpose. Some fundamentalists, such as Michelle and Jim Bob Duggar, would say that they cannot be expected to curb their numbers because they are morally committed to following the word of God. Indeed, the Duggars state repeatedly that they want as many children as God sends them, and on their Web site they proclaim, "We believe that each child is a special gift from God and we are thankful to Him for each one" (Duggar and Duggar 2011).

Enthusiastic viewers also point out that the Duggar children are seemingly happy and healthy.[8] The family is prosperous, at least in part because of substantial revenues from their reality television appearances. This very large family seems not to be a result of the victimization of the wife;[9] it is evident that Michelle Duggar knows what she is doing, and her husband, Jim Bob Duggar, says he leaves it up to her whether to have more children. Moreover, we can't say that children are *entitled* to be part of a small family, and there may be some advantages to being a member of a large one (provided there are sufficient resources for them to live well), such as a ready source of playmates and plenty of personal support. What, then, is the moral problem with a large family such as the Duggars?

To say that the children are well cared for is an inadequate defense of the adult Duggars' procreative behavior. If each Duggar child in turn has 19 children, then there will be 361 grandchildren. If each of those children has 19 children, there will be 6,859 great-grandchildren. The next generation would number 130,321. Just as worrying, the Duggars may well serve as role models and inspiration to at least some other prospective parents. As research psychologist Michael Ashton says (ironically), "In a few years we will all be Duggars" (personal communication, July 2010). With the example set by the Duggars, there would be no hope of population stabilization, let alone reduction. Despite their claims to "buy used and save the difference," the family presumably consumes resources at a rate more than five times that of the average family in North America. And, frankly, it is highly doubtful that the genes of Michelle and Jim Bob Duggar (or the genes of any human being at all) are so valuable as to need or deserve to be so often reproduced.

The justification for having many children that is derived from God's alleged command does not exempt individuals from reevaluating their procreative behavior in light of the dangers of overpopulation. The argument I am making is not about compelling people to toe certain reproductive lines, nor is it about forcing morality on anyone. I simply suggest that even religious believers who think God mandates repeated procreation have a responsibility to consider whether in light of the social, environmental, and even personal costs of overpopulation it really is morally acceptable to have more than two children. I have no illusions that religious fundamentalists are likely to give up their beliefs. But if some human beings claim to know in some detail what is God's will, then they can also reconsider whether there are good grounds for believing that their God wants them to procreate (and consume) to a degree that degrades the planet and destroys the environment that makes human life possible. The simple moral question—and one that religious believers can and should ask themselves—is this: Assuming that God's command to procreate is directed at everyone, is it possible for every (heterosexual) couple to follow God's supposed mandate and have 5, 10, 15, or 20 children (Bob Cadman, personal communication, December 2009)? The obvious answer is no; the outcome is not sustainable. It is wrong to consider oneself a moral exception, and scripture provides no basis for supposing that some parents are more entitled than others to procreate. Large families are parasitical on small ones in the sense that some families' lower fertility rate gives parents of large families the illusion that their procreative choices are not environmentally costly.

There is, however, one further counterargument to my one-child-per-adult proposal that is different from any of those discussed so far. This counterargument is intended to show that adopting a moral responsibility to limit procreation to one child per adult would in fact be ineffective and even counterproductive to the aim of containing population growth. Ashton asks us to imagine a scenario in which some people accept a responsibility to limit their procreation:

The more socially responsible people end up having fewer children, on average, than do the people who don't have much sense of social responsibility. Therefore, to the extent that "social responsibility" is transmitted from parents to children, then the next generation will be somewhat lower in social responsibility than the current generation. (Note that it doesn't matter if social responsibility is mainly transmitted genetically or through social learning [culture].)

The next generation will therefore have a smaller proportion of people who will voluntarily have fewer children (or who will do anything else) out of a sense of social responsibility. This cycle then repeats, so that there are fewer socially responsible people with each generation. (Note that the total population might not decline at all, if the less socially responsible people have many children.) This in turn means a lower likelihood of avoiding the kinds of "commons dilemmas" that were supposed to be solved by telling people to have fewer children.

. . . [T]his process might be slow: It depends on *(a)* the extent to which the more socially responsible people have fewer children and *(b)* the extent to which social responsibility is transmitted from parents to children. If either *(a)* or *(b)* is not strong, then the problem will be relatively small. Now, based on what we know about the transmission of traits and attitudes, *(b)* is probably pretty substantial, though far from a perfect link. I think *(a)* is likely to be smaller, so there might not be a problem in the next few generations. But the more "successful" one is in encouraging socially responsible people to have only one child or no children at all, the less socially responsible the next generation will be, and the less successful one will be in getting that next generation to have fewer children. So the policy defeats itself. (email message to the author, August 17, 2009)[10]

Perhaps the social supports widely found in developed countries make Ashton's predicted outcome more likely. Richard Dawkins writes that "in nature" at least or in times when there is no state support for children or families, "individuals who have too many children are penalized, not because the whole population goes extinct, but simply because fewer of their children survive. Genes for having too many children are just not passed on to the next generation in large numbers, because few of the children bearing these genes reach adulthood" (1989, 117). But with the advent of good medical care, free public education, and at least minimal welfare payments and unemployment insurance, the offspring of individuals who have many children are quite likely to survive, along with the tendency to have more children.

Ashton's argument depends on a number of empirical predictions. To assess the argument's strength adequately, it would be necessary to test its predictions by widely (and successfully) promulgating the idea that there is a moral responsibility to limit the number of one's children and then seeing whether the adoption of the moral responsibility is, as predicted, self-defeating. This informal experiment is worth trying both because we need to know whether an attempt at individual ethical regulation of population growth is effective and because by publicizing the concept of a moral duty to limit procreation, we would be taking the action that seems morally justified by the problems facing our planet. The evidence that people *can* change in this way is that they *have*—the number of babies born has declined precipitously in the West over the past century, although probably not primarily out of apprehension of global overpopulation. Concern for the planet is both a simple and a significant reason for people to evaluate carefully their procreative goals, but if Ashton's prediction turns out to be correct, then appeals to immediate personal benefit rather than to planetary preservation might be the most effective way of persuading people to change their reproductive behavior.

Wisor less plausibly uses an argument similar to Ashton's to assert that "individuals concerned about the environment" ought to have even *more* children rather than fewer on the grounds that their influence can then counterbalance the effects of people who don't care about the environment (2009, 29). It just seems counterproductive and rhetorically implausible, if not crazy, to promote having more children in an effort to reduce the impact of population growth on the environment. One cannot count on one's children sharing one's own views, especially when they are seemingly contradicted by one's own behavior. It seems just as likely that a child born into a large family will reject her parents' environmentalism—or at the very least regard it as a manifestation of bad faith. (Of course, that being so, we might also anticipate that the offspring of persons indifferent to planetary depredation might turn out to be environmentalists.)

If having more children is counterproductive, then at least at the level of individual ethics there is no alternative for those concerned about the future of the planet than to limit their own procreation. If we have a responsibility to limit our consumption and our environmental footprint, then surely we also have a responsibility to limit the birth of new human beings who will otherwise contribute both to that consumption and to the despoliation of our planetary home.[11]

The Extinction of the Human Species

Having discussed our moral responsibilities in the face of drastic population growth, I now want to consider the other extreme: the possible extinction of the human species. Some people predict that the world population, despite its frightening growth, will eventually reach a maximum and then decline (Vallely 2008). According to Statistics Canada, 17.1 percent of Canadian women and 18.3 percent of Canadian men age 30 to 34 said in 2006 that they did not plan to have any children at all. According to the U.S. National Center of Health Statistics, "The number of American women of childbearing age who define themselves as 'child-free' rose sharply in the past generation: 6.2 per cent of women in 2002 between the ages of 15 and 44 reported that they don't expect to have children in their lifetime, up from 4.9 per cent in 1982" (statistics cited in Kingston 2009, 38). The fear is much bruited that declining populations mean an insufficiency of workers to maintain a nation's gross domestic product or even to support a dependent aging population.

Elisabeth Nickson writes, "Japan's drop [in birthrate] is catastrophic: at 1.25 births per woman, Japan is at the rate at which demographers believe a cataclysmic downward spiral is inevitable. Korea? Even worse at 1.08 births per woman. Russia? Dying.[12] And don't even mention Europe. Demographers project that the European Union will lose between 24 million and 40 million people during each coming decade unless fertility is markedly raised. . . . Nor will immigration help. It takes less than a generation for an immigrant family in Canada to accept local norms and stop reproducing" (2006, A21).

If these tendencies were to continue far into the future and spread to even more nations, we as a species might face the prospect of extinction. What, if anything, would such a prospect imply about our procreative responsibilities?

The Value of the Human Species

In the face of threatened extinction, it might seem that fertile human beings would have a moral obligation to reproduce. According to Torbjörn Tännsjö, for example, we do have such responsibilities:

> Even if Adam and Eve were leading fantastic lives in the Garden of Eden, the world was not perfect. Not only could the world have been made better through mere addition of people, if God had bothered to create more of our kind. Even at some cost, Adam and Eve themselves should replenish the earth.
>
> The very idea of a universe without sentient life strikes us as terrible. A world with human life, and other kinds of sentient life on Earth only, is better than a universe with no life at all. (2004, 231)

The question is whether human beings truly are such assets to the universe (or even to the solar system or just the planet) as to make it imperative to stave off human extinction.

Some people see having children as in effect our species' vote of confidence in itself. They see procreation as an expression of hope and of our belief in our collective value. For example, Vangie Bergum writes, "In the act of conceiving a child . . . we show confidence in the world as a good place to be. . . . We see the world as a world for children and are prepared to conceive a child. Or it may be the converse: In deciding on children we come to accept the world as a place for children and begin to take responsibility for it in a different way" (1997, 32). Rex Sayers similarly writes, "Having children is an act of great hope, an affirmation that no matter how chaotic and tragic the world seems to be, it is still worth living in. That no matter how much we adults screw things up, what we leave behind will be a little better than what we started with. That we trust our children to do even better than we've done" (2007, C3).

A skeptic would find it easy to be critical of these ideas. It is hard to have confidence in the procreative plans of someone who counts himself among people who "screw things up." Taken literally as claims about reality, Bergum's and Sayers's statements are founded on faith rather than on anything more solid. It is not clear that they have *good reasons* to have hope or that the planet is in fact a good place to be. In fact, they beg the question at issue by taking it for granted that there are positive answers to the question of whether human existence matters and the human species deserves to be perpetuated.

One possible explanation of why our existence matters and is worth perpetuating points to the human capacity for happiness. Thus, John Leslie writes that if you did *not* see a world of very happy people, with only a small number of unhappy persons, as "remarkably good," "then you'd have fairly strong grounds for thinking it right to annihilate the human race in some quick and painless fashion." "Just as a planet of utterly miserable people could be worse than nothing, so also a planet of happy people could be better than nothing. If a philosopher had a chance to create the first planet simply by lifting a finger, then prima facie the finger oughtn't to be lifted. . . . Similarly with the second planet. Assuming that creating it wouldn't produce harm elsewhere, it ought to be created." Leslie writes of there being a "moral need," wherever possible, to replace miserable people with happy people. He asks "what our duty would be in a situation where absolutely nothing could be done to help the miserable, no matter how hard we tried," and he draws an analogy to "miserable" individuals who are born ill or impaired and cannot be helped. His implication is that because such individuals cannot be changed, one must instead go on and create new ones who will not be ill or impaired and hence will be happy. Indeed, once the science and technology are developed, he postulates that humanity might have "a very strong duty" to spread right across our galaxy (1996, 181, 178, 182, 183).

Because no amount of "finger lifting" will in reality create and sustain human populations, the human situation is of course much more complex than Leslie's hypothesis acknowledges. Similar to the writings of other philosophers on procreation that we have already encountered, Leslie's otherwise rather engaging thought experiments consistently ignore women's role, for they never mention the people who will inevitably have the job of carrying out the purported duty to create happy people. Contrary to Leslie, we can recognize that there may be a "moral need," wherever possible, to try to assist miserable people to become happy, but *without* admitting a "moral need" to create new happy people. To suppose there is a "moral need" to create new happy people is implicitly to endorse a version of the Repugnant Conclusion. Recall that, according to the Repugnant Conclusion, "compared with the existence of very many people—say, ten billion—all of whom have a very high quality of life, there must be some much larger number of people whose existence, if other things are equal, would be better, even though these people would have lives that are barely worth living" (Parfit 2004, 10). Leslie's version would have us go on creating human beings and spreading them throughout the galaxy (a monumental task), provided they are happy. As I argued in chapter 5, however, for a number of reasons (including supererogation, obligations to one's existing children, and respect for women and their autonomy), women do not have any obligation to create happy people. A woman with one happy child does not have a responsibility to have a second child who, if created, will also be happy.

Hence, the fact that some people are happy or have the potential to be is not a sufficient reason to require that we prevent the extinction of humanity. Our situation is very different from God's (imagined) position, which I described in chapter 6. If the work of procreation and rearing were the product of God's effortless magic, then the absence of good (happy people) would be bad, and we might readily assent to the creation of entire planetfuls of happy people. In the real world, however, to assume that a galaxy of happy people *must* be created is to put unconscionable requirements on women, who are the ones who must do the reproductive labor, for wherever women become more educated and more prosperous, they choose to have fewer children, not more.

Another possible answer to the question why our existence is worth perpetuating might be that sheer human life has *intrinsic* value.[13] Some writers have claimed that because of the value of existence itself, we have a moral responsibility to bring as many human beings into existence as possible. Sahin Aksoy, for example, says that human existence "is essential and prerequisite to everything good or bad." He adds, "Every life is worth living, even if it is worse than some other lives, if the only alternative is non-existence." "Life and existence is [*sic*] always better than non-existence," and "therefore, it is irrational and immoral to 'sentence' someone to non-existence while you have the chance to bring them into life and existence" (2004, 382, 383).

Postulating that human life has intrinsic value can be morally useful and can serve as a basis for important moral limits on how human beings may be treated, both at the level of individuals and at the level of communities and even nations. If human life is assumed to have intrinsic value, then it is never acceptable to enslave any human beings, to torture them, to assault them, or to treat them in any way that suggests that their life is not valuable.[14] At the same time, there is danger in the idea of the intrinsic worth of human life if it leads—as Aksoy so enthusiastically concludes—to another version of the Repugnant Conclusion. Aksoy appears to believe that human beings have an ethereal existence, in which they wait for their potential parents to call them into the material world. In Aksoy's formulation, the Repugnant Conclusion is changed from its original formulation as a duty to maximize the good and becomes a duty to maximize sheer human life. From his perspective, we have a responsibility to create indefinitely many human beings not because we have a utilitarian duty to create as much good as possible, but because we have a duty to create as much human existence as possible.

This conclusion is, if anything, even more repugnant than the utilitarian duty. On utilitarian grounds, there would at least be some foreseeable limit to the number of human beings we should create because the sheer numbers of human beings would eventually start to prevent any good whatsoever from being achievable. But if human life itself is intrinsically valuable and must be produced for that reason only, then we might have a duty to go on procreating without limit and without regard to the condition of the human beings created. There would be nothing about the intrinsic value of human life to put an end to the sheer numbers that instantiate it.

Indeed, Michael N. Mautner, for one, believes that there should be no limits. He writes, "The shared drive for self-propagation can . . . define a human purpose: To safeguard and perpetuate life. To this effect, we can expand life and seek to advance it into a controlling force in nature." He estimates that the resources of our solar system "can support, at high standards, human populations of thousands of trillions, more than one hundred thousand times the Earth's present population." What he calls "panbiotic ethics" supports the further multiplication of human beings in "billions of solar systems" (2009, 436, 437).

James Lenman draws from a hypothesis about intrinsic value a very different and more plausible conclusion. He focuses not, like Aksoy, on the alleged intrinsic value of human *life*, but on the alleged intrinsic value of individual human *beings*. And he says that even if human beings are intrinsically valuable, that fact does not imply that we must create more human beings. He uses an analogy with white rhinoceroses. Lenman suggests that even if we assume, for the sake of argument, that white rhinos are intrinsically valuable, it does not follow that it is better that there be *more* rhinos and that they should be spread all over the planet. No one laments the fact that there are no white rhinos in Scotland, for example. And just as the intrinsic value of individual white rhinos does not imply that there should be more of them spread out over the planet at any given time, it also does not imply that there should be more of them spread out *through* time. "If it is unclear how it would make things better to stretch out, synchronically, in a single generation, the numbers of white rhinos, it is unclear why it should make things better to stretch them out diachronically by having more generations." We need not regret that there are no white rhinos in Scotland, and we also need not regret that there may be no white rhinos a million years from now (2004b, 138–139).

In other words, contrary to what Aksoy and Mautner appear to believe, the fact (if it is a fact) that y is intrinsically valuable does not imply that there should be more of y, whether simultaneously or serially. Even if possible human beings will be intrinsically valuable, we do not have a duty to bring them into existence. The very fact that they are only possible shows that we are not being unjust or ungenerous by failing to create them. As a result, even if we assume that human life or human beings themselves are intrinsically valuable, it does not follow that the extinction of our species would be bad and that we are morally obliged to prevent it.[15]

Biodiversity

Humanity is unique—yet so is every species. In that respect, humanity is paradoxically not special. Indeed, we have come to feel a pang of regret when we learn that a species has become extinct under our watch, and many of us feel alarm when informed that members of a certain species have been reduced to a critically minimal number. If there is a duty to prevent our own extinction on grounds of our species' uniqueness, then there is arguably a duty to protect other species and try to prevent their extinction. However, in staving off our own extinction, we would also have to take into account the effects of maintaining human beings on the perpetuation of members of other species.

Why is species uniqueness an argument for its preservation? Perhaps a species is worth preserving simply because of its unique contribution to biodiversity, the variety of forms of life that exist on our planet. Mautner goes so far as to suggest that "new lines of evolution, rich biodiversity" (2009, 437) justify the spread of human beings not just in our own solar system, but throughout the universe. It is disconcerting to suppose that our mere contribution to biodiversity might be the reason to prevent our own extinction. In order for this to be the case, however, we would have to have grounds for believing either that biodiversity itself is intrinsically valuable or that biodiversity is instrumentally valuable. Both possibilities raise problems.

It is, first, unpersuasive to think of biodiversity as being intrinsically valuable; to borrow a term from Benatar, it is far from clear that this feature of our world has value *sub specie aeternitatis* (Benatar 2006, 199). Sheer variety is not necessarily good in itself—dangers, diseases, pollutants, and crimes are not made better by being diverse. A variety of anything is valuable usually because of what it causes or facilitates. A variety of sports allows people with different abilities and interests to obtain physical exercise. A variety of Web sites allows one to learn more and to compare the information provided. Biodiversity is likely to be valuable not for its own sake, but because it contributes to the health of the natural environment and thus to the preservation of species.

But notice, now, that this attempt to show that human extinction would be bad and should be resisted culminates in circularity. We tentatively attributed value to the survival of our own species just because it contributes to biodiversity—the sheer variety of species in a particular area or on the planet as a whole. And we value biodiversity because biodiversity supports the survival of species (presumably including our own). Species survival and biodiversity mutually support each other, but if the value of each is justified by reference to the other, we have no additional, external reason to value either one. Nor is there is an independent reason to resist our own extinction.

Moreover, although our species is genetically unique and its disappearance would by definition reduce biodiversity, our continued existence, with its destructive effects on the planet, tends to hasten the extinction of multiple other species and thus to *diminish* biodiversity. In that re-spect, members of other species might very well be better off without us: "our own extinction would very likely do more good than harm to natural biodiversity" (Lenman 2004b, 140). The International Union for Conservation of Nature, which describes itself as the world's oldest and largest global and environmental organization, reports that 17,291 out of 47,677 assessed species are threatened with extinction. Those threat-ened include "21 percent of all known mammals, 30 percent of all known amphibians, 12 percent of all known birds, . . . 28 percent of reptiles, 37 percent of freshwater fishes, 70 percent of plants, [and] 35 percent of invertebrates" (2009).

The implacable fact is that the planet and its other inhabitants got along fine without human beings in the distant past and probably will again in the distant future. Trees, plants, insects, birds, and wild animals will not miss us; indeed, most of them are likely to thrive in our absence. Some domestic animals might miss us, although there is evidence that domestic animals such as cats and dogs are able to survive in a feral existence without human beings if they have to. In fact, although some individual companion animals might grieve their lost relationship to hu-man beings, many domestic animals would be better off because they would avoid the hardships of factory farming and the torments of the slaughterhouse. Cows, sheep, chickens, and pigs might have more dif-ficulty fending for themselves, but they would suffer less without us be-cause they would no longer be raised in mostly execrable conditions and killed by human beings for food. Some people have argued to me that if, for whatever reason, human beings ceased to create and factory-farm immense numbers of pigs, sheep, cows and chickens, then many possible animals would never have the opportunity to live. That is, of course, true, provided we always remember that a merely possible animal is not an animal at all. Without human beings, there would be billions fewer food animals, but because there are no ethereal cows, sheep, chickens, and pigs waiting in the metaphysical wings of the planetary drama to be brought onstage into existence, the real reduction in suffering by domestic animals would be significant and the losses (in terms of animals never born) non-existent. In short, the extinction of human beings would be a hardship for very few other beings. Thus, the human species' purported contribu-tion to biodiversity fails as an argument against human extinction both because the argument is circular and because the human species' presence on the planet does not contribute to biodiversity at all; instead, it compromises biodiversity.[16]

Do Human Beings Matter?

We saw earlier that a moral duty to resist human extinction cannot be founded on the basis of our collective happiness or the alleged intrinsic value of human life; the familiar problems with the Repugnant Conclusion defeat these arguments. I have also shown that a moral duty to resist human extinction cannot be founded on humanity's uniqueness or supposed contribution to biodiversity.

Some people think it must be human beings' special characteristics that make us valuable. When we fear human extinction, what we fear is the extinguishment of certain important capacities that are definitive of human beings. These capacities include rationality or, more broadly, intelligence and creativity; the use of language or, more broadly, the ability to communicate; self-awareness, the ability to see oneself as an individual and to contemplate one's past and future; and moral agency, the ability to make deliberate choices to do good or to cause harm.

Of course, human history suggests we should be careful not to overestimate the extent and value of human abilities because doing so often leads to human and environmental domination and indifference to the well-being of members of other species (and even to certain groups of our own species) apart from their capacity to enhance our own well-being. Moreover, these characteristics are not necessarily unique to human beings. As Young points out, whatever traits one chooses as valuable will exclude some human beings if pitched too high or include nonhuman beings if not pitched so high (2001, 189). Not all human beings possess these traits—neither fetuses nor persons in a persistent vegetative state are self-conscious or rational, for example. In addition, however, many nonhuman beings possess intelligence and the capacity to communicate, and although self-awareness and moral agency may be unusual among species on this planet, we cannot assume that there are no beings elsewhere in the galaxy—let alone the universe—that also have these abilities. We may, by a combination of cunning and brute force, be at the top of the food chain on our own planet, but we can't assume we'd be at the top elsewhere.

Centuries of religious dogma have claimed that we are a superior species, but the universe is a big place, and the conditions for development of intelligent self-conscious beings may very well exist elsewhere. So there should be no illusions that human extinction would be bad because it would *necessarily* be the end of rationality, self-awareness, communication, and moral agency.[17]

However, it might be objected that it is not so much the sheer exercise of rationality, self-awareness, communication, and moral agency that is important about human beings. Rather, it is the *products* of these capacities: the distinct culture (or range of cultures) of and the myriad creations by human beings—scientific, artistic, intellectual, educational, athletic, moral—are what matter.

I agree wholeheartedly that despite all the errors we human beings have made and all the disasters and cruelty we have perpetrated, our cultures are worth preserving. The question, however, is whether the existence of human beings in perpetuity is necessary in order to preserve these cultures. Some of my own undergraduate students claim not to be distressed at the prospect of human extinction—first, because they believe human beings are highly destructive of other species, and, second, because they believe that human beings are subject to evolution just like members of other species on this planet. We can imagine that (with a great deal of luck) there may be one or more successor species to human beings. These successor species, let us hope and expect, will preserve all of our cultures.

If we can be reasonably confident about such a future, is it enough to reconcile us to extinction? *Should* it reconcile us? I suspect it definitely is not and perhaps should not. The reason is that cultures are living processes, not just historical artifacts. We want to go on as a species because we are deeply engaged in all our collective enterprises—aesthetic, scientific, philosophical, religious, athletic, entrepreneurial, and so on. They are not merely of historic value, and they are much bigger than any one or even any subset of us. Those enterprises are immeasurably important to us; they help to define and express who we are as a species. We resist our own extinction because we matter to ourselves.

The issue whether human extinction is a bad thing, an outcome that we should actively resist, arises in the context of this book because it raises questions about the morality of our procreative choices: If we were facing species extinction, would we then have a special moral responsibility to

procreate in order to perpetuate our own kind? If all fertile human beings collectively and gradually decided not to reproduce, ought they to be
urged to change their minds—or even be compelled to?

I have not found adequate reasons to show that the extinction of the
human species—provided it is voluntary—would inevitably be a bad
thing. We human beings have a sentimental attachment to our own species and cultures. We matter to ourselves, of course, but it is in no way
evident that humanity matters to anyone else. If we were to disappear,
members of other species would soon forget us and get along without us.
In the absence of convincing evidence for a Supreme Being or even for the
existence of beings elsewhere in the galaxy that are aware of us, it seems
that human beings do not have value for anyone else in the universe. And
if we cease to matter to ourselves, we have no duty to continue to breed
just for the sake of facilitating more breeding. Because human beings are
valuable only from the perspective of human beings, then when human
beings cease to exist, our value will cease to exist.

Human beings, like any other species, are part of the natural order and
with no more entitlement than any other to go on existing forever. All
other species, to our knowledge, eventually go extinct. Just as individual
immortality is both undesirable and impossible (Overall 2003), so also
species immortality is both undesirable and impossible. As Lenman sensi-
bly points out, the question is not *whether* the human species will become
extinct; "the Second Law of Thermodynamics [resulting in the maximization of entropy] will get us in the end in the fantastically unlikely event
that nothing else does first" (2004b, 137).

All of this is *not* to say that we human beings should either hasten our
extinction or be indifferent to it. I think we do have a duty to prevent any
extinction that is aimed at through unilateral acts, such as nuclear attack
or biological terrorism, that involve deliberately destructive behavior by a
minority resulting in massive suffering and deaths. We would avoid such
extinction not by putting moral pressure on women to reproduce, but
by preventing and guarding against nuclear attacks, biological terrorism,
and other globally destructive acts. Human beings do not want to suffer,
and they do not want to die prematurely; that is reason enough not to
hasten our own extinction.

But if the human population drastically declines as a collective result
of many individual procreative decisions not to reproduce, I don't think

people should be compelled to procreate, nor would they be morally obligated to do so. It is a great hardship to be required to reproduce when doing so is not part of one's life plan. In such a situation, women are expected to acquiesce to being used as reproductive machines. And even when women are not compelled by force or by law to procreate, unwilling reproductive labor that is undertaken only out of a sense of obligation is a kind of enslavement. The woman's body is taken over by another living entity not as part of her own project, but in response to what is perceived as an overriding moral requirement.[18] An individual might feel it is virtuous to contribute to continuing the human community in a case of impending gradual extinction, but she would not be wrong if she chose not to.

I conclude that we do not have a moral obligation to procreate simply in order to prevent our own extinction. We might even have an obligation *not* to stave off extinction if it turns out that our posterity will not have lives that are worth living (Lenman 2004b, 148). That is, we ought not to go on reproducing if we might somehow know that the future for members of our species will be unalterably bleak and unremittingly miserable. Although we cannot know this future for sure, our apparent commitment to the despoliation of our planet makes it more likely than not that our descendants will have a very hard time—so hard that extinction may someday look preferable. I, however, prefer to hope that when the human species becomes extinct, it will be for a potentially much more positive reason: that we will have gradually evolved into another species. I hope, too, that despite the undeniable talents and abilities of our kind, we will be replaced by a species with considerably greater intellectual, psychological, and moral capacities than those that human beings now possess.

10

Procreation, Values, and Identity

In this book, I have presented no general formula for handling the ethics of choosing to have children; there cannot be one. In cases of ethical ambiguity, there are often no obvious, easy, mechanical answers. We can only attempt to figure out which purported solutions don't work, and we can assess the weight of the evidence on different sides. To suppose ethics is or can be much more than this is to ask for what we cannot have.

When we are trying to decide what is right and wrong, what we have a responsibility to do, and what we ought to avoid, all we have to work with is the reality around us—multiple societies of diverse human beings, all of them situated in a nonhuman material world with many other living and in some cases sentient beings. We get better at ethics as we learn more about those with whom we interact. For example, a better understanding of the harms of sexism and racism and how to respond to them has developed as human beings have learned more about gender and race as well as about gendered and racialized people (that is to say, about everyone—but especially those who have been victimized by virtue of their gendering and racialization). People (and other sentient beings) suffer, and they do not like to suffer. This we know. People are capable of joy, happiness, pleasure, well-being, satisfaction, achievement, and fulfillment. This we also know. That's our main evidence collectively for any ethical conclusions we may draw. Inadequate ethics arises, at least in part, from inadequate knowledge.

Hence, instead of standing back at a great distance from the procreation issue and pronouncing upon it, as a number of philosophers (mostly male) have tended to do, we must engage in close examination of the various issues and arguments, examining the strengths and weaknesses of different claims, and in particular remaining very aware that it is women who gestate and deliver babies, not machines, not society, not men, and not simply some gender-unspecified "reproducers." That is what I have attempted to do in the previous nine chapters.

Despite my own religious doubts, I began this book with a biblical quotation: "I call heaven and earth to record this day against you, that I have set before you life and death, blessing and cursing: therefore choose life, that both thou and thy seed may live" (Deuteronomy 30:19). When this quotation is hijacked by the antiabortion movement, it is dangerous to women. But as guidance to people wondering whether to procreate, it may be inspiring.

People sometimes ask me whether I would advise them to have children. I often say, "Don't miss it!" My response sounds excessively pronatalist, but I would argue that it is not. I certainly do not say it to people who have told me or of whom I know that they have already decided not to have children; nor do I say it to someone who has not raised the procreation question with me. I do not actively go around promoting procreation. But in response to people who have thought about it, who are weighing their choices, who are imagining life as a parent and life as a nonparent, I usually encourage them to take the plunge.

Given all that I have said so far in this book, readers might wonder how I can possibly defend such advice. Earlier chapters demonstrated that it is not easy to find sound arguments to justify the individual choice to procreate. Reproductive rights are certainly not enough on their own to make having children something not to be missed. Both the deontological and consequentialist arguments for procreation are weak and inadequate. In addition, the sheer giving of life is not self-justifying, and creating a child does not automatically make one a good person. We cannot say that choosing to have a child is vindicated merely by the fact that the child now exists. Children are not brought into the world for their own sake because they do not preexist their conception. Coming into existence can turn out to be a benefit or a burden, depending on how the child's life goes. Indeed, as I showed in chapters 7 and 8, there are some situations in which it is difficult to justify procreation. And the dangers of overpopulation and planetary despoliation imply that we should be especially cautious about making more babies. It is not at all clear that the extinction of the human species would be so bad as to morally obligate fertile human beings to procreate if they did not want to. If we all have children just so that they can have children and their children can have children, ad infinitum, we are rooted in a Sisyphean process that appears to have no foundation and no clear value.

Choosing the Nonrational: The Wager

Is there any other way to justify choosing to be a parent? Some might think the approach to the question up to this point is misguided. Deciding to have or not to have a child is not simply a matter of counting up the pluses and subtracting the minuses of parenthood. As Elizabeth Harman remarks, "Reasons interact in many different ways. While it is sometimes useful to talk of one reason being stronger than another, it by no means follows that all reasons have strengths that can be compared, or that reasons simply add up with the stronger one winning out" (2004, 109 n. 8). One possibility, then, is that the "why have children?" decision ought not to be approached as a question of rational decision making.

Matti Häyry advises against having children on the grounds that there is simply a *chance* that the child will suffer, and "it is morally wrong to cause avoidable suffering to other people" (2004, 378). (But, of course, with most things we do there is a chance of causing suffering to someone.) To Häyry, procreation is both immoral and *irrational*. In response, Rebecca Bennett agrees that having children is irrational: "In most cases we choose to bring to birth children on the basis of unquantifiable and unpredictable ideas of what they will bring to our lives and the lives of those around us" (2004, 379). Yet she does believe that most human lives are worth living.[1] She writes, "Many of what are considered to be the most valuable experiences in life, such as love, sex, dancing, creating children, recreational drug/alcohol use, etc., may have little or no rational justification . . . but life without such irrational pleasures and freedoms for many would be unbearable" (2004, 379).

Bennett's list is uneven: it is hard to think of recreational drug use as on a par with creating children or drinking alcohol as in the same category as love. Recreational drug and alcohol use may indeed be irrational if it is self-destructive, but feeling love or going dancing doesn't seem irrational at all: they may very well be entirely consistent with one's interests, purposes, and well-being. Perhaps Bennett ought to be making the point that certain activities are *non*rational rather than irrational. That is, some activities, such as falling in love or dancing all night, may be worthwhile, but choosing them is not simply the result of reasoning about what is most logical to do in one's life. At the same time, they are neither foolish nor unfounded. Maybe, as Bennett assumes, procreation is similar in that way to falling in love. Vangie Bergum writes, "The choice to mother is not a strictly rational one, where one can just add up all the items on one side of the ledger, compare it to the other side, and get a definitive answer": "Instead of the deliberate, rational making of a decision, which sounds like a technical process, there is a sense that deciding on a child is like a coming to a decision that may not be rational at all. Perhaps it is like Kierkegaard's 'leap of faith'—a realization that having a child opens one to life's possibilities—which can only be taken with 'fear and trembling'" (1997, 18, 30).

Is procreation nonrational—not susceptible to a straightforward tally of pros and cons—but at the same time not necessarily irrational? The seventeenth-century philosopher Blaise Pascal provides one model for thinking about a major life choice in a situation where, he believes, the relevant truth cannot be discerned via logical reasoning.

Pascal regards the decision whether to believe in God or not as nonrational. Choosing whether to believe in God is instead, he argues, like making a wager. One cannot know whether God exists or not; the very nature of the question is, according to Pascal, such that it does not admit of arguments. Reason cannot decide the question of what to believe ([1662] 1966, 150). But whether to believe in God or not is nonetheless a momentous and life-changing decision. Therefore, in choosing whether to believe in God or not, according to Pascal, one is in the metaphorical position of making a bet on a race whose outcome one does not know.

But one *must* decide, says Pascal; it is not optional. That is, unlike the situation of a horse race, one cannot simply walk away from the wager. In religion, the choice not to decide is in itself a choice not to believe in God. Therefore, because reason cannot decide the issue, one should wager on the basis of an assessment of the well-being that will be yielded if one outcome or the other turns out to be correct. Pascal's idea is that if God exists, eternal life is the reward for belief in God, and eternal suffering is the punishment for failure to believe. By contrast, if God does not exist, then one wins and loses nothing. Given the stakes, one should therefore wager that God exists because one thereby becomes eligible for an eternal life (and avoids eternal punishment) if one's wager is correct, whereas there is no comparable payoff if one wagers that God does not exist and one is correct (Pascal [1662] 1966, 151).

In certain ways, the decision about whether to procreate or not is similar to the decision whether to believe in God or not, as Pascal describes it. First, the outcome of the "why have children?" decision is unknown. By the nature of the situation, one cannot know what it is like to have one's own child unless and until one has a child. Nor, despite all the advances in prenatal screening and diagnosis, is it possible to know much about the child herself—what she will be like, how she will develop, the state of her health, or what kind of person she will become. Second, it appears difficult to make the choice on the basis of weighing the reasons for and against procreation. Although there are plenty of arguments on both sides, many people find that an assessment of the supposed evidence is inadequate to make the choice. Third, as in the case of whether to believe in God or not, one cannot merely sit on the fence with respect to procreation. If one decides not to decide, then the decision is made—either by not having a child at all or by allowing "nature" to take its course and running the risk of becoming pregnant or making another person pregnant without intending to.

Given these similarities, should the decision whether to procreate also be treated as a Pascalian wager? It is important to note that, despite Pascal's disclaimer, his wager *is* in a certain way based on logical thought. The wager is admittedly not concerned with the truth value of belief in God's existence, for Pascal thought that truth with respect to theism is not attainable. Nor is it based on the epistemic or moral justification of believing or not believing in God, for justification is precisely what we cannot have, according to Pascal. Pascal instead is looking for the option that is best for the individual person confronting the wager; he recommends the choice that in his view is most likely to produce the biggest payoff. So if we use a comparable process with respect to procreation, we must weigh not the reasons for and against reproducing, but rather the potential payoff of the procreation bet—the "winnings" both from having children and from not having children.

The likely payoff for not having children includes greater disposable income (the money saved by not having children), more leisure, less housework (children are messy), more personal freedom, less responsibility, more spontaneity, less conflict in the relationship with one's partner, if any, and fewer worries (about children's health, safety, education, and so on). The payoff, however, may also include the possibility of future regrets if the individual changes her mind, along with (possibly) an unfulfilled longing for a child. By contrast, one can assume that having children will mean less disposable income, less leisure, more housework, less personal freedom, more responsibility, less spontaneity, more conflict in the relationship with one's partner if one has a partner, and many more worries. Of course, it may also include the joy and rewards of rearing one's children, helping them, interacting with them, and learning with and from them.

I don't know whether the choice about procreation is made any clearer or easier by regarding it as a Pascalian wager. Anyone who chooses to become a parent either for the love of taking a risk or solely as a gamble about her own individual well-being may very well be disappointed. Of course, parenthood can and often does contribute to happiness and well-being, both one's own and that of others. Yet, as I pointed out in chapter 5, it also involves a great deal of hard work as well as discomfort, anxiety, and sacrifice.

But I am more interested in whether it is even *legitimate* to regard procreation as a wager at all. Consider the following problem. Although Pascal recommends belief in God, he recognizes that people might not simply be able to believe on demand. He therefore urges his readers to deliberately turn off their rational facilities and "stupefy" their minds in order to induce and sustain religious belief if they are not otherwise able to believe ([1662] 1966, 152). Yet there is something highly questionable about this approach to the religious life. It makes belief in God a prudential rather than a moral or spiritual decision. The individual who accepts the terms of Pascal's wager comes to believe in God not because of arguments based on evidence for God's existence, not out of a sense of piety, not out of acquiescence to God's will, not through revelation, prayer, scriptures, reverence, respect for religious leaders, or awe at creation, but simply out of an egoistic gamble that believing will pay off infinitely in the afterlife. It is hard to imagine that a Supreme Being, if there is one, would be pleased with these methods and motives.

In the decision whether to procreate or not, if the individual's only concern—on the model of Pascal's wager—is whether the decision will pay off *personally* in the long as well as the short term, then she is similarly making a merely prudential and self-regarding decision and ignoring the moral dimensions of the choice. From the very first chapter of this book, I have argued that deciding whether to procreate *is* a moral decision and that it is a moral decision because it affects so many people—not only the prospective parent(s), but also the prospective child, other family members, and other members of the community. Although one is certainly entitled to take into account the effects of having a child on oneself, if one decides *only* on the basis of a gamble about one's future well-being, then one is refusing to treat procreation as a fully moral matter.

And that, I suggest, is a mistake—although the potential implications of the mistake are much greater if one chooses to procreate than if one does not. One ought not to treat a moral decision as if it were merely a pragmatic one, a bet that one makes based on one's chances of winning personal gains. If we were to ask someone why he is childless, and he said, "There just wasn't enough in it for me," we might not be impressed by his approach, but we would likely commend him for his honesty and self-understanding, and we would be glad he did not become a parent. But if we asked someone else why she became a parent, and she said, "I just took a gamble that it would pay off better for me personally than being child-less," there would be nothing in that reply to give us confidence about her abilities as a mother or about the nature of her relationship with her child.

Whether to procreate is a life-changing and far-reaching decision; it ought not to be treated as merely a wager and especially not a wager about the odds of benefit for oneself. Wagering for or against procreation fails to handle the issue—or one's own life—with the respect it deserves. A life well lived is not just a matter of personal payoff.

The Kind of Beings We Are and What Parenting Is About

Yet when I tell people who seek my advice about having children, "Don't miss it!" it sounds as if I'm recommending a Pascalian wager or at the very least a leap of faith.

That is not at all what I'm advising. Instead, when I advocate parenting to people who have already thought about it for a long time, I am endorsing a particular vision of who we are as human beings and what parenting is about. Throughout this book, I have argued that there is no moral obligation to have children. But even if there is no obligation to do *x*, *x* may still be a good thing to do. We don't have an obligation to become highly educated, but getting as much education as one can manage is usually a good thing to do. We don't have an obligation to engage in volunteer activities in our community, but doing so is almost always a good thing. It is possible that having one or two children may in many cases be good, even if not morally obligatory—and even if it is hard to justify in the way in which more straightforward moral decisions are. Perhaps we should look not only at the prospect of overpopulation or extinction, nor merely at the reasons people give for and against procreation, but rather at the *meanings* people attribute to reproduction and to children and at the significance of procreation for the kinds of beings that we are.

Imagine a person, Isabella, who does not have children and who commends herself on her environmental sensitivity and her desire not to overload the planet. Isabella also claims to be a social benefactor, giving money to support various good causes. Yet Isabella nonetheless leads a self-centered life, enjoying lots of luxuries, international travel, and the most-recent model cars, while at the same time being indifferent or even nasty to her nieces and nephews, the children who play next door, and the students who pass by on their way to school.

By contrast, consider the case of Carla, who is the mother of three children. Carla has more children than can be ecologically justified. The second one was an "accident." Carla worries about having enough money to support them all. But Carla loves her children, listens to them, and can be counted on as a reliable and responsible parent. Carla takes a keen interest in their education, prepares nutritious meals, and plays with her kids at the local playground.

I am by no means claiming that either Isabella or Carla is typical. My point is just this: Carla is arguably at least as good a person as Isabella and perhaps even better. Isabella's decision not to procreate does not automatically make her a good person, given her other characteristics. Carla's decision to have more than two children does not make her a bad person, given her other characteristics. Choosing to have children and raise them is about the kind of person we want to be and about the kinds of persons we want there to be on this planet. As a society, we would no more want to convince good people like Carla never to procreate than we would want to convince musicians not to make music.

Some people would go further and say that having children is genuinely analogous to making art. Recall from chapter 4 that Rosalind Hursthouse sees bearing children as "intrinsically worthwhile." Hursthouse also says that a woman who has a child "can look upon her children as *her* achievements, her works of art, the result of her efforts and suffering" (1987, 315, her emphasis). Should we see being a parent as valuable because it is like being an artist?

Creating art is worthwhile, but some of us either can't do it or are not interested in it; our strengths and interests lie elsewhere. Human society is definitely better off for having people who can and do make art, people who are motivated to do so. But if someone who is artistically talented nonetheless chooses to be a mountain climber, it seems odd to say that she is making a *moral* mistake or that she ought to make art for the benefit of others even if she does not want to and would much prefer to be exploring the Antarctic. A person with potential gifts for child rearing is similarly not making a moral error if she nonetheless prefers to be a chef or an architect.

A healthy pregnancy and delivery are an important achievement, and successfully raising children is an admirable accomplishment. Nonetheless, I am uneasy about seeing children as a product—even a valuable product such as art. Parenting can go wrong when parents see their offspring as objects they can and should mold to suit their own purposes. Of course, parents must train their children, set rules, and enforce limits. But a child, unlike a work of art, is a self-conscious, autonomous entity with her own abilities, preferences, and needs. Children are not property. Children are persons, and respect for children both individually and collectively is ethically essential both to society as a whole and to individuals. As I argued in chapter 4, children should not be treated only or primarily as a means to the attainment of deontological values such as the perpetuation of lineage, name, and property; the fulfillment of religious, marital, or familial duties; or the discharge of duties to the state. As I argued in chapter 5, they should also not be treated only or primarily as a means to consequentialist goals. Children, like adult women and men, should be treated as ends that are valuable in themselves. If we ask ourselves "What are children for?" the most important answer must be that they are for themselves, not for their parents or for their society.

Thus, children are not artifacts, and parents are not artists. What, then, makes being a parent valuable? Parenting is a *relationship*, not a set of actions directed at an object. The lifetime of parent-child interactions is, I believe, key to understanding what is good about procreation. Although the outcome of procreation and child rearing cannot be foreseen—much can go wrong, children can disappoint, and offspring sometimes delight in becoming what their parents do not want—what matters is the *process* of procreation and parenting, that is, the relationship between parent and offspring. In this relationship lies the best reason for choosing to have a child.

The Parent-Child Relationship

Since his arrival, through all the exhaustion and preoccupation, I have grown another part of myself: another whole heart that dwarfs any preexisting organ, this one the size of [a] sperm whale's, a brand-new gargantuan muscle, developed by strange and powerful paternal steroids. It will beat inside me until I die. (Nichols 2006, 145)

Rex Sayers writes, "There is only one real reason to have children, which is to love them, deeply and madly" (2007, C3). And according to Elizabeth Anderson, "Parental love can be understood as a passionate, *unconditional* commitment to nurture one's child, providing it with the care, affection, and guidance it needs to develop its capacities to maturity" (quoted in Gibson 1995, 238, emphasis added by Gibson). These statements suggest that the essence of the parent-child relationship is *unconditional love* and that the possibility of giving (and usually receiving) pure, unadulterated, unqualified love provides the best possible reason for having a child.

But the idea of unconditional love deserves further examination. In many ways, it seems genuinely attractive. We all want to be loved, and we hope that people will continue to love us even when we are irritable, impatient, rude, careless, or unkind. We want our parents, our children, our lovers, and our close friends to overlook our faults and focus on our good qualities. We want them to cherish us, even—or maybe especially—on our bad days. The idea of unconditional love implies that we should treasure the loved one no matter what he or she does and that all behavior, no matter how abominable, should be forgiven and forgotten.[2]

The idea of unconditional love is a cultural platitude. Unfortunately, however, it sets a standard that is almost unattainable. No one except perhaps a saint or a fully enlightened being can be entirely unmoved by hateful words and harmful actions directed at oneself. But more important philosophically, I suggest that unconditional love is, with only a few exceptions, not desirable.

The exceptions are people who are not yet or not any longer autonomous and hence not responsible for their behavior. Thus, toward an infant or young child, unconditional love may be an appropriate goal. One loves one's baby or toddler through colic, tantrums, diaper changes, vomiting, and inconsolable wailing—*whatever* the child may do. But as the child grows up, behavior that was formerly appropriate and tolerable becomes much less so. Babyish behavior in a two-year-old is not unexpected; in a ten-year-old, though, it becomes a problem. Unless the child has developmental problems, unconditional love as a response to inappropriate behavior is not desirable. Once the child is past six or seven and is acquiring both autonomy and responsibility for his actions, I suspect that even the fans of unconditional parental love are doing little more than paying lip service to the concept. At that point, parental love is not really unconditional, and, more important, it should not be.

Here is the problem with unconditional love: babies and children do grow up.[3] The idea of having unconditional love for an individual who is older than six or seven suggests that it does not really matter *who* the loved one is. If love for a person is truly unconditional, then it is unrelated to the loved one himself. According to the ideal of unconditional love, no matter what someone says or does, no matter who someone is, no matter what attitudes, beliefs, values, or emotions the person has, the loving parent is supposed to love him or her. Unconditional love is a god's-eye perspective that is independent of the individual's unique characteristics.

But who the loved one is *does* matter. Real human love is love for particular human beings. We love people for who they are. And most people want to be loved for who they are, not loved in a way that is indifferent to their particularities. They want their own personal characteristics to be appreciated. They hope that it is their individual features, values, and behavior that are lovable. From the parent's point of view, a child is loved and lovable precisely because of who the child is.[4]

There are, then, real limits to unconditional love, especially after early childhood, and it seems implausible that adults should have children in order to have someone to whom they can forever give unconditional love.[5] The parent-child relationship lasts a lifetime, and after early childhood unconditional love is no longer appropriate or even possible.

But having said that unconditional love is inappropriate after a certain point in the child's life, we are apparently left only with "conditional" love. Conditional love sounds like a feeble basis for the parent-child relationship. Must the child, after the age of seven, earn his parent's love? Is love the product of a contract?

I suggest there are two kinds of conditional love. One kind is related to the behavior on some school playgrounds: "If you share your candy with me, I'll be your best friend." This kind of conditional love is what some parents offer their unfortunate children when they give their kids the message that they will be loved only if they behave according to the parents' standards, if they achieve in school, or if they become outstanding athletes. This kind of conditional love says, "I will love you if you do what I want, say what I think you should say, and become the kind of person that I favor." That kind of love is conditional on the love object's conformity to the parent's demands and decrees.

But another and much better kind of conditional love is the kind that says, "I love you for who you are; I love you *because* you are you. I love you because of what you do, what you say, and what you are becoming. Your needs, hopes, and choices endear you to me." I suggest that it is conditional love in this second sense that makes procreation worthwhile. This kind of conditional love is conditional on who the child is; it values the child for what he chooses to be. It is compassionate—it sees the child realistically, not as a doll to be played with or a pet to be manipulated, but as a person in his own right. This kind of conditional love is also forgiving. It accepts that the child is fallible and will make mistakes, as everyone does. It sees the forest and not only the trees—the long-term life of the child, not just the headaches and problems of the now. But this kind of conditional love is not "unconditional" toward the child's behavior. This kind of love recognizes that cruelty, dishonesty, manipulativeness, and violence are not to be embraced or loved unconditionally. Instead, the parent loves the child enough to help the child become a better person.

This conditional love of a parent for her offspring is different from the conditional love she may have for another adult, for, unlike most adult–adult relationships, the parent-child relationship is crucially asymmetrical.

In one way, it is inherently asymmetrical; in another way, it is only contingently asymmetrical.

The parent-child relationship is inherently asymmetrical because the child never chooses her parents; indeed, she does not choose to come into existence. By contrast, the parents do choose the child, at least to the extent that they choose to become parents. Even though the child cannot be brought into existence for her own sake—that is, to maximize her interests (because she does not preexist her own conception)—we can ask whether the child, once born, is *wanted by her parents for her own sake*, whether she is valued for herself, not just valued for the benefits that she may bring to her parents and sibling(s). The developing relationship between parent and child is significantly different from developing a friendship or other love relationship with another adult. The difference in procreation is that the parents not only start to build a relationship with the child but actually *create* the person with whom they have the relationship. They choose to have *their child*. Of course, they do not know much about the child they are choosing to have, only that she will be biologically related to them, a fact that may foreclose on some characteristics but also leave open many others. To choose to have a child is, at best, to choose to love and care for an unknown but related person, a person whom one will gradually get to know better and better even as that child goes through all the changes generated by maturing and growing up. This relationship is different from a connection between two adults or two children, where in the usual case each one chooses the other, and each one consents to be in the relationship. Hence, the parent-child relationship is inherently asymmetrical.

The parent-child relationship is also contingently asymmetrical. In the beginning and for many years of the child's life, the child is vulnerable, dependent, and needy. Without the parents or other responsible adults, the child cannot survive. By contrast, the parents are more or less self-sufficient prior to the child's arrival; the child certainly does not keep them alive. To choose to have a child is thus to choose to nurture and care for an initially helpless being—to be a literal life preserver for many years, committed to helping the child to achieve her own self-sufficiency.

The child's dependence gradually diminishes; indeed, one of the signs of good parenting is that it enables the child to become more and more autonomous. That is why I say that the relationship is also contingently asymmetrical. In addition, the parent also discovers sooner or later—often sooner than expected—her own vulnerability in the relationship, the vulnerability that is her need for the child. If she is breastfeeding, she may discover it very early on. But whether she breastfeeds or not, her attachment to the child makes her need him, and this fact also applies to loving fathers. It is a kind of dependence—the sort we have when our own flourishing is contingent upon another person's flourishing. The parent is vulnerable to the child because the parent's life cannot go well unless the child's life goes well.

As the child grows up, and if the relationship works reasonably well, the parent and child eventually relate to each other as adult equals. They are not equal because they have the same amount of experience—they don't—but rather because they both are self-determining and can contribute to choosing the relationship's future direction. They are tied to each other by their shared history, the dependency of love, and the need for the other's well-being as a condition for their own well-being. A contingent asymmetry may eventually return to the relationship if the parent becomes frail, impaired, or ill and needs to depend on the care of her adult children.

It is this kind of "conditional" love, a love that is both inherently and contingently asymmetrical and is focused on the child's true being, that is the strongest reason for having a child. To become the biological parent of a child whom one will raise is to *create a new relationship*: not just the genetic one, but a psychological, physical, intellectual, and moral one. The parents seek out a connection to a new human being, a connection that not only will serve the needs of that new human being but will also make the parents themselves needy and vulnerable in a way they have never been before.

Susanne Gibson says something similar: "I hold that reasons for having a child may be judged morally desirable or undesirable according to the extent to which they enhance or detract from the possibility of forming a particular kind of relationship with that child. The goals of this relationship will be many, although one of the most important goals will be to aid the child in developing a sense of her own value, regardless of her value to anyone else" (1995, 238). It is, however, a little misleading to speak of "the goals" of the parent-child relationship. Parents do not form loving relationships with their children only to achieve some outcome farther down the road. Parents are, of course, vitally interested in and devoted to their children's future, but the best reason for having a child is not to produce an adult or even to create a specific kind of child. To choose to have a child is to set out to create a relationship, a relationship that gives a particular meaning to one's own life and to the life of the being that is created. This kind of relationship may well have certain goals, but the value of the relationship is not derived only from its having goals or even from achieving them. The relationship is valuable for its own sake. The best reason to have a child is simply the creation of the mutually enriching, mutually enhancing love that is the parent-child relationship. In choosing to become a parent, one sets out to create a relationship, and in a unique way one also sets out to create the person with whom one has the relationship.

Identity

Now why would the creation of a new relationship be the best reason for having a child? A critic might point out that human beings can and do create new relationships at any time—we meet potential friends, colleagues, and lovers at work, in leisure activities, and even as we go about ordinary activities such as shopping. We don't need to have a child in order to create a new relationship. In fact, the critic might say, having a child for this reason is selfish[6] and places a burden on the child.

I don't deny that much of this is true. Of course many kinds of relationships are possible, and of course one need not procreate in order to have new relationships. There is no obligation to procreate, and many people feel no desire to do so. Moreover, procreation *is* sometimes just an expression of egotism and selfishness, although it need not and ought not to be. In chapters 4 and 5, we saw that when procreation is undertaken for reasons that simply seek to benefit the parents, it is morally unjustifiable.

Nonetheless, procreation cannot be entirely altruistic either: potential parents cannot have a child for the child's sake because before being created, the child does not exist to have a sake, an interest, in anything. Procreation is the parents' project, but it is not a project they can undertake to benefit a potential baby. As a result, procreating is, for the parents, *self-oriented*. But it is not inevitably *selfish* if one is seeking a relationship with the child that will be based on the kind of love that I described in the previous section.

For some people, being a mother or a father is integral to their concept of self. It is a matter of their individuality—who they are and how they want to be connected to the world. Their sense of personal authenticity and integrity draws them to parenthood. For some people, parenthood is a "calling" (Kingston 2009, 39). Bergum gives the following example:

Joan is forty-six. Time is running out for her to exercise all the possibilities of life, which, for her, included time to have her own baby. To her, having a baby is part of a whole life, of living one's life to its fullest, of exercising the talents and capacities that one has. . . . For Joan, "being a mother and having a family is exercising a whole set of domestic capacities that you never exercise if you live on your own." She believes that it is totally wrong to say that a woman has missed something out of life because she doesn't have a child. Rather, "I think I'll have missed something out of *my life* if I don't. It is something that I want to do. Having a baby is not like getting some smart job. Having a baby is part of *having a life*." (1997, 77, her emphasis)

Hursthouse similarly remarks that "parenthood in general . . . [is] . . . among the things that can be correctly thought to be partially constructive of a flourishing life" (1987, 241). When people like Joan become parents, they find not only that their "domestic capacities" are exercised, but also that many other abilities have a chance to flourish: their ability to observe; their understanding of human development and psychology; their courage and tenacity; their appreciation for play; their artistic, musical, scientific, or athletic abilities; and their understanding of their own place in the social world.

In choosing to have a child, one is deciding both to fulfill one's sense of who one is and at the same time aspiring to be a different person than one was before the child came along. In becoming a parent, one creates not only a child and a relationship, but oneself; one creates a new and ideally better self-identity. To choose to have a child is to take on a life-changing project. This is the case even with subsequent children; each child opens up a new world of experiences and challenges and changes the existing configuration of relationships of parent to parent and parent to child. The parent grows the child (and the child will eventually outgrow the parent), but, just as important, the child also grows the parent. Because becoming a parent is creating a relationship, the child shapes the parent even while the parent shapes the child.

The process can be challenging. Emily Grosholz writes: "There is nothing more delicious than a baby, nothing funnier than a little kid, nothing more mysterious, bracing, and beautiful than a teenager. Raising children is the best way I know to locate oneself in time, to bring the past and future into relationship, which is also the way we continue to grow up" (2009, A55). As novelist Anne Lamott describes her own experience as the single mother of a son, "Having a child, loving a child deeply in a daily way, forces you to connect with your mortality, forces you to dig into places within that you have rarely had to confront before. . . . What I found way down deep . . . by having a child is a kind of eternity, a capacity for—and reserves of—love and sacrifice that blew my mind. But I also found the stuff inside me that is pretty miserable. I was brought face-to-face with a fun-house mirror of all the grasping, cowardly, manipulative, greedy parts of me, too" (2007, 184–185).

Parenthood provides the opportunity for the growth of experience, the expansion of knowledge, and perhaps even the development of humility. One comes to know one's limits—and then stretches them. Although one can't really know what it means to be a parent until one is already embarked upon it, having a child is an opportunity for self-transformation. Perhaps it is the very unknown nature of parenthood itself that has the potential to make it transformative.

There are of course many paths to self-transformation and a good life—through artistic creativity, scientific discovery, athletic striving, teaching, practicing medicine, nursing, farming, animal care, gardening, building, designing, fixing things, being a worthy political leader, and so on. Children are not essential to all good lives, nor are having and rearing children prerequisites to becoming a good person. Moreover, there are many childless persons who support, love, care for, and teach other people's children. Chosen childlessness has as much potential for the good life as chosen parenthood has. In fact, the individual who chooses childlessness has made a decision that is easier to justify morally than is choosing to procreate. Such an individual takes the less-risky path; no new, vulnerable human beings are created. The genuinely unselfish life plan may sometimes be the choice not to have children, especially in the case of individuals who would otherwise procreate merely to please others, to conform to convention, or to benefit themselves based on the delusion that children will fix their problems.

As I stated in chapter 1, the burden of justification rests primarily on those who choose to have children. Having children is morally risky. And the ideas I have explored in this chapter must not by any means be interpreted as a claim that parenthood is the only or even the primary path to a flourishing life. But it *is* one such path.

Who am I to say this? What makes my opinion worth considering? I first wrestled with the question of whether to have children or not almost four decades ago. I am now the mother of two adult children, and my experiences undoubtedly influence what I say. I hope the evidence that I have presented and the arguments I have evaluated reveal the complexity and difficulty of the procreation decision. But if, after taking account of all the issues in this book, you are still considering whether to have a child, I continue to say, "Don't miss it!" Yet I also say, "Please consider having no more than one each."

Notes

Chapter 1

1. I am also very interested in questions about parents' role, the nature of parental rights and responsibilities, and children's rights and responsibilities. But these issues do not form part of this book.

2. In general, I am reluctant to use the term *child free*. Although I recognize that the term has libratory implications for some people who do not have children, whether by choice or not, I think it is too much like words such as *pest free* and *virus free* to be used justifiably. Because children are persons, it is no more appropriate to use a term such as *child free* than to use in other contexts terms such as *woman free* or *disabled free*.

3. Whether it makes sense for a father to be proud of his newborn is an interesting philosophical question. He has not, after all, performed the labor of gestation and birth. Nor has he yet done much, if any, fathering—although he may well have cared for the mother during her pregnancy and interacted indirectly with her fetus.

4. I am grateful to Kassy Wayne for drawing my attention to this part of Hursthouse's work.

5. Thanks to Lynda Ross for drawing my attention to this article.

6. In this book, for the sake of simplicity, I use language that assumes that all human persons who gestate and give birth are female and identify as women. I acknowledge that there have been a handful of transmen who have also given birth—hence, the media phenomenon of the "pregnant man." I intend my comments about moral issues pertaining to conception, gestation, labor, delivery, and parenthood to apply to these transmen also, although I recognize that their gender identification will affect, often profoundly, their individual experiences of procreative and parental events and conditions.

7. When a woman chooses to have an abortion, it might be argued that it is not appropriate to refer to her as a "mother."

8. Maier also adds later in her book that "a man no longer *decides* to become a father. Fifty years ago it was the men who turned women into mothers, often against their wishes. Nowadays the power relationship is reversed: only moth-

erhood is voluntary, not fatherhood. A man becomes a father only when he is accepted as such" (2007, 110, her emphasis). It is odd to suggest that women suddenly have this much power, and Maier provides no evidence for it.

9. The zeitgeist is changing, but perhaps more for men than for women. There are recognized forms of male personhood that are quite independent of children yet are considered fully acceptable and, indeed, even commendable or enviable. For women, the expectation tends to be that they will simply add the role of mother to their roles of paid employee and forever sexually attractive playmate.

10. So-called surrogate motherhood, or what should be called "contract pregnancy," cuts across procreation and adoption. A contract is made by the commissioning person (usually a man) to create a baby who will be adopted by the man's partner, usually but not always a woman.

11. Many "classic" works in feminist bioethics include sections on reproductive issues (e.g., Holmes and Purdy 1992; Sherwin 1992; Mahowald 1993; Callahan 1995; Tong 1997). I have also contributed two books on reproductive technologies (Overall 1987, 1993).

12. James Lenman suggests that the reason for this disconnect might be that "our ordinary motivation is not sufficiently moral—or it might be because so much of contemporary ethical theory is simply disconnected from the realities of human moral experience" (2004b, 147). I suspect the disconnect to which he refers may exist because so few women are writing about population ethics.

13. I am not enthusiastic about the development of ectogenesis. It would be potentially risky for the fetus, and it may well encourage contempt for and devaluing of women—the idea that the contingent problems of women's procreative capacities can be overcome by sterile and efficient science.

14. In this book, I use the terms *obligation, responsibility*, and *duty* interchangeably. Although in some contexts it may be worthwhile to assign them different meanings, such differences are not relevant to this project.

15. I have attempted to make this distinction as clear and straightforward as possible, but in fact I have had to ignore some of the complexities of this way of categorizing ethical arguments. In some respects, deontology and consequentialism are closely related, both generally in ethical theory and specifically in regard to the ethics of having children. As an example of the latter, consider a culture in which carrying on the male lineage is regarded as a good deontological reason for having children. Whether that claim is morally justified or not, the women of that culture will likely also experience pronatalist pressures to reproduce, the alleviation of which provides a consequentialist reason (whether sound or not) for procreating.

16. Cannold's subjects listed the following reasons for not having children: "the fear of and the desire to avoid the all-encompassing nature of maternal responsibility and commitment, the fact that children are hard work and women's work, an unwillingness to parent without either a (currently lacking) husband or family support, the desire to remain at the centre of and in control of their emotional and/or working lives and the irreversibility of the childbearing decision (i.e. the fear of being 'trapped')" (2003, 279).

Chapter 2

1. For a history of the development of the concept of reproductive rights, see Kates 2004.

2. How such services should be funded is a separate issue that I cannot explore here. Nonetheless, it seems plausible to me that if these services are part of the health-care system and especially if prospective patients are not wealthy, then the state should pay for them. (It is also often argued that public financing of IVF, in particular, will reduce the incidence of gestation of HOMs [triplets, quadruplets, and so on], and hence of all the medical problems [including blindness, cerebral palsy, and death] and resulting costs borne by the public that are associated with such infants [Barwin 2009] because if women do not have to pay for IVF themselves, then they will be less likely to expect that, to increase the odds of becoming pregnant, large numbers of fertilized eggs be implanted at each attempt but will be content with the implantation of only one or two at a time.)

3. In Canada, for example, the overall live birth rate with IVF is 27 percent per cycle (Bouzayen and Eggertson 2009, 243).

4. Another moral reason for rejecting commercial contract pregnancy is that it is the sale of babies (Overall 1993). However, I set this argument aside.

5. Philosopher Elisabeth Gedge has suggested that my position may compromise an analogous claim on behalf of a positive right to general health care (personal communication, June 19, 2008), and such an implication is morally problematic. However, there are always limits that must be placed on the availability of services, even if those services are essential to life itself. For example, a system of blood and organ donation is highly desirable, but no individual, no matter how needy, has a right to the use of the blood or organs from another person if the latter person does not want to donate them. If there is a system of blood and organ donation in which donors participate willingly, knowledgeably, and consensually, then a needy patient is of course entitled to be served by that system if he or she meets the criteria of medical eligibility. But the system cannot compel donors to participate, and there is not a right to the use of other persons' body parts.

6. Note, however, that I am *not* saying that women (or men, for that matter) are not entitled to set, as a condition for their participation in heterosexual sexual activity, the requirement that their partner use contraception. We are entitled to do so in order to protect (insofar as the effectiveness of contraception permits) our procreative future. In such cases, the use of contraception is not coerced: because each participating partner is entitled to say "no" to the sexual activity if he or she does not want to use contraception, there is no compulsion.

7. In this book, I do not discuss the general arguments for and against the justification of abortion. First, there is a huge body of literature about the abortion issue, so attempting to summarize it here would take me too far from my original topic. Second, I think the question whether to abort an embryo or fetus that has already come into existence is different from the question primarily at issue in this book, which is whether to conceive that embryo or fetus in the first place. How-

ever, in chapter 7 I make a few comments about the possibility that there may be an obligation to *have* an abortion.

Chapter 3

I am grateful to the audiences at the University of Western Ontario Colloquium Series, October 24, 2008, and the Queen's University Department of Philosophy Colloquium Series, March 26, 2009, for their interesting and intensely challenging feedback on this chapter. I also thank Kassy Wayne for her comments.

1. For an early description of this issue, see Levy 1980.

2. What I have to say here does not, however, deal with the situation of two male partners—not because that situation does not raise interesting questions, but because I am focusing on cases in which one of the two persons is the actual gestator of the prospective offspring.

3. Questions have been raised (indeed, I have contributed to the discussion) about whether respect for women's reproductive freedom requires the death of the fetus (e.g., Ross 1982; Overall 1987; Mackenzie 1992; Reader 2008). This issue is sufficiently complex that it cannot be discussed here.

4. An early discussion of this issue can be found in a paper by Wesley Teo (1975), who argues that husbands have constitutionally recognized rights in an abortion decision. I do not discuss his work because his claim is rooted primarily in American law rather than in moral theory and because Laura Purdy (1976) convincingly sets forth the many errors in his arguments.

5. One wonders why some male philosophers are so worried about women who become pregnant by deceit. One must be careful not to suppose that this occurrence is frequent, standard, or normal. Ho and Hubin's concerns about deceptive women remind me of some men's equally overwrought fears about women who supposedly lie about having been raped or sexually assaulted.

6. A partially related case is where sperm is removed from a man's body shortly after his death and used to inseminate the man's female partner (Bard 2006, 154). The moral question in this case is thought to revolve around consent: whether and when it occurred, whether it was freely and competently given, and what was consented to.

7. Male pregnancy has been suggested as another imaginable option. Even if possible, it would encounter the same problems as those I describe for ectogenesis.

8. Thanks to Sue Donaldson for drawing my attention to this issue.

9. The following thought experiment has been suggested to me: Suppose a woman becomes pregnant and seeks an abortion. A physician performs the abortion but keeps the fetus alive and then subsequently reimplants it, either in an artificial uterus or in the uterus of a different woman, and the child comes to term. In effect, this would be a case of a "purloined fetus." The question is whether the original woman is then financially responsible for the child. Consistency seems to require that I say yes. However, it is also important to remember that there is a huge material difference between the man in the purloined sperm case and the

woman having the abortion. The former is presumably conscious throughout the activity and is in control of it—he can end the sexual activity if he chooses and can dispose of the used condom. The latter may not be conscious or fully conscious; to that extent, she is disadvantaged vis-à-vis responsibility for what happens to her body and her fetus, and she has no way of stopping the abortion partway through.

10. It is better for men both because men were once children and because men, as human beings, have needs to be close to other persons, including their own children. They might well regret any hasty decision to abandon the children they have fathered.

11. But suppose the woman completes the pregnancy and then decides that she cannot or does not want to rear the child? Is the decision about adoption hers alone to make? If the inseminator has no interest in helping to rear the child, then he cannot prevent her from putting the child up for adoption. If, however, the inseminator is committed to being involved in the child's life in the role of father and not just in the role of financial support, then the adoption decision arguably should be different (cf. Brake 2005, 63). If the father is willing to rear the child on his own and demonstrates that willingness, I think he should be allowed to—even though I do not think that the woman has any obligation to sustain the pregnancy in the first place in order to give the baby to him. That is, provided he is competent, his wish to raise his child would trump her wish to have the child adopted by a stranger. But if the inseminator is committed only to financial support and nothing more, he should not be able to prevent the mother from putting the child up for adoption if that is what she needs or wants to do.

12. See Shanley 1999 for discussion of the situation in which a mother and an "unwed father" disagree about whether to surrender an infant for adoption.

13. Kassy Wayne has pointed out to me that Manninen's "virtuous" woman is reminiscent of what Judith Jarvis Thompson says about women who are refused abortions: that such women are required to be Good Samaritans (or more than good) to the fetuses they carry (personal communication, March 2009).

14. It may be as important or more important to note that the power involved in pregnancy is power over the fetus and ultimately the infant insofar as what happens during pregnancy strongly influences the infant's health.

15. Manninen also says that a woman is acting nonvirtuously if she uses obtaining an abortion as a method of revenge against the inseminator (2007, 13).

16. An unwanted pregnancy may be experienced very differently than a wanted pregnancy (Lundquist 2008).

17. I also set aside the prospective social policy issues raised by ectogenesis, such as whether it should be available; to whom it should be available; whether it should be included within a socialized health-care system; and whether it is worth funding and promoting compared to all our other competing health-care needs.

18. I suppose another alternative is to remove ova from female aborted fetuses, but such a process raises a number of issues about the source of, authority over, and treatment of fetuses that I cannot examine here. In any case, there still remains the general problematic issue: How would the fetuses be obtained?

19. As far as I can see, the only way that ectogenesis might be a neutral process as between two progenitors would be if it were possible to create a fetus using two ova. In such a situation, if it were possible, each of the two ovum providers would have exactly the same physical "investment" in the fetus and therefore exactly the same authority to determine whether the fetus continues to be gestated within an artificial uterus.

20. There are, of course, limits on bodily autonomy, and those limits are defined in part by the effects that the expression of our bodily autonomy may have on other persons. Thus, for example, bodily autonomy is not a defense for a gestator's deliberately harming her fetus if she intends to bring the fetus to term. As Catriona Mackenzie suggests, "In pregnancy the assumption of parental responsibility necessarily involves a certain commitment of one's body. In other words, the decision to continue a pregnancy . . . is a decision to assume responsibility (even if only for nine months) for the well-being of the foetus and this entails providing bodily nurture for it, perhaps even at some bodily risk to yourself" (1992, 146). The reason for the assumption of this responsibility is that harming the person whom the fetus will become is wrong.

21. It might be suggested that the inseminator should be responsible for the costs of extrauterine gestation. If acted upon, this approach would ensure, for good or ill, that the ectogenesis solution to the problem of disagreement between gestator and inseminator would be available only to the wealthy few.

22. Indeed, there are many complex questions about which fetuses, if any, should be saved and on what grounds (Bard 2006, 154–155).

Chapter 4

1. See, for example, Gould 2002.

2. People still tend to call reproductive technologies "new," but given that the first successful use of IVF was in 1978, in this fast-moving time they no longer qualify as "new."

3. The potential pressure to be a replica, by the way, may be part of what is wrong with cloning. I am not rabidly anticloning; I don't think it is as radical a process as some people believe, but I do think it might be bad for the children because of the pressure of expectation that the child will be just like the individual from whom he or she was cloned.

4. The pressure to perpetuate the family is also ageist if the (usually male) firstborn is considered most important and has the privilege of inheritance and (in the case of royalty and nobility) carrying on the title.

5. There is not much danger that most nations will run out of productive citizens. Even people sixty-five and older are not all mere dependents. The medical treatments, policy changes, lifestyle improvements, and technologies that enable people to live longer lives also permit them to remain in a healthy condition, with a reduced incidence of disability, for a longer period. We should not assume that old people do not and will not continue to work and pay taxes. Many of them also make a large contribution to society through their volunteer labor.

6. What if a woman were allowed to immigrate to a country only after her agreement to have children there? This agreement once again creates some prima facie responsibility, but it is countered by the fact that it might be bad for the child if it is born simply as a means to fulfill a contract.

Chapter 5

I am grateful to Chris Lowry, Queen's University, for his thoughtful and inspiring comments on an early draft of this chapter and to the audience at the Fourteenth International Association of Women Philosophers Symposium, "Feminism, Science, and Values," University of Western Ontario, London, Ontario, June 25, 2010, where an early version of part of this chapter was presented.

1. I return in chapter 6 to the idea that there is an obligation to avoid bringing suffering people into existence.

2. The debate is exemplified, to take just one example, by an anthology suitably titled *The Repugnant Conclusion* (Ryberg and Tännsjö 2004).

3. This point comes up again in chapter 7, when I discuss Julian Savulescu's claim that we have a moral obligation to maximize the quality of our children by employing genetic tests to select the "best possible" child (2001, 415).

4. It may also be a point of personal honor for this woman to raise any babies that she does create; hence, she cannot countenance any alternative that involves birthing babies and giving them away.

5. If the point is simply that disease-free existence is valuable for its own sake or inevitably better than a life with disease (both of which assumptions are dubious), then we seem to be approaching a kind of modified Repugnant Conclusion in which women would have an obligation to create as many children as they possibly can, provided the children are not ill. I have already pointed out the fallacies of this type of argument.

6. Will the parents then go on to have yet another child in the hope that it will be the right one? The moral problems are then reiterated.

7. Thanks to Tabitha Bernard for alerting me to information about the effects of early cord clamping.

8. Sheldon and Wilkinson believe that opponents of creating savior siblings worry about a slippery slope leading to "designer babies"—infants selected through PGD on the basis of hair and eye color (2004, 534). "Designer babies" are different from savior siblings in that the latter are created to be used as a medical resource. Whether selecting babies on the basis of appearance (or other characteristics such as intelligence or athletic ability) is morally justified is a separate issue. It is morally troubling in its own right, as I show in chapter 7.

9. It has also been suggested to me that there might be medical reasons for having a child that would benefit the would-be mother. For example, it's been speculated that some women might become pregnant as a way to improve their own health—if, for example, they believe that breastfeeding reduces one's risks of breast cancer or that it puts multiple sclerosis into remission. This plan is not as bad as having a

savior sibling because the child born to reduce its mother's cancer risks is presumably not subjected to further medical use after birth. But it is nevertheless still a scheme that uses a child primarily as a means.

10. Mianna Lotz, for example, raises the worry that a savior sibling will come to see his own value as entirely instrumental regardless of whether his parents see him in that way. He may interpret his creation as "entirely conditional upon his possession of particular attributes or a capacity to fulfil predetermined and designated roles and expectations. . . . This may lead to feelings of subordination and inferiority" (2008a, 299).

Chapter 6

I am grateful to Jackie Davies, Department of Philosophy, Queen's University, for her commentary on an earlier version of this chapter at the Queen's University Department of Philosophy Colloquium Series, February 14, 2008. I am also grateful for extensive comments from Sue Donaldson, Adèle Mercier, and the rest of the audience. Thank you also to the audience at the conference "Bearing and Rearing Children: The Ethics of Procreation and Parenthood," University of Cape Town, South Africa, May 28, 2008, and especially to David Benatar for his comments.

1. Thank you to Narnia Worth for drawing this article to my attention.

2. I am grateful to Adèle Mercier for alerting me to this article.

3. That is the very advice that philosopher Matti Häyry also gives to would-be parents: because the individual whom we create might have a bad life, and because it is rational "to avoid the possible negative outcome, when the alternative is zero," it is rational to choose not to have children (2004, 377).

4. The underlying assumption of this book is agnosticism with respect to the existence of God. Here I am using the idea that God exists only as a device to enable the thought experiment.

5. Adèle Mercier pointed out to me a troubling implication here: if the absence of bad is good, then under every single actual and possible condition, there is an infinite amount of bad, constituted by the absence of all the good that might but does not exist. (Equally, of course, there is also an infinite amount of good, constituted by all the bad that might but does not exist.)

6. In his introduction to his edited anthology *Life, Death, and Meaning*, Benatar writes, "To say that *coming* into existence is always a harm does not entail that death—*ceasing* to exist—is always better than *continuing* to exist. One can claim consistently that it would be better not to come into existence, but, all things being equal, that it is nonetheless bad, once one has started to exist, to cease to exist" (2004a, 10, his emphasis). This type of principle obviously does not hold in other contexts. For example, would we say that a party is so dull and boring that it's a bad idea to go to it, but, once there, the dullness and boredom are not sufficient to warrant leaving? Would we say that it's bad to become a bureaucrat, but having become one, the compelling reasons not to become a bureaucrat aren't necessarily strong enough to justify quitting? I'm not convinced. In these cases,

it would seem that the reasons for not going or not becoming, as the case may be, are also strong enough to justify leaving or quitting. Yet Benatar assumes that "the view that death is a harm to the one who dies is not an unreasonable view" (2006, 196). That is, even though, according to him, it is always a harm to come into existence, it is not automatically a benefit to end one's existence. But based on the preceding analogies to the party and the bureaucrat, we might wonder whether his theory suggests rather strongly that suicide is almost always a good thing, despite his denials (2006, 212–213).

7. It is genuinely possible to regret the nonexistence of certain people. Thus, an impoverished mother might regret that she did not have the time or resources to have a second child. A father might regret that his son never had children of his own.

8. What might Benatar say if human beings were immortal? Immortality presumably would not, from his standpoint, make existence better than nonexistence. As far as I can tell, only if we were invulnerable to pain or suffering of any kind might Benatar's argument not (in his view) be justified.

9. In some cases, they can also have meaning by reference to other animals that are sentient but are not persons. But I stress the person-referring meaning here because, although Benatar is willing to apply "better never to have been" to sentient nonpersons, he is most concerned with persons.

10. Benatar's theory is reminiscent of the ontological argument for the existence of God, but he attributes the opposite valence to existence. The ontological argument suggests that a being that is omniscient, omnipotent, and all good is very great, but that being would be even better if it also existed. In the ontological argument, existence is a property that adds value to an entity. In Benatar's theory, existence is a property that subtracts value from (sentient) entities.

11. Benatar seems surprised that within almost every country the poor are just about as happy as the rich. The implication appears to be that they are irrational. Is he saying that because poor people have much less money than the rich, they should be miserable? On the contrary, it may be entirely rational to make the best of difficult circumstances if it is impossible to change them.

12. I am not advocating that people in effect should take a happiness pill and distance themselves entirely from reality. I am not advocating false beliefs across the board, for, among other reasons, such beliefs may make one's life go worse. Instead, in the case of the subjective quality of one's life, it is evident that one's life is often better if one focuses on the good than if one focuses on the bad. That is, there is a genuine benefit from making a positive present-time assessment about one's life.

13. Benatar concedes that "some people do enjoy the process of fulfilling some desires" (2006, 78).

14. I owe most of the argument, up to the end of criticism 3, to Matthew Kersten, a student in Philosophy 204 at Queen's University in fall 2009. He communicated his arguments to me in an email message dated November 16, 2009. I am grateful to Matt for his permission to use his arguments here.

15. I'm grateful to Matthew Kersten and Rian Dewji, also an undergraduate student in Philosophy 204 in fall 2009, for the inspiration for this analogy.

16. I return in chapter 7 to the idea that there is an obligation to avoid bringing suffering people into existence. For now, I want to concentrate on the idea that there is no obligation to create happy people.

17. A major example of this obliviousness is Benatar's chapter on abortion, which makes no reference to arguments in favor of abortion access that are based on women's entitlement to make decisions about their own bodies, arguments that would obviate the need for discussions of the status of fetus, on which Benatar focuses.

18. Consider the following quotation: "Whether or not one reproduces can have a profound impact on the character and quality of one's life. . . . It can affect the quality of one's sense of self. (For example, some people feel inadequate if they are unable to produce children of their genetic own)" (Benatar 2006, 104).

19. In an oral response to an earlier version of this argument, Benatar claimed that his thesis would "liberate women" because they would no longer be expected to reproduce. However, there is a difference between respecting women's reproductive freedom and telling women that they need not and even should not reproduce because all the results of their reproduction are bad.

Chapter 7

1. Maier herself regrettably failed to live up to this responsibility and has had two hapless offspring, now in their teens.

2. Two of Parker's criticisms are that it is impossible to rank embryos with respect to their chances of the best life possible and that the best possible life cannot be "lived by a person with no flaws of character or biology" (2007, 281–282). Savulescu answers these criticisms in Savulescu 2007 and in Savulescu and Kahane 2009.

3. Savulescu and Kahane also mention the possible use of prenatal diagnosis, followed in some cases by abortion (2009, 275), but I focus on the use of PGD and IVF.

4. Savulescu oddly writes, "I understand morality to require us to do what we have most reason to do" (2001, 415). Such a capacious understanding of morality will make far more actions *morally required* than common sense would ordinarily accept. I have "most reason" to turn on both lights in my office rather than just one. But surely I do not have a moral obligation to do so.

5. Thanks to Herissa Chan for pointing out this issue.

6. Then there are the social costs: providing IVF and PGD to all women who procreate would undoubtedly require a huge investment of resources, medical expertise, time, and technology, most of which are completely unnecessary to ordinary procreation.

7. A case can be made that Suleman's obligation not to procreate also rested on the needs and well-being of the six children she already had, at least one of whom

has impairments. Because she has scant material resources and only her two aging parents to count on, her decision to have additional children looks irrational as well as immoral.

Chapter 8

I am grateful to the audience at the Fourteenth International Association of Women Philosophers Symposium, "Feminism, Science, and Values," University of Western Ontario, London, Ontario, June 25, 2010, where an early version of part of this chapter was presented.

1. This solution is similar to Elizabeth Harman's solution to the Non-Identity Problem, although she retains Parfit's genetic version of identity: if the mother has an alternative action in which she provides parallel benefits (the creation of a life that will be reasonably good) without parallel harms (such as injury from the mother's drug use), then the action that causes the harm is wrong, even if the identity of the resulting offspring is dependent on it (2004, 95).

2. This claim about what pregnant women ought to do during pregnancy is not the same as the slippery-slope requirements of complying with the PPB (discussed in chapter 7), in which the woman would have to engage in extreme self-sacrifice in order to produce the best child possible. Instead, I am advocating behavior that is good for the fetus and good for the pregnant woman herself.

3. Julian Savulescu and Guy Kahane note that if at least some parents act on the PPB, they may eventually have children who are "far more intelligent, empathetic or healthier than existing people." "In comparison to such possible future persons, most existing persons may count as suffering from disability" (2009, 290).

4. I think Jack's circumstances are like those of many people with Down syndrome who live in a supportive environment.

5. As I show in chapter 10, the formation of a relationship is a profound and morally valuable reason for choosing to have a child.

6. However, I also believe that when women have a choice, they are entirely justified in aborting fetuses with potential physical or cognitive impairments. They are obviously justified when it is known that the future child will suffer, but there are several other reasons that can also make abortion for fetal impairment the right choice. First, in some cases one cannot know ahead of time whether a particular impairment or set of impairments will cause suffering and whether they will be a misfortune for the person who has them. Given these unknowns, potential mothers are entitled to be cautious with respect to their procreative behavior. The responsibility of nonmaleficence mandates procreative precaution. Second, women who choose to abort a fetus with potential physical or cognitive impairments have the right to make the judgment as to whether they, along with the rest of their family, are capable of raising a child with impairments, for a child with impairments may have care, development, and medical needs that demand great courage, strength, and sacrifices so that he will not suffer and will have a happy and fulfilled life. The mother is more likely than any other to be the one who cares for the child, and she is entitled to decide that she cannot and will not do it.

Chapter 9

I am grateful to Chris Lowry for his helpful comments on parts of this chapter. I am also appreciative of the students in my Queen's University Philosophy 204 course, "Life, Death, and Meaning," especially those in the fall 2007 class, for pushing me to rethink my ideas about the extinction of the human race.

1. My thanks to Narnia Worth and Michael Ashton for suggesting Dawkins's book to me.

2. As I have argued elsewhere (Overall 2003), it is unjust to seek population control by expecting aging persons to step aside and abandon their lives to make room for more human beings. The obvious reason is that they themselves are persons, and they already exist. It is immoral to expect them to deprive themselves prematurely of their own existence. In contrast, when we consider procreation, we are contemplating people who do not yet exist; so no beings will be deprived of existence if we make a moral commitment to limit procreation.

3. Scott Wisor states a less extreme version of the argument: "Since having more children will likely cause more environmental destruction and having fewer children will likely reduce contributions to environmental destruction, individuals ought to limit family size for environmental reasons" (2009, 27).

4. I am not speaking here of laws to compel people not to procreate. I think such laws would be both unenforceable and unconscionable. What I am considering is the possibility that we can legitimately say that people in developed nations have *moral* responsibilities to limit their procreation because of the global dangers of overpopulation to all of us.

5. It is a separate practical and moral question how a single man or a pair of men would go about having children. I am not hereby condoning commercial contract motherhood, which I think is morally problematic (Overall 1987, 1993). I am, however, reiterating the point from chapter 7 that neither one's sex/gender nor one's sexual orientation make it morally impermissible to have a child.

6. Of course, those with sufficient wealth and connections may also use sex selection and sex preselection to try to ensure that they get the desired sex/gender in their offspring on their first try. I do not endorse these methods, nor do I think that a desire for a child of a particular sex/gender is easy to justify. I think it's better for children and parents if the parents are accepting of and pleased about the kinds of children they end up with. Even worse are those parents who keep "trying" for a child of the right sex/gender and end up with, say, four girls before finally landing the much-desired son.

7. I set aside criticisms of the idea that limiting one's procreation is a type of consumer activism, although it appears to assume unwisely that children are consumer products.

8. The exception may be their youngest child, number 19, Josie Brooklyn, who was born four months premature, in December 2009, and weighed only one pound six ounces (Duggar and Duggar 2011).

9. However, the large family may victimize the children or at least the daughters because they are expected to raise their own siblings and to marry young, with no education beyond their limited "home schooling." Moreover, it is possible that women with less freedom and access to the outside world than Michelle Duggar may have little choice (given their fundamentalist beliefs, their embeddedness in a religious culture with a commitment to complete male power, and their lack of access to contraception and abortion) about how many children to have and may have no opportunity to learn ways of thinking that might lead them to question their submissive position.

10. Lonnie Aarssen makes a similar prediction, at least for the long term: "We can expect that the males and females who leave the most descendents in the long-term future will necessarily be those with the strongest parenting drive (2007, 1775). Compare David Benatar's comment: "Those with reproduction-enhancing beliefs are more likely to breed and pass on whatever attributes incline one to such beliefs" (2006, 205).

11. Of course, although individual choice is the focus of this book, truly global change cannot happen only through changes in individual behavior. It must be supported by national and global efforts to reduce poverty, lower infant and maternal mortality, eliminate hunger and illiteracy, increase education and employment, and drastically reduce nonsustainable industry and agriculture.

12. With a 2008 fertility rate of 1.4, Russia's population is projected to decline from 140 million in 2009 to 128.5 million in 2025 and 109.4 million in 2050 ("Russia's Demographic Profile" 2010).

13. Note that this claim is different from the idea critiqued in chapter 4, that *bearing children* is intrinsically worthwhile.

14. Even so, there are limits to how far this principle should be taken. Respect for members of the human species should not, for example, rule out abortion, although I do not have room here to argue for this claim.

15. Despite his skepticism, Lenman mentions one positive argument indicating that human extinction would be bad: he suggests the possibility that our *premature* extinction at least might be bad if it cuts off the human narrative before it has run its course, perhaps while human beings are, so to speak, only in their species childhood (2004b, 141). The question, then, is whether there is any such species-encompassing narrative and, even if there is, how we might discern it (and thus decide when it is complete and extinction no longer bad). We have no knowledge of a grand, overarching purpose toward which our species is moving; in the absence of a religious framework and a God who is involved in human life, it is hard to see how there can be one. We do not know whether we are in the childhood, the adolescence, the early adulthood, the middle adulthood, or the late adulthood of our species. We also do not know whether these life-stage concepts even apply to the trajectory of the human species.

16. Mautner is insouciant about this kind of problem. He says, for example, that we need not worry about fouling the universe as we spread throughout it: "Seeding other planetary systems could prevent the study of pristine space but seeding

a few hundred new solar systems will secure and propagate life while leaving hundreds of billions of pristine stars for exploration" (2009, 437).

17. For some reason, certain other philosophers who have written on these issues are rather less impressed than I am by the vast possibilities of a seemingly limitless universe. Leslie, for example, writes that human beings might be unique: "Humans could easily be the only intelligent living beings who would ever have evolved in our galaxy, or in all the galaxies observable by our telescopes" (1996, 178). And Mautner, despite his belief in hundreds of billions of stars, not only agrees that human beings might be the only intelligent life but also says that our planet might be the only site of any life at all in the entire universe (2009, 437).

18. As noted in previous chapters, many who write on this issue blithely overlook this drawback to morally obligated procreation. Torbjörn Tännsjö, for example, goes so far as to remark that if the universe (rather implausibly) turns out to be empty of intelligent beings other than those on Earth, then "no sacrifice will seem too hard" to colonize as much of the universe as we can (2004, 232).

Chapter 10

1. Bennett also thinks implausibly that unless a life is not worth living, "it will always be in [the] child's interests to be brought into being" because "it is, after all, that child's only chance of existence" (2004, 379). As I have shown in previous chapters, she's wrong about this. Many of our lives are indeed worth living, but unless individuals enjoy some sort of ethereal preconceptual existence, it cannot be in their interest to come into existence; they have no interests before they come into existence.

2. The concept of unconditional love is related to the Christian tradition of turning the other cheek. The Book of Matthew in the New Testament exhorts the reader to "love your enemies, bless them that curse you, do good to them that hate you, and pray for them which despitefully use you, and persecute you" (5:44).

3. Maybe that's why some people are attracted only to babies: as a child becomes autonomous and develops a mind of his own, he must be seen as an independent person, not simply an object to be enveloped in unconditional love.

4. The parent loves the whole child, and of course who he is will include faults and weaknesses in addition to endearing qualities. But if a dearly loved child somehow grows up to become a vicious batterer, an unrepentant rapist, an unfeeling terrorist, or a serial murderer—an identity quite inconsistent with who he previously was—no parent should be expected to love him still. A parent who abuses or exploits his child should similarly not expect his offspring to continue to love him. People are responsible for what they do, and if what they do is consistently cruel and vicious, then there is not much to love in them.

5. Perhaps "loving children" in general is as morally suspect as "loving" any other group of people would be. We do not speak of "loving" people with blue eyes, people who are left-handed, or people who are six feet tall. The idea of loving an entire subset of humanity just because they are very young is uncomfortably akin

to loving kittens. Love is for a particular person, not for the entire group to which the person belongs.

6. Lenman concedes the charge of selfishness but makes a further statement about it: "The desire to have children is a selfish sort of sentiment, to be sure, but in a peculiar and complicated way. Partly it is a matter of wanting there to be a constituency for that range of our moral and altruistic instincts that we bring to bear on our immediate successors." Procreation is the expression of "a desire that there be objects for certain central other-regarding emotions to engage with and a desire both to have certain projects and commitments that transcend the limits of one's own lifetime's efforts and to have those projects and commitments flourish" (2004b, 144, 146). I believe that Lenman's somewhat ponderous statement fails to capture what is at the heart of the parent-child relationship. Prospective parents probably do not and ought not to think, "I want to have a child so that I can have a focus for my altruism and my other-regarding emotions."

References

Aarssen, Lonnie W. 2007. Some Bold Evolutionary Predictions for the Future of Mating in Humans. *OIKOS: Synthesizing Ecology* 116 (10): 1768–1778.

Aksoy, S[ahin]. 2004. Response to: A Rational Cure for Pre-Reproductive Stress Syndrome. *Journal of Medical Ethics* 30: 382–383.

Allen, Jeffner. 1983. Motherhood: The Annihilation of Women. In *Mothering: Essays in Feminist Theory*, ed. Joyce Trebilcot, 315–330. Totowa, NJ: Rowman & Allanheld.

American Society of Clinical Oncology. n.d. Donating Bone Marrow. http://www. asco.org/portal/site/patient/menuitem.169f5d85214941ccfd748f68ee37a01d/?vg nextoid=ac9b04a3c5982110VgnVCM100000ed730ad1RCRD&vgnextchannel =95d5bf8f21e3a010VgnVCM100000f2730ad1RCRD.

Ariès, Philippe. 1962. *Centuries of Childhood: A Social History of Family Life*. Trans. Robert Baldick. New York: Vintage Books.

Bard, Jennifer S. 2006. Immaculate Gestation? How Will Ectogenesis Change Current Paradigms of Social Relationships and Values? In *Ectogenesis: Artificial Womb Technology and the Future of Human Reproduction*, ed. Scott Gelfand and John R. Shook, 149–157. New York: Rodopi.

Barker, David. n.d. The Barker Theory: New Insights into Ending Chronic Disease. http://www.thebarkertheory.org/science.php.

Barwin, Norman. 2009. A Private Issue in Need of a Public Solution. *The Globe and Mail*, May 21, IC2.

Bayles, Michael D. 1979. Limits to a Right to Procreate. In *Having Children: Philosophical and Legal Reflections on Parenthood*, ed. Onora O'Neill and William Ruddick, 13–24. New York: Oxford University Press.

Benatar, David. 2004a. Introduction. In *Life, Death, and Meaning: Key Philosophical Readings on the Big Questions*, ed. David Benatar, 1–16. Lanham, MD: Rowman & Littlefield.

Benatar, David. [1997] 2004b. Why It Is Better Never to Come into Existence. In *Life, Death, and Meaning: Key Philosophical Readings on the Big Questions*, ed. David Benatar, 155–168. Lanham, MD: Rowman & Littlefield.

Benatar, David. 2006. *Better Never to Have Been: The Harm of Coming into Existence*. Oxford, UK: Clarendon Press.

Bennett, R[ebecca]. 2004. Human Reproduction: Irrational but in Most Cases Morally Defensible. *Journal of Medical Ethics* 30: 379–380.

Bennett, Rebecca. 2008. The Fallacy of the Principle of Procreative Beneficence. *Bioethics* 23 (5): 265–273.

Bergum, Vangie. 1997. *A Child on Her Mind: The Experience of Becoming a Mother*. Westport, CT: Bergin & Garvey.

Bouzayen, Renda, and Laura Eggertson. 2009. In Vitro Fertilization: A Private Matter Becomes Public. *Canadian Medical Association Journal* 181 (5) (September 1): 243.

Bova, Ben. 1998. *Immortality: How Science Is Extending Your Life Span—and Changing the World*. New York: Avon Books.

Bowe, John. 2009. The Octomom and Her Babies Prepare for Prime Time. *New York Times Magazine,* November 12. http://www.nytimes.com.

Boyle, Robert J., and Julian Savulescu. 2001. Ethics of Using Preimplantation Genetic Diagnosis to Select a Stem Cell Donor for an Existing Person. *British Medical Journal* 323 (November 24): 1240–1243.

Brake, Elizabeth. 2005. Fatherhood and Child Support: Do Men Have a Right to Choose? *Journal of Applied Philosophy* 22 (1): 55–73.

Callahan, Joan C., ed. 1995. *Reproduction, Ethics, and the Law: Feminist Perspectives*. Bloomington: Indiana University Press.

Cannold, Leslie. 2003. Do We Need a Normative Account of the Decision to Parent? *International Journal of Applied Philosophy* 17 (2): 277–290.

Caplan, Bryan. 2010. The Breeders' Cup: The Case for Having More Kids. *Wall Street Journal*, June 19. http://online.wsj.com/article/SB10001424052748704289 504575313201221533826.html.

Card, Claudia. 1996. Against Marriage and Motherhood. *Hypatia* 11 (3): 1–23.

Casey, Maud. 2006. The Rise from the Earth (so Far). In *Maybe Baby: 28 Writers Tell the Truth about Skepticism, Infertility, Baby Lust, Childlessness, Ambivalence, and How They Made the Biggest Decision of Their Lives*, ed. Lori Leibovich, 66–75. New York: HarperCollins.

Cassidy, Lisa. 2006. That Many of Us Should Not Parent. *Hypatia* 21 (4): 40–57.

Children's Hospital Boston. n.d. Bone Marrow Transplant. http://www.children shospital.org/az/Site2169/mainpageS2169P0.html.

Davies, Jacqueline. 2008. Better to Affirm Life? Some Remarks on Christine Overall's "*Not* 'Better Never to Have Been.'" Commentary presented at the Queen's University Department of Philosophy Colloquium Series, February 14.

Dawkins, Richard. 1989. *The Selfish Gene*. Oxford, UK: Oxford University Press.

DeVille, Kenneth. 1997. Adolescent Parents and Medical Decision-Making. *Journal of Medicine and Philosophy* 22: 253–270.

Devolder, Katrien. 2005. Preimplantation HLA Typing: Having Children to Save Our Loved Ones. *Journal of Medical Ethics* 31: 582–586.

Donaldson, Susan. 2000. Boycotting Motherhood. Unpublished paper.

Duggar, Jim Bob, and Michelle Duggar. 2011. The Duggar Family. http://www. duggarfamily.com.

Ebenstein, Avraham. 2010. The "Missing Girls" of China and the Unintended Consequences of the One Child Policy. *Journal of Human Resources* 45 (1): 87–115.

Fertile, Candace. 2006. Alien Invasion. In *Nobody's Mother: Life Without Kids*, ed. Lynne van Luven, 181–188. Victoria, Australia: Touch Wood Editions.

Firestone, Shulamith. 1970. *The Dialectic of Sex: The Case for Feminist Revolution*. New York: Bantam Books.

Floyd, S. L., and D. Pomerantz. 2004. Is There a Natural Right to Have Children? In *Should Parents Be Licensed? Debating the Issues*, ed. Peg Tittle, 230–232. Amherst, NY: Prometheus Books.

Frankena, William K., and John T. Granrose, eds. 1974. *Introductory Readings in Ethics*. Englewood Cliffs, NJ: Prentice-Hall.

Gartrell, Nanette, and Henny Bos. 2010. US National Longitudinal Lesbian Family Study: Psychological Adjustment of 17-Year-Old Adolescents. *Pediatrics* 126 (10): 28–36.

Gibbs, Nancy. 2006. A Man's Right to Choose? *Time*, March 15. http://www. time.com/time/nation/article/0,8599,1173414,00.html.

Gibson, Susanne. 1995. Reasons for Having Children: Ends, Means, and "Family Values." *Journal of Applied Philosophy* 12 (3): 231–240.

Gilbert, Daniel. 2005. *Stumbling on Happiness*. New York: Vintage Books.

Gimenez, Martha E. 1983. Feminism, Pronatalism, and Motherhood. In *Mothering: Essays in Feminist Theory*, ed. Joyce Trebilcot, 287–314. Totowa, NJ: Rowman & Allanheld.

Grosholz, Emily. 2009. Letter to the editor. *Chronicle of Higher Education*, September 4, A55.

Gould, Steven Jay. 2002. Carrie Buck's Daughter. *Natural History* 111 (6): 12–16.

Guillebaud, John, and Pip Hayes. 2008. Population Growth and Climate Change. *British Medical Journal* 337: a576.

Hales, Steven D. 1996a. Abortion and Fathers' Rights. In *Reproduction, Technology, and Rights*, ed. James M. Humber and Robert F. Almeder, 5–26. Totowa, NJ: Humana Press.

Hales, Steven D. 1996b. More on Fathers' Rights. In *Reproduction, Technology, and Rights*, ed. James M. Humber and Robert F. Almeder, 43–49. Totowa, NJ: Humana Press.

Hanck, Beverly. 2009. Canada Needs More Babies. *Globe and Mail,* May 16, IC2.

Hannan, Sarah, and Richard Vernon. 2008. Parental Rights: A Role-Based Approach. *Theory and Research in Education* 6 (2): 173–189.

Harman, Elizabeth. 2004. Can We Harm and Benefit in Creating? *Nous-Supplement: Philosophical Perspectives* 18: 89–113.

Harris, George W. 1986. Fathers and Fetuses. *Ethics* 96 (3): 594–603.

Harris, John. 2007. *Enhancing Evolution: The Ethical Case for Making Better People*. Princeton, NJ: Princeton University Press.

Häyry, M[atti]. 2004. A Rational Cure for Prereproductive Stress Syndrome. *Journal of Medical Ethics* 30: 377–378.

Ho, Dien. 2006. Leaving People Alone: Liberalism, Ectogenesis, and the Limits of Medicine. In *Ectogenesis: Artificial Womb Technology and the Future of Human Reproduction*, ed. Scott Gelfand and John R. Shook, 139–147. New York: Rodopi.

Ho, Dien. 2008. How Unilateral Abortion Rights Helps [*sic*] Identify the Limits of Procreative Autonomy. Paper presented at the conference "Bearing and Rearing Children: The Ethics of Procreation and Parenthood," University of Cape Town, Cape Town, South Africa, May 27.

Hollingworth, Leta S. 1916. Social Devices for Impelling Women to Bear and Rear Children. *American Journal of Sociology* 22 (1): 19–29.

Holmes, Helen Bequaert, and Laura Purdy, eds. 1992. *Feminist Perspectives in Medical Ethics*. Bloomington: Indiana University Press.

Horrobin, Steven. 2007. Natural Processes: On the Nature of Aging, Persons, and the Value of Life Extension. Paper presented at the Second International Workshop on the Extension of Life Span, San Raffaele University, Cesano Maderno, Italy, May 17.

Hubin, Don. 2008. Procreators' Duties. Paper presented at the conference "Bearing and Rearing Children: The Ethics of Procreation and Parenthood," University of Cape Town, Cape Town, South Africa, May 27.

Hursthouse, Rosalind. 1987. *Beginning Lives*. Oxford, UK: Blackwell.

Hutchinson, D. S. 1982. Utilitarianism and Children. *Canadian Journal of Philosophy* 12 (1): 61–73.

Hutchon, David J. R. 2006. Letter to the editor. Delayed Cord Clamping May Also Be Beneficial in Rich Settings. *British Medical Journal* 333 (November 18): 1073.

International Union for Conservation of Nature. 2009. Extinction Crisis Continues Apace. November 3. http://iucn.org/about/work/programmes/species/red_list/?4143/Extinction-crisis-continues-apace.

Kaposy, Chris. 2009. Coming into Existence: The Good, the Bad, and the Indifferent. *Human Studies* 32: 101–108.

Kates, Carol A. 2004. Reproductive Liberty and Overpopulation. *Environmental Values* 13: 51–79.

Kingston, Anne. 2009. No Kids, No Grief. *Maclean's* (August 3): 38–41.

Lamott, Anne. 2007. *Grace (Eventually): Thoughts on Faith*. New York: Riverhead Books.

Leibovich, Lori. 2006. Introduction. In *Maybe Baby: 28 Writers Tell the Truth about Skepticism, Infertility, Baby Lust, Childlessness, Ambivalence, and How They Made the Biggest Decision of Their Lives*, ed. Lori Leibovich, xiii–xvii. New York: HarperCollins.

Lenman, James. 2004a. Immortality: A Letter. In *Life, Death, and Meaning: Key Philosophical Readings on the Big Questions*, ed. David Benatar, 323–330. Lanham, MD: Rowman & Littlefield.

Lenman, James. 2004b. On Becoming Extinct. In *Life, Death, and Meaning: Key Philosophical Readings on the Big Questions*, ed. David Benatar, 135–153. Lanham, MD: Rowman & Littlefield.

Leslie, John. 1996. *The End of the World: The Science and Ethics of Human Extinction*. London: Routledge.

Levy, Steven R. 1980. Abortion and Dissenting Parents: A Dialogue. *Ethics* 90: 162–163.

Lotz, Mianna. 2008a. Procreative Reasons-Relevance: On the Moral Significance of *Why* We Have Children. *Bioethics* 23 (5): 291–299.

Lotz, Mianna. 2008b. Rethinking Procreative Motivations: Why It Matters *Why* We Have Children. Paper presented at the conference "Bearing and Rearing Children: The Ethics of Procreation and Parenthood," University of Cape Town, Cape Town, South Africa, May 27.

Lundquist, Caroline. 2008. Being Torn: Toward a Phenomenology of Unwanted Pregnancy. *Hypatia: A Journal of Feminist Philosophy* 23 (3): 136–155.

Mackenzie, Catriona. 1992. Abortion and Embodiment. *Australasian Journal of Philosophy* 70 (2): 136–155.

MacKinnon, Mark. 2009. China's Second Thoughts on the One-Child Policy. *The Globe and Mail*, August 22, A1, A12, A13.

Mahowald, Mary Briody. 1993. *Women and Children in Health Care: An Unequal Majority*. New York: Oxford University Press.

Maier, Corinne. 2007. *No Kids: Forty Good Reasons Not to Have Children*. Toronto: McClelland & Stewart.

Manninen, Bertha Alvarez. 2007. Pleading Men and Virtuous Women: Considering the Role of the Father in the Abortion Debate. *International Journal of Applied Philosophy* 21 (1): 1–24.

Mautner, Michael N. 2009. Life-Centered Ethics, and the Human Future in Space. *Bioethics* 23 (8): 433–440.

McLaren, Leah. 2010. Maybe Teen Mums Are on to Something. I'm Just Saying. *The Globe and Mail*, March 6, L3.

Meyers, Diana Tietjens. 2001. The Rush to Motherhood. *Signs: Journal of Women in Culture and Society* 26 (3): 735–773.

Mills, Claudia. 2005. Are There Morally Problematic Reasons for Having Children? *Philosophy and Public Policy Quarterly* 25 (4): 2–9.

Moriarty-Simmonds, Rosaleen. 2006. Just Crash through It. In *Defiant Birth: Women Who Resist Medical Eugenics*, ed. Melinda Tankard Reist, 239–257. North Melbourne, Australia: Spinifex.

Myers, David G. 2000. The Funds, Friends, and Faith of Happy People. *American Psychologist* 55 (1): 56–67.

Nedelsky, Jennifer. 1999. Dilemmas of Passion, Privilege, and Isolation: Reflections on Mothering in a White, Middle-Class Nuclear Family. In *Mother Troubles: Rethinking Contemporary Maternal Dilemmas*, ed. Julia Hanigsberg and Sara Ruddick, 304–334. Boston: Beacon Press.

Nichols, Peter. We'll Always Have Paris. In *Maybe Baby: 28 Writers Tell the Truth about Skepticism, Infertility, Baby Lust, Childlessness, Ambivalence, and How They Made the Biggest Decision of Their Lives*, ed. Lori Leibovich, 137–146. New York: HarperCollins.

Nickson, Elizabeth. 2006. Bags or Babies: Women Don't Have to Choose. *The Globe and Mail*, October 14, A21.

O'Neill, Onora. 1979. Begetting, Bearing, and Rearing. In *Having Children: Philosophical and Legal Reflections on Parenthood*, ed. Onora O'Neill and William Ruddick, 25–38. New York: Oxford University Press.

Orwin, Clifford. 2009. Go Ahead, Have Kids—the Patter of Little Feet Leaves Few Footprints. *The Globe and Mail*, August 11, A11.

Overall, Christine. 1987. *Ethics and Human Reproduction: A Feminist Analysis*. Boston: Allen & Unwin.

Overall, Christine. 1993. *Human Reproduction: Principles, Practices, Policies*. Toronto: Oxford University Press.

Overall, Christine. 2003. *Aging, Death, and Human Longevity: A Philosophical Inquiry*. Berkeley and Los Angeles: University of California Press.

Parfit, Derek. 1984. *Reasons and Persons*. Oxford, UK: Oxford University Press.

Parfit, Derek. 2004. Overpopulation and the Quality of Life. In *The Repugnant Conclusion: Essays on Population Ethics*, ed. Jesper Ryberg and Torbjörn Tännsjö, 7–15. Dordrecht, Netherlands: Kluwer Academic.

Parker, Michael. 2007. The Best Possible Child. *Journal of Medical Ethics* 33: 279–283.

Parks, Jennifer A. 1999. On the Use of IVF by Post-Menopausal Women. *Hypatia* 14 (1): 77–96.

Pascal, Blaise. [1662] 1966. *Pensées*. Harmondsworth, UK: Penguin Books.

Patel, Vishaal. 2007. Liquorice Jellybeans. Paper written for Philosophy 204, Queen's University, fall term.

Peck, Ellen, and Judith Senderowitz, eds. 1975. *Pronatalism: The Myth of Mom and Apple Pie*. New York: Thomas Y. Crowell.

Picoult, Jodi. 2004. *My Sister's Keeper*. New York: Washington Square Press.

Plato. 1941. *Euthyphro*. In *The Collected Dialogues of Plato*, ed. Edith Hamilton and Huntington Cairns, 169–185. New York: Pantheon Books.

Plotz, David. 2001. The Myths of the Nobel Sperm Bank. *Slate* (February 23). http://www.slate.com/id/101318.

Powdthavee, Nattavudh. 2009. Think Having Children Will Make You Happy? *Psychologist* 22 (4): 308–310.

Purdy, L[aura] M. 1976. Abortion and the Husband's Rights: A Reply to Wesley Teo. *Ethics* 86 (3): 247–251.

Purdy, Laura M. 2000. Loving Future People. In *Readings in Health Care Ethics*, ed. Elisabeth Boetzkes and Wilfrid J. Waluchow, 313–329. Peterborough, Canada: Broadview Press.

Purdy, Laura M. 2004. Can Having Children Be Immoral? In *Should Parents Be Licensed? Debating the Issues*, ed. Peg Tittle, 143–156. Amherst, NY: Prometheus Books.

Reader, Soren. 2008. Abortion, Killing, and Maternal Moral Authority. *Hypatia: A Journal of Feminist Philosophy* 23 (1): 132–149.

Reist, Melinda Tankard, ed. 2006. *Defiant Birth: Women Who Resist Medical Eugenics*. North Melbourne, Australia: Spinifex.

Richards, Norvin. 2010. Lives No One Should Have to Live. *Social Theory and Practice* 36 (3): 463–477.

Robertson, John A., Jeffrey P. Kahn, and John E. Wagner. 2002. Conception to Obtain Hematopoietic Stem Cells. *Hastings Center Report* 32 (3): 34–40.

Ross, Steven L. 1982. Abortion and the Death of the Fetus. *Philosophy and Public Affairs* 11 (3): 232–245.

Ruddick, Sara. 1993. Maternal Thinking. In *Women and Values: Readings in Recent Feminist Philosophy*, 2nd ed., ed. Marilyn Pearsall, 368–379. Belmont, CA: Wadsworth.

Russia's Demographic Profile. 2010. *The Chronicle Review*, February 14. http://chronicle.com/article/Russias-Demographic-Profile/64116.

Ryberg, Jesper, and Torbjörn Tännsjö, eds. 2004. *The Repugnant Conclusion: Essays on Population Ethics*. Dordrecht, Netherlands: Kluwer Academic.

Savulescu, Julian. 2001. Procreative Beneficence: Why We Should Select the Best Children. *Bioethics* 15 (5–6): 413–426.

Savulescu, Julian. 2007. In Defence of Procreative Beneficence. *Journal of Medical Ethics* 33: 284–288.

Savulescu, Julian, and Guy Kahane. 2009. The Moral Obligation to Create Children with the Best Chance of the Best Life. *Bioethics* 23 (5): 274–290.

Sayers, Rex. 2007. The Kid Question: Does Having Children Offer Any Advantage to an Academic's Professional Career? *Chronicle of Higher Education* 54 (17): C3.

Schiltz, Elizabeth. 2006. Living in the Shadow of Mönchberg. In *Defiant Birth: Women Who Resist Medical Eugenics*, ed. Melinda Tankard Reist, 182–195. North Melbourne, Australia: Spinifex.

Senior, Jennifer. 2010. All Joy and No Fun: Why Parents Hate Parenting. *New York Magazine*, July 4. http://nymag.com/print/?/news/features/67024.

Shanley, Mary L. 1999. Fathers' Rights, Mothers' Wrongs? Reflections on Unwed Fathers' Rights and Sex Equality. In *Having and Raising Children: Unconven-*

tional Families, Hard Choices, and the Social Good, ed. Uma Narayan and Julia J. Bartkowiak, 39–63. University Park: Pennsylvania State University Press.

Sheldon, S[ally], and S[teven] Wilkinson. 2004. Should Selecting Saviour Siblings Be Banned? *Journal of Medical Ethics* 30: 533–537.

Sherwin, Susan. 1992. *No Longer Patient: Feminist Ethics and Health Care*. Philadelphia: Temple University Press.

Shiffrin, Seana Valentine. 1999. Wrongful Life, Procreative Responsibility, and the Significance of Harm. *Legal Theory* 5: 117–148.

Smart, J. J. C., and Bernard Williams. 1973. *Utilitarianism: For and Against*. Cambridge, UK: Cambridge University Press.

Smilansky, Saul. 1995. Is There a Moral Obligation to Have Children? *Journal of Applied Philosophy* 12 (1): 41–53.

Spriggs, M[erle]. 2005. Is Conceiving a Child to Benefit Another Against the Interests of the New Child? *Journal of Medical Ethics* 31 (6): 341–343.

Spriggs, M[erle], and J[ulian] Savulescu. 2002. Saviour Siblings. *Journal of Medical Ethics* 28: 289.

Steinbock, Bonnie, and Ron McClamrock. 1994. When Is Birth Unfair to the Child? *Hastings Center Report* 24 (6): 15–21.

Sullivan, Rosemary. 1998. *The Red Shoes: Margaret Atwood Starting Out*. Toronto: HarperCollins.

Tännsjö, Torbjörn. 2004. Why We Ought to Accept the Repugnant Conclusion. In *The Repugnant Conclusion: Essays on Population Ethics*, ed. Jesper Ryberg and Torbjörn Tännsjö, 219–237. Dordrecht, Netherlands: Kluwer Academic.

Teo, Wesley D. H. 1975. Abortion: The Husband's Constitutional Rights. *Ethics* 85 (4): 337–342.

Thomson, Judith Jarvis. 1975. A Defense of Abortion. In *Moral Problems: A Collection of Philosophical Essays*, 2nd ed., ed. James Rachels, 89–106. New York: Harper & Row.

Timson, Judith. 2010. So You Expected Kids to Make You Happy? Get Real. *The Globe and Mail*, July 9, 1 and 3.

Tittle, Peg, ed. 2004. *Should Parents Be Licensed? Debating the Issues*. Amherst, NY: Prometheus Books.

Tong, Rosemarie. 1997. *Feminist Approaches to Bioethics: Theoretical Reflections and Practical Applications*. Boulder, CO: Westview Press.

Tremain, Shelley. 2001. On the Government of Disability. *Social Theory and Practice* 27 (4): 617–636.

United Nations. 2008. *World Population Prospects: The 2008 Revision*. http://www.un.org/esa/population/publications/wpp2008/wpp2008_highlights.pdf.

Vallely, Paul. 2008. Population Paradox: Europe's Time Bomb. *The Independent*, August 9. http://www.independent.co.uk/news/world/europe/population-paradox-europes-time-bomb-888030.html.

Vehmas, Simo. 2002. Is It Wrong to Deliberately Conceive or Give Birth to a Child with Mental Retardation? *Journal of Medicine and Philosophy* 27 (1): 47–63.

Velleman, J. David. 2005. Family History. *Philosophical Papers* 34 (3): 357–378.

Weeks, Andrew. 2007. Umbilical Cord Clamping after Birth. *British Medical Journal* 335 (August 18): 312–313.

Wendell, Susan. 1996. *The Rejected Body: Feminist Philosophical Reflections on Disability*. New York: Routledge.

Wennerholm, U-B. 2004. Obstetrical Risks and Neonatal Complications of Twin Pregnancy and Higher Order Multiple Pregnancy. In *Assisted Reproductive Technologies: Quality and Safety*, ed. Jan Gerris, Francois Olivennes, and Petra de Sutter, 23–38. London: Taylor & Francis.

Wente, Margaret, and David Eddie. 2006. Who Needs Grandchildren? *The Globe and Mail*, July 22, F7.

Whitaker, Leisa. 2006. I Wouldn't Swap Them for Anything. In *Defiant Birth: Women Who Resist Medical Eugenics*, ed. Melinda Tankard Reist, 212–223. North Melbourne, Australia: Spinifex.

Wise, Jennifer. 2006. Who Wants to be a Mommy? In *Nobody's Mother: Life without Kids*, ed. Lynne van Luven, 119–131. Victoria, Australia: Touch Wood Editions.

Wisor, Scott. 2009. Is There a Moral Obligation to Limit Family Size? *Philosophy and Public Policy Quarterly* 29 (3–4): 26–31.

Wong, Sophia Isako. 2002. At Home with Down Syndrome and Gender. *Hypatia: A Journal of Feminist Philosophy* 17 (3): 89–117.

World Health Organization. 2010. Disabilities. http://www.who.int/topics/disabilities/en.

Worth, Jennifer. 2002. *The Midwife: A Memoir of Birth, Joy, and Hard Times*. New York: Penguin Books.

Young, Thomas. 2001. Overconsumption and Procreation: Are They Morally Equivalent? *Journal of Applied Philosophy* 18 (2): 184–192.

Index

Basic Bioethics

Arthur Caplan, editor

Books Acquired under the Editorship of Glenn McGee and Arthur Caplan

David H. Brendel, *Healing Psychiatry: Bridging the Science/Humanism Divide*

Jonathan Baron, *Against Bioethics*

Michael L. Gross, *Bioethics and Armed Conflict: Moral Dilemmas of Medicine and War*

Karen F. Greif and Jon F. Merz, *Current Controversies in the Biological Sciences: Case Studies of Policy Challenges from New Technologies*

Deborah Blizzard, *Looking Within: A Sociocultural Examination of Fetoscopy*

Ronald Cole-Turner, ed., *Design and Destiny: Jewish and Christian Perspectives on Human Germline Modification*

Holly Fernandez Lynch, *Conflicts of Conscience in Health Care: An Institutional Compromise*

Mark A. Bedau and Emily C. Parke, eds., *The Ethics of Protocells: Moral and Social Implications of Creating Life in the Laboratory*

Jonathan D. Moreno and Sam Berger, eds., *Progress in Bioethics: Science, Policy, and Politics*

Eric Racine, *Pragmatic Neuroethics: Improving Understanding and Treatment of the Mind–Brain*

Martha J. Farah, ed., *Neuroethics: An Introduction with Readings*

Books Acquired under the Editorship of Arthur Caplan

Sheila Jasanoff, ed., *Reframing Rights: Bioconstitutionalism in the Genetic Age*

Christine Overall, *Why Have Children? The Ethical Debate*